What Really ~~Works in~~ Special and Inclusive Education

Teachers around the globe are anxious to develop genuine, evidence-based policies and practices in their teaching of children with special educational needs, yet this field is notorious for the significant gap that exists between research and practice.

What Really Works in Special and Inclusive Education presents educators of learners with special educational needs with a range of strategies they can implement right away in the classroom. David Mitchell, a leading writer in special and inclusive education, has distilled a huge range of recent studies that have the most genuine potential for improving the practices of teachers and schools, in order to help them produce high-quality learning and social outcomes for all.

Each of the 24 strategies included in the book has a substantial research base, a sound theoretical rationale, clear practical guidelines on how they can be employed, as well as cautions about their use.

The book covers:

- strategies for arranging the context of learning, such as inclusive education, cooperative group teaching and the classroom climate
- cognitive strategies, including self-regulated learning, memory enhancement and cognitive behavioural therapy
- behavioural strategies, addressing issues of functional assessment and direct instruction
- formative assessment and feedback
- assistive technology and opportunities to learn.

While the book focuses on learners with special educational needs, most of the strategies are applicable to all learners.

This ground-breaking book will be welcomed by any teacher working in special and inclusive education settings who has neither the time nor the inclination to engage with theory-heavy research, yet wants to ensure that their teaching strategies are up-to-the-minute and proven to be the most effective best practices. Researchers, teacher educators and psychologists will also find this book informative and unique in its scope.

David Mitchell is an Inclusive Education Consultant in Hamilton, New Zealand, and an Honorary Research Fellow at Manchester University. Most recently he edited *Special Education Needs and Inclusive Education* and *Contextualising Inclusive Education*, both by Routledge.

What Really Works in Special and Inclusive Education

Using evidence-based teaching strategies

David Mitchell

Routledge
Taylor & Francis Group

LONDON AND NEW YORK

First published 2008
by Routledge
2 Park Square, Milton Park, Abingdon, Oxon OX14 4RN

Simultaneously published in the USA and Canada
by Routledge
270 Madison Ave, New York, NY10016

Routledge is an imprint of the Taylor & Francis Group, an informa business

© 2008 David Mitchell

Typeset in Times New Roman by
Florence Production Ltd, Stoodleigh, Devon
Printed and bound in Great Britain by
Antony Rowe Ltd, Chippenham, Wiltshire

British Library Cataloguing in Publication Data
A catalogue record for this book is available from the British Library

Library of Congress Cataloging in Publication Data
A catalog record for this book has been requested

ISBN 13: 978–0–415–36926–8 (hbk)
ISBN 13: 978–0–415–36925–1 (pbk)
ISBN 13: 978–0–203–02945–9 (ebk)

ISBN 10: 0–415–36926–6 (hbk)
ISBN 10: 0–415–36925–8 (pbk)
ISBN 10: 0–203–02945–3 (ebk)

For my mother,
Adelaide Margaret (Addie) Mitchell (1918–2006)

Contents

Preface   ix
Acknowledgements   xii

1 Introduction   1

2 A learning and teaching model   14

3 Strategy 1: Inclusive education   27

4 Strategy 2: Cooperative group teaching   43

5 Strategy 3: Peer tutoring   52

6 Strategy 4: Collaborative teaching   60

7 Strategy 5: Parent involvement   68

8 Strategy 6: School culture   78

9 Strategy 7: School-wide positive behaviour support   83

10 Strategy 8: Indoor environmental quality   92

11 Strategy 9: Classroom climate   103

12 Strategy 10: Social skills training   113

13 Strategy 11: Cognitive strategy instruction   122

14 Strategy 12: Self-regulated learning   132

15 Strategy 13: Mnemonics and other memory strategies   139

16 Strategy 14: Reciprocal teaching   147

17 Strategy 15: Phonological awareness and phonological
                 processing   154

18 Strategy 16: Cognitive behavioural therapy   163

19 Strategy 17: Behavioural approaches   173

20 Strategy 18: Functional behavioural assessment   182

21 Strategy 19: Direct instruction   188

22 Strategy 20: Review and practice   195

23 Strategy 21: Formative assessment and feedback   201

24 Strategy 22: Assistive technology   207

25 Strategy 23: Augmentative and alternative communication   216

26 Strategy 24: Opportunities to learn   224

    Index   232

Preface

In most countries, children are required to spend 10–15,000 hours in learning spaces we call 'schools' and 'classrooms'. During that significant period of their development they will interact with many educators and peers, as well as with a large range of learning materials, and be exposed to many different teaching strategies.

For these experiences to yield effective learning it is essential that the environments we create are safe, challenging and educative. It is essential that they ensure that all children actually learn what is expected of them, that their education contributes to enhancing their quality of life, that they achieve a balance between independence and interdependence, and that they are prepared to lead full and satisfying lives as citizens and as members of their cultures.

These challenges are no less important for those children who, for a variety of reasons, we consider to have special educational needs and who face significant barriers to their learning and development. These children comprise perhaps 10–15 per cent of the school population. Their special needs arise from diverse factors: sensory, physical, intellectual and emotional. They are expressed in difficulties in making academic progress in the school curriculum, in acquiring the physical and social skills appropriate to their cultures, and in achieving a fulfilling sense of self-esteem. Their special needs range from major to minor, and they reflect physiological and environmental factors. These children are the focus of this book, although, as you will discover, many of the teaching strategies are universally applicable.

In this book I will describe and present the evidence and underlying ideas for a total of 24 teaching strategies. Some of the strategies are to do with arranging the context of learning (for example, inclusive education, cooperative group teaching and the classroom climate). Another group looks at cognitive strategies such as self-regulated learning, memory strategies and cognitive behavioural therapy. A third group focuses on behavioural strategies such as functional assessment and direct instruction. As well, consideration is given to such strategies as formative assessment and feedback, assistive technology and opportunities to learn.

In all of these strategies I have thoroughly examined the research evidence (much of which is not readily available to classroom educators) and have attempted to interpret it in a user-friendly manner. I am keenly aware that in most countries the drive for accountability means that educators are increasingly being expected to be responsible not only for the learners' outcomes, but also for using the most scientifically valid methods to achieve them. I hope this book helps in this regard.

The book had its origins in several sources. First, I drew upon over 2,000 research articles on teaching learners with special educational needs at the primary and secondary school levels. In an endeavour to ensure that the book is international in scope, I have included reference to studies carried out in countries as diverse as the USA, the UK, New Zealand, Australia, Canada, Spain and the Netherlands. Second, I reflected on my experiences in teacher education programmes in many countries. Third, I drew upon my own research and publications.

In approaching the task of selecting strategies for inclusion in the book, I resolved from the outset to 'follow the evidence'. Apart from a commitment to evidence-based teaching, I had no theoretical axe to grind and no pre-conceived ideas about where the evidence might lead me. In some cases, it took me into areas that were initially quite unfamiliar to me (for example, indoor environmental quality and augmentative and alternative communication), while in others I was on familiar grounds (for example, cognitive strategy instruction and behavioural approaches).

Another decision I made very early on was to focus on teaching strategies first, and special educational needs second, as the framework for the book. I will explain my reasons for this in the introduction.

In writing the book, my primary aim is to help educators (practicing and trainee teachers, principals, assistant teachers/paraprofessionals) and the professionals who advise them (e.g., school psychologists, special education needs coordinators, special education advisers) to become more effective in teaching learners with special educational needs, whether in a special education setting or in a regular classroom. In these days of widespread commitment to inclusive education, every teacher is a teacher of learners with special educational needs. I recognize that, as a busy educator, it is virtually impossible for you to keep up with the ever-expanding research literature, and then translate it into your teaching practices.

Finally, let me introduce myself. I am David Mitchell, a New Zealander who has worked as a consultant in inclusive and special education in many countries. My education career commenced as a primary school teacher, with a particular focus on gifted and talented children, from which I moved to become an educational psychologist assisting educators to work with learners with special educational needs. My next career step was to work as a teacher educator in universities, mainly in New Zealand, but also as a visiting professor and UNESCO consultant in countries as diverse as the

USA, Canada, the UK, Japan, Singapore, Kazakhstan, South Africa and Uzbekistan. I have carried out extensive research into special and inclusive education and have co-directed a professional development programme on inclusive education for teachers and principals. My most recent publications (also published with Routledge) include a four-volume series, *Special Education Needs and Inclusive Education* (2004), and *Contextualizing Inclusive Education: evaluating old and new international perspectives* (2005).

David Mitchell
Hamilton, New Zealand

Acknowledgements

I should like to acknowledge the crucial and critical role played by my wife, Dr Jill Mitchell, for accessing sources, acting as a sounding board and giving editorial advice, as well as exercising considerable patience as I completed the writing of this book.

Kathy Wilson, Peter Gillies and Glennis Ericksen, special education practitioners, also gave me helpful feedback on early drafts of the book.

I also acknowledge with gratitude the ideas I obtained from my class EDPI – 341, Instruction in Inclusive Schools, which I taught as a visiting professor at McGill University, Montreal, Canada in Fall 2004: Stefania Audi, Shannon Beauce, Naomi Benizri, Kathryn Brereton, Sarah Breton, Veroniki Buchmann, Bernadett Burger, Jennifer Caro, Angela Caza, Tanya Caza, Jane Cooper, Josie D'Adamo, Cristina Del Torto, Cheryl Demcoe, Marivie Dube-Simard, Melissa Duheme, Lisa Fazio, My Na Hang, On Ki Hui, Claudia Janezic, Emilie Lapointe, Andrea Lee, David Lewkowich, Laura Malizia, Emile McCaig, Lisa McMartin, Tamsin Morrell, Vanessa Mustillo, Pinky Patel, Christine Piercy, Marina Rendina, Stephanie Smyth, Sabrina Trottier, Laura Vallelonga, Loretta Varano, Sandra Vineberg-Martel, Rebecca Waterhouse and Suet-Ying Wong.

Chapter 1

Introduction

Along with parents, teachers are at the heart of ensuring a good quality of life for learners with special educational needs, regardless of where their education takes place. The central idea in this book is that, to enhance their performance, teachers could, and should, be drawing upon the best available evidence as they plan and implement their teaching. Indeed, in the United States, the No Child Left Behind (NCLB) law requires teachers to use 'scientific, research-based programs', defined as: '(1) grounded in theory; (2) evaluated by third parties; (3) published in peer-reviewed journals; (4) sustainable; (5) replicable in schools with diverse settings; and (6) able to demonstrate evidence of effectiveness'. As well, NCLB requires each state to ensure that all learners (including those with disabilities) make 'adequate yearly progress', i.e., 'continuous and substantial improvement'.[1] In a similar vein, although not explicitly targeting education, the UK government requires that 'policy makers should have available to them the widest and latest information on research and best practice, and all decisions should be demonstrably rooted in this knowledge'.[2] While the concern for basing practices on research evidence has long characterized such fields as medicine, agriculture and technology, its emergence in education has largely occurred in the past decade. Welcome to the twenty-first century![3]

Although the body of evidence in education is not without problems and much remains to be investigated, it has produced a useful and reliable knowledge base about effective teaching practices for learners with special educational needs. Unfortunately, it is clear that there is a significant gap between what researchers have found and what educators practise.[4] At least in part, this gap is due to the fact that much relevant research is not available to educators in a readily accessible form – a situation that I hope this book will go some way to rectifying.

Briefly, I define evidence-based teaching strategies as:

clearly specified teaching strategies that have been shown in controlled research to be effective in bringing about desired outcomes in a delineated population of learners.[5]

My aim is to assist you, as an educator, to increase your effectiveness by using the best available evidence to help your students to become effective learners. Ultimately, the effectiveness of your teaching is judged by:

- the value you add to your learners' store of information, concepts, skills and values;
- the degree of independence your learners are able to exercise in managing their own learning now and in the future; and
- the extent to which you develop a sense of well-being in learners.

As an educator you play a vital role in helping learners to develop these attributes. For example, one writer recently estimated the following influences on learners' development:

Individual students – who account for about 50 per cent of their achievement, and possibly more in the case of those with special educational needs.
Teachers – who account for about 30 per cent of achievement, hence the importance of using well-founded teaching strategies, as described in this book.
Schools – which account for about 5–10 per cent of achievement. This influence is mediated mainly through principals.
Peers – who account for 5–10 per cent of achievement.
Homes – which account for 5–10 per cent of achievement, especially through parents' expectations and encouragement.[6]

In drawing up the 24 strategies described in this book, I should like to emphasize from the outset that I am not arguing for a single strategy or blueprint that all educators should use with learners with special education needs. Indeed, their needs are so varied (even within particular categories of disability) that one size will *not* fit all. Rather, the most effective programmes are those that incorporate a variety of best practices. My strong advice is that you develop a repertoire of such strategies nested within your own philosophy, personality, craft knowledge, professional wisdom and, above all, your knowledge of the characteristics and needs of your students and your knowledge of local circumstances.

A word about terms and other things

In deciding what terminology to use in the book, I had to make three decisions. First, should I refer to 'students', 'children' or 'learners'? Since the focus of the book is on children *and* youth, and 'students' can suggest a narrower focus on academic learning, I have generally opted for *learners*. Second, should I refer to learners with 'disabilities', 'special educational needs' or 'barriers to learning'? Although my main focus is on learners with disabilities (thus excluding gifted learners except where they may also have a disability), I will also be referring to other special needs. While I am very attracted to the concept of 'learners with barriers to learning and development', for ease of reference I have opted for *special educational needs.* (Please note that when I summarize the evidence for the various strategies, I will use the terminology employed in the original articles, even though this sometimes goes against my 'people first' sensibilities.) Third, I had to choose between 'teachers' and 'educators'. Although I will be directing most of my attention to teachers, I also want to include others who have educative roles, such as school psychologists, paraprofessionals and parents, hence my choice of *educators.*

By now you will have noted that I have chosen to write often in the first person, a somewhat unusual style for someone steeped in academic traditions. My reason for this is simply that I want to connect with you, the reader, on a personal level as far as it is possible via the printed word.

Another point I would like to mention is my approach to referencing sources: I have attempted to minimize possible distractions by including them in endnotes, rather than in the body of the text. Unless you are seeking further information on the studies I have consulted or wanting technical information, you should be able to read the text without constantly referring to the endnotes.

How do we know what works?

As an educator of learners with special educational needs, I guess that you have come across many teaching strategies, but that you have been unsure of how effective they are. I would guess, too, that you have been frustrated by ideas that turn out to be no more than fads and fancies and that you have often asked yourself what is the evidence that this or that idea really works? As an educator, you are faced with making choices among an ever-increasing list of intervention options. I hope this book will help you make good choices of strategies you could use with the learners in your charge.

Ideally, evidence that a particular strategy works should be based on carefully designed research studies that meet the following criteria:[7]

Treatment fidelity. The intervention strategy is fully described in a treatment manual (which is available, if not published in the research article) and there is evidence that the intervention has been closely adhered to. Two related issues arise. First, when trying to accumulate evidence of the effectiveness of particular strategies, one has to ask are they consistent across studies? Second, are they 'pure' treatments or are they combined with other treatments? (With regard to the latter point, this is not to say that the aim should be to develop some form of 'pure' treatment. It could well be that with some students a mixed form of intervention might be necessary; if that is the case, the precise mix should be carefully described.)

Behavioural outcomes. The study should include reliable and valid measures of the behavioural outcomes: after all, we must be sure that a particular strategy has a positive effect on the behaviours we want to change. Here, I must refer to two technical matters.

First, in my selection of teaching strategies that 'really work', I will be relying heavily on various *meta-analyses* that have been carried out. Briefly, a meta-analysis synthesizes the results from a range of similar studies to determine the average effect of a particular intervention.[8] Its originator referred to it as 'the analysis of analyses'.[9]

Second, meta-analyses usually produce a numerical indicator, referred to as *effect size* (ES). This tells you the magnitude of the effect of the treatment[10]: the larger the ES, the greater the impact of the treatment.[11]

In allocating stars to the various strategies I will be describing in this book, I will follow the grading system outlined below. With the exception of one two-star strategy, I have confined myself to three- and four-star strategies.[12]

★★★★   *Convincing, or conclusive, evidence.* For example, an effect size of 0.7 or greater, which shows that learners with special educational needs undoubtedly benefit from the strategy. Such effect sizes show that the percentile scores of learners would increase from 50 to at least 76.

★★★☆   *Good, or preponderant, evidence.* For example, an effect size of 0.31–0.69, which shows that learners with special educational needs probably benefit from the strategy. These effect sizes indicate that the strategy results in improvements in percentile scores from 50 to a band of 62–75.

★★☆☆   *Modest, or suggestive, evidence.* For example, an effect size of 0.2–0.3, which shows that learners with special educational needs benefit somewhat from the strategy. These effect sizes indicate that the strategy results in improvements in percentile scores from 50 to a band of 58–61.

        Note: where no effect size data are available I will use other ways to determine the value of the research, particularly the criteria I outline in the rest of this section.

Learner characteristics. Studies should include clear descriptions of the learners' ages, developmental levels, and the nature and degree of any disabilities they might have. Also, it is desirable that the learners' family characteristics such as ethnicity be reported. Ideally, research studies should focus on learners who are as homogeneous as possible. The more heterogeneous the sample studies, the more difficult it is for educators to decide which learners would benefit from the strategy.

Control of variables. The research should be designed in such a way as to ensure that the outcomes are due to the intervention and not to any confounding variables such as the simple passage of time or a placebo effect. We would also want to be confident that the outcomes were not due to the effects of additional attention to the learners in the study or to the effects of repeated testing. This can be achieved in several ways, two of which I will mention here.

First, there are *randomized controlled studies* in which learners are randomly assigned to an experimental group that receives the intervention or to a control group that does not receive the intervention, but is in all other significant ways similar to the experimental group. Here, it is important that the two groups should be equivalent at baseline, i.e., before the intervention commences. It is also important that there be acceptable levels of attrition between the pre- and post-intervention phases.

Second, there are *single-case studies* in which there are repeated measurements of a single learner in different conditions over time. Here, in order to establish that a strategy changes a target behaviour, a stable baseline must also be achieved. There are two main designs of single-case studies.

In an ABAB design, the first task is to establish a stable baseline (Time A). This involves repeated observations of the target behaviour, as it occurs without the new intervention, until there are consistent scores. The new intervention is then introduced and new measurements of the target behaviour are taken throughout this phase (Time B). The process is then repeated, with the new intervention taken away and a return to baseline (second Time A). At this point you might expect to see a reversal or levelling out of the earlier improvement. The intervention is then re-introduced, and you might expect to see a resumed improvement (second Time B).

On the other hand, in a multiple-baseline design, variants include multiple baselines across settings, behaviours or participants. For example, two behaviours of a single subject are selected for study and a treatment is applied to one of them. The behaviour that is not treated serves as a baseline against which the effects of the treatment can be determined. This approach does not require returning the target behaviour to baseline, as in the ABAB design, when such a procedure may be undesirable.

Freedom from contamination.   There should be no, or minimal, 'contamination' which might affect the results of the study. In other words, it is important that nothing happens (outside of the intervention) that could affect the outcomes for either the experimental group or the control group. Of course, if events occur that affect *both* the experimental and the control groups, these are acceptable.

Acceptable side effects.   Possible side effects should be assessed and should be positive, or at least not negative. For example, coercive means might be used to control certain learner behaviours, but they might cause heightened anxiety or even fear.

Theory-based.   The psychological mechanisms or learning processes underlying the strategy should be clearly explained, thus enabling us to generalize it to other situations. While I am giving priority to scientifically conducted research, I also recognize the validity and value of strategies that have a strong theory base (which, of course, have been based on thorough testing in the first place), but which themselves might not have been rigorously evaluated.[13]

Follow-up.   There should be adequate follow-up after, say, six months, but preferably longer, to ascertain if the behavioural gains are maintained over time.

Research versus natural conditions.   Ideally, the research should be carried out in everyday teaching environments, not just in research conditions. This is because it could well be that the research conditions are dramatically different from the actual conditions you, as an educator, work in. However, while studies that have been conducted in real conditions (often referred to as 'effectiveness' studies) usually have higher credibility to educators, those that have been conducted in controlled research settings ('efficacy' studies) will not be overlooked in this book.[14]

Peer review.   The research should have been published in reputable journals after rigorous peer review. It is worth noting here that, by and large, studies are more likely to be published if significant effects have been demonstrated than if no effects were found. In other words, there is a bias towards publishing positive results and we might never know the results of studies that *don't* support a particular strategy.

While I give priority to peer-reviewed academic journals, I do recognize that there are other legitimate sources of knowledge in the field of education, for example, practitioner journals, student theses, report literature and, increasingly, Internet publications.

Replication.   The research should contain at least two studies (more for single-case studies) that have shown positive effects for the strategy; i.e., the research has been replicated, preferably by independent researchers. Even better, there is a wide base of support for the strategy, as reflected in meta-analyses, described above.

Cost effectiveness.   Clearly, for an intervention to be adopted it must not be excessively expensive. For example, the more the intervention depends on one-to-one treatment over a prolonged period, the less likely it is considered to be cost effective, especially in poorer countries.

Practical significance.   It is possible for research to yield statistically significant results, but the actual effects of the treatment might not be practically
meaningful and would have limited appeal to educators looking for strategies
that make a big difference to learner outcomes.[15]

Accessibility.   Finally, it is important that educators can readily access in a
usable form those teaching strategies that have been researched. I see this
as my main responsibility in writing this book.

Unfortunately, only relatively few studies have used the rigorous methodology
referred to above.[16] While I will be paying close attention to these criteria,
I will be including studies that do not meet all of them, but which, nevertheless,
provide credible evidence.[17] That is simply the current state of the art of
research into what constitutes effective teaching for learners with special
educational needs – indeed, for all learners.

Do learners with special educational needs require distinctive teaching strategies?

The answer to this question is both 'Yes' and a qualified 'No'.

First, *yes*: some learners – especially those with high or very high needs
– do require significantly different teaching strategies to those that educators
in regular classes might usually employ. For example, some learners

- with visual impairments are reliant on their tactile and auditory senses
  for learning and will require specialized techniques such as Braille and
  orientation and mobility training;
- who are deaf will require specific adaptations such as total communication
  (including signing), FM listening systems and assistance with maintaining
  hearing aids;
- with speech and language difficulties will require specialized speech/
  language therapy to deal with such errors as substitutions, distortions
  and omissions in their speech;
- with intellectual disabilities will require tasks to be broken down into
  very small steps and will need assistance with such matters as self-care;
- with physical disabilities will need assistance with positioning and
  movement normally provided by specialists such as physiotherapists and
  occupational therapists, or with toileting;
- with autistic spectrum disorder will need adjustments to their educational
  programme to take account of their 'triad of impairments': social interactions, social communication and imagination.[18]

In most instances, specialist teachers or therapists undertake these specialized
teaching strategies and these will not be discussed further in this book.

Second, *no*: for the most part, learners with special educational needs simply require good teaching. As some writers argue, there is little evidence to support the notion of disability-specific teaching strategies, but rather that all learners benefit from a common set of strategies, even if they have to be adapted to take account of varying cognitive, emotional and social capabilities.[19] What is required is the systematic, explicit and intensive application of a wide range of effective teaching strategies – day-by-day, minute-by-minute – in classrooms. As a successful educator of learners with special educational needs, you will have many strategies at your disposal that are appropriate for *all* learners, as will become apparent as you read about the strategies I have selected for this book.

How is the book structured?

I have selected 24 strategies for you to consider. In doing so, I have taken account of the above criteria and sought strategies that meet as many of them as possible. I have focused on those strategies that have been used with learners with special educational needs at the elementary and secondary school level. I have not included pharmacological treatments (e.g., Ritalin and anti-depressants), or dietary treatments, or highly specialized interventions such as physiotherapy or Braille.

In the next chapter, I will show how most of the strategies fit into an overall learning and teaching model. This will show the relationship between a learner's biological functions, motivation, cognition and memory, as well as indicating how you can create a learning environment that responds to these factors.

For ease of reference, I have structured the presentation of the strategies in a consistent format, as follows:

 The strategy: definition of the strategy.

 The underlying idea: theoretical basis for the strategy and its brief history.

 The practice: an outline of the strategy and its variants, with examples. Note that the next section on evidence also includes examples of strategies used in controlled conditions.

 The evidence: a brief review of the research on the strategy, with a discussion of its pros and cons and its applicability to different categories of learners with special educational needs. Since most of the strategies presented in this book have an extensive literature, I will outline only a representative sample. Mainly, I have selected only those that have involved learners with special educational needs.

Addressing risks: an indication of any problems in implementing the strategy, including ethical issues and contraindications.

 Conclusion: a succinct summary of the value of the method.

 Further reading: suggestions for readings, including Web sites, which supplement the description.

Key references: the references noted in the text.

What behaviours are affected by the strategies?

In each of the 24 strategies I will select a representative sample of supportive evidence. Space limitations allow me to select only a few such studies – around six to ten per strategy. In each item of evidence I will describe the age of the learners involved, their special educational needs, the nature of the intervention that was employed and the behaviours that were affected.

Table 1.1 presents a matrix showing what behavioural outcomes have been achieved for each strategy, arranged according to improved outcomes in desired behaviours and decreases in undesired behaviours. For example, by reading down the table you can see that **Strategy 3: Peer Tutoring** leads to improvements in nine learner behaviours, including general achievement and learners' self-concepts, and to decreases in two behaviours in such areas as dropping out from school. Reading across the table, you can see, for example, that four of the 24 strategies are associated with improved outcomes in interactions with peers, while two are associated with decreases in social and general anxiety.

As mentioned earlier, because of the space limitations, I could include only a small fraction of available studies in each strategy. Therefore, you should not assume that gaps in the matrix mean that a particular strategy is not relevant to a particular outcome. Rather, you could extrapolate the information shown in the table. For example, you could be fairly sure that if a strategy is effective in improving mathematics achievement, it would probably also work for spelling achievement, etc. In making this point, I would like to emphasize that although the 24 strategies are described separately, they are interconnected, with the common theme of helping students to become more effective and efficient learners.

The context is important

Although I hope that this book will be a valuable resource for educators in many countries, I do recognize the importance of different contexts. Most significantly, the vast bulk of the research I will be referring to has been conducted in developed countries, especially the USA, and therefore might

Table 1.1 Teaching strategies related to selected outcome areas

Column key:
1. Inclusive education
2. Cooperative group teaching
3. Peer tutoring
4. Collaborative teaching
5. Parent involvement
6. School culture
7. School-wide positive behav support
8. Indoor environmental quality
9. Classroom climate
10. Social skills training
11. Cognitive strategy instruction
12. Self-regulated learning
13. Mnemonics & other memory strats
14. Reciprocal teaching
15. Phonological awareness
16. Cognitive behavioural therapy
17. Behavioural approaches
18. Functional behavioural assessment
19. Direct instruction
20. Review and practice
21. Formative assessment & feedback
22. Assistive technology
23. Augmentative & alternative communic
24. Opportunities to learn

Improved:	1	2	3	4	5	6	7	8	9	10	11	12	13	14	15	16	17	18	19	20	21	22	23	24
General achievement	■		■				■				■						■		■	■	■	■	■	■
Reading achievement	■	■	■					■			■		■	■	■									■
Writing/spelling achievement	■	■									■													
Math/sci/soc st achievement								■			■		■				■							
Communication skills																							■	
Study/test skills											■													
Engagement in lessons/attention			■					■																
Attitude towards subjects			■						■															
Task engagement												■				■								
Interactions with peers		■												■									■	
Social skills/interactions	■		■							■						■								
Self-control/determination												■				■								
Classroom behaviour						■											■							
Self-concepts/esteem																		■						
Teacher percpetions				■																				
Parent-child relationships					■																			
Inclusion						■				■														
Decreased:	1	2	3	4	5	6	7	8	9	10	11	12	13	14	15	16	17	18	19	20	21	22	23	24
Competing behaviours			■				■																	
Disruptive behaviour				■			■					■					■							
Anti-social behaviour						■										■	■							
Social & general anxiety				■												■								
Autistic behaviours																	■							
Requirement for special education			■	■																				

not be readily transferable to developing countries with different cultural practices, resources and levels of teacher training. Such factors as large classes, extreme poverty, cultural and linguistic diversity, the presence of HIV/AIDS, poor buildings, inadequate teacher training and little or non-existent support may limit the uptake of evidence-based teaching. Where possible, I will address the challenge of implementing the strategies in such contexts, but I do recognize that much remains to be researched in these important areas.

How to use the book

I am sure you will have your own strategy for using a book such as this one, but here are my suggestions. Having read this introductory chapter, I strongly suggest that you read the next one on my learning and teaching model to see how the various teaching strategies are connected. For an overview of the 24 strategies outlined in the book you could then turn to the final chapter, particularly the section on providing high-quality instruction. After that, I would think it is a matter of exploring strategies that appear most relevant to the challenges you are facing. Here, you could refer to the table in this chapter that summarizes the strategies according to the behaviours you want to improve in the learners you are responsible for. If your starting point is your need to know ways of teaching learners with particular special needs, the index will provide you with some entry points. However, please remember my earlier caution that, with some exceptions, there are no disability-specific teaching strategies. Most of the strategies I present in the book are relevant to all learners with special education needs, indeed to all learners.

A final point: be your own researcher

I hope that this book will 'tune' you into how sound research will enhance your teaching of learners with special educational needs. This does not mean simply being a 'consumer' of research, but also being a 'producer'. Thus, I hope that you will find opportunities to collaborate with professional researchers to advance the evidence base for good teaching practice. At the very least, I hope that you will bring a scientific approach to your teaching by designing innovative programmes, carefully evaluating their outcomes, re-designing them until their effectiveness is proven, and then disseminating the results among your colleagues.

Key references

1 No Child Left Behind Act of 2001, Pub. L. No. 107–110, 115 Stat. 1425. (Part A, Subpart 1, Sec. 1111, 2[c]). URL: www.ed.gov/legislation/ESEA02/ (accessed 17 January 2007). But note recent criticisms of the extent to which practices occurring since the passage of NCLB actually follow scientific evidence: Slavin,

R.E. (2006). 'Evidence-based reform and No Child Left Behind: Next time use what works'. *Teachers College Record*, 12 December 2006: URL: www.tcrecord. org ID Number 12887 (accessed 10 February 2007).

2 www.policyhub.gov.uk (accessed 11 February 2007).

3 For discussions of evidence-based practices, see, for example, Slavin, R.E. (2002). 'Evidence-based education policies: Transforming educational practice and research'. *Educational Researcher*, 31(7), 15–22; *Exceptional Children*, 2005, 71(2) for several relevant articles; Best Evidence Encyclopedia. URL: www. bestevidence.org (accessed 11 February 2007); and What Works Clearinghouse. URL: www.whatworks.ed.gov (accessed 11 February 2007).

4 See, for example, Heward, W.L. (2003). 'Ten faulty notions about teaching and learning that hinder the effectiveness of special education'. *The Journal of Special Education*, 36(4), 186–205; Mostert, M.P. and Crockett, J.B. (1999–2000). 'Reclaiming the history of special education for more effective practice'. *Exceptionality*, 8(2), 133–143; Mostert, M.P. and Kavale, K. (2001). 'Evaluation of research for usable knowledge in behavioural disorders: Ignoring the irrelevant, considering the germane'. *Behavioral Disorders,* 27(1), 53–68; and Sasso, G.M. (2001). 'The retreat from inquiry and knowledge in special education'. *The Journal of Special Education*, 34(4), 178–193.

5 Based on a definition of 'empirically supported therapies' by Chambless, D.L. and Hollon, S.D. (1998). 'Defining empirically supported therapies'. *Journal of Consulting and Clinical Psychology*, 66(1), 7–18.

6 Hattie, J. (2003). 'Teachers make a difference: What is the research evidence?' Paper presented at Australian Council for Educational Research Conference on Building Teacher Quality.

7 See, for example, Brestan, E.V. and Eyberg, S.M. (1998). 'Effective psychosocial treatments of conduct-disordered children and adolescents: 29 years, 82 studies, and 5,272 kids'. *Journal of Clinical Child Psychology*, 27(2), 180–189; Eddy, J.M., Dishion, T.J. and Stoolmiller, M. (1998). 'The analysis of intervention change in children and families: Methodological and conceptual issues embedded in intervention studies'. *Journal of Abnormal Child Psychology*, 26(1), 53–69; Goldstein, H. (2002). 'Communication intervention for children with autism: a review of treatment efficacy'. *Journal of Autism and Developmental Disorders*, 32(5), 373–396; Hargreaves, D. (1997). 'In defence of research for evidence-based teaching: a rejoinder to Martyn Hammersley'. *British Educational Research Journal*, 24(4), 405–419; Van de Wiel, N., Mattys, W., Cohen-Kettenis, P.C. and Van Engeland (2002). 'Effective treatments of school-aged conduct disordered children: Recommendations for changing clinical and research practices'. *European Child and Adolescent Psychiatry*, 11(2), 79–84; and Wolery, M. and Garfinkle, A.N. (2002). 'Measures in intervention research with young children who have autism'. *Journal of Autism and Developmental Disorders*, 32(5), 463–478.

8 While meta-analysis is undoubtedly a powerful tool, it is not without weaknesses. For critiques, see, for example: Lipsey, M.W. and Wilson, D.B. (1993). 'The efficacy of psychological, educational, and behavioral treatment: Confirmation from meta-analysis'. *American Psychologist*, 48(12), 1181–1209; Lloyd, J.W., Forness, S.R. and Kavale, K.A. (1998). 'Some methods are more effective than others'. *Intervention in School and Clinic*, 33(4), 195–200; and Mostert, M.P. (2001). 'Characteristics of meta-analyses reported in mental retardation, learning disabilities, and emotional and behavioural disorders'. *Exceptionality*, 9(4), 199–225.

9 Glass, G. (1976). 'Primary, secondary, and meta-analysis of research'. *Educational Research*, 5, 3–8.

10 See, for example, the comprehensive meta-analysis in Lipsey and Wilson, op. cit.
11 To explain further, an effect size of 1.0 indicates an increase of one standard deviation, which means that the average learners receiving the treatment would achieve better than 84 per cent of those who did not receive the treatment. To put it another way, an effect size of 1.0 would increase scores from the 50th to the 84th percentile. To illustrate further, an effect size of 0.8 indicates a rise from the 50th to the 79th percentile, 0.7 to the 76th percentile, 0.6 to the 73rd percentile, 0.5 to the 69th percentile, 0.4 to the 66th percentile, and 0.3 to the 62nd percentile. (Best Evidence Encyclopedia. URL: www.bestevidence.org (accessed 11 February 2007)).
12 See the notion of 'levels of certainty' discussed by Simeonsson, R.J. and Bailey, D.B. (1991). 'Evaluating programme impact: Levels of certainty'. In D. Mitchell and R. Brown (eds) *Early intervention studies for young children with special needs* (pp. 280–296). London: Chapman and Hall.
13 See Hirsch, E.D. (2002). 'Classroom research and cargo cults'. *Policy Review*, No. 115.
14 See Kratochwill, T.R. and Stoiber, K.C. (2000). 'Empirically supported interventions and school psychology: Conceptual and practice issues. Part II'. *School Psychology Quarterly*, 15(2), 233–253.
15 Lipsey and Wilson op. cit., pp. 1198–1199.
16 For example, in a comprehensive review of research on inclusive education programmes involving learners with low-incidence disabilities, US scholars McGregor and Vogelsberg (1998) found that only 36 of 112 studies met their criteria of valid scientific evidence. In a European analysis, Van Wijk and Meijer (2001) reported an even lower proportion, noting that only 13 of over 100 studies they reviewed were evidence-based. Similarly, writing from a UK perspective, Dockrell, Peacey and Lunt (2002) noted that there have been few attempts to evaluate outcomes of provisions for learners with special educational needs and that there are considerable methodological problems in comparing outcomes of different forms of provisions for such students (Dockrell, J., Peacey, N. and Lunt, I. (2002). 'Literature review: Meeting the needs of children with special educational needs'. In Audit Commission. *Special educational needs: a mainstream issue* (pp. 36–43). London: Audit Commission; McGregor, G. and Vogelsberg, R.T. (1998). *Inclusive schooling practices: Pedagogical and research foundations*. Baltimore, MD: Paul H. Brookes; and Van Wijk, C.J.F. and Meijer, C.J.W. (2001). 'International literature review'. In C.J.W. Meijer (ed.) *Classroom and school practice Report of the first phase: effective practices* (pp. 19–33, 244). Middelfart, Denmark: European Agency for Development in Special Needs Education).
17 I recognize that these criteria tend to favour quantitative, or positivistic, over qualitative research studies. I will, however, give consideration to studies carried out in the latter tradition, where I judge them to provide trustworthy evidence. For the most part, however, qualitative research's main value is in providing rich insights into educational processes in natural settings and in suggesting testable hypotheses for future empirical research (Wheldall, K. (2005). 'When will we ever learn?' *Educational Psychology*, 25(6), 573–584). My own research has straddled both methodologies and has often included a mix of both.
18 New Zealand Ministry of Education (2006). *Autism Spectrum Disorders (ASD): A resource for teachers*. URL: www.minedu.govt.nz/index.cfm?layout=document &documentid=7357&data=l (accessed 12 February 2007).
19 See, for example, Lewis, A. and Norwich, B. (2001). 'Mapping a pedagogy for special educational needs'. *British Education Research Journal*, 27(3), 313–329; and Norwich, B. (2003). 'Is there a distinctive pedagogy for learning difficulties?' *ACCP Occasional Papers*, No. 20.

Chapter 2

A learning and teaching model

In this chapter I will describe a learning and teaching model that sets the scene for the teaching strategies outlined in the remainder of the book.[1]

Two key questions are addressed:

1 How do learners acquire, process, store, retrieve, link and use information so that it can be applied to carrying out tasks?
2 How can learners who experience difficulties in learning be helped to become more efficient and effective in solving problems?

The model outlines the relationship between the requirements of various tasks and a learner's performance. This relationship is influenced by several factors. If these are not operating at an optimal level, they can impede the quality of a learner's performance. In broad terms, these factors comprise the learner's:

- biological structures and functions;
- motivational states;
- cognitive strategies; and
- memory.

All of these factors require a responsive environment, which you as an educator can create.

One writer[2] described how these factors relate to each other with the following 'formula', where 'motivation' refers to goals, emotions and personal agency beliefs, and 'skill' refers to cognitive strategies and memory.

$$\text{Competence} = \frac{\text{Motivation} \times \text{Skill}}{\text{Biology}} \times \text{Responsive environment}$$

Overview of model

In brief, the learning and teaching model, as shown in Figure 2.1, has several features, which occur in approximately the following sequence:

1 A learner is confronted with the demands of a *task*, or a problem to solve. This might be externally sourced or it might arise internally from the learner's own thought processes.

2 Information from the external world is filtered by a *sensory register*, which, because of biological differences, varies in efficiency from learner to learner.

3 Some elements of the task will automatically elicit associations with past experiences. This automatic memory, known as *primary memory*, frees our cognitive processing resources for more important activities.

4 At about this point, the learner's '*motivational headquarters*' will be deciding if he or she really wants to engage with the problem. This decision will reflect the learner's goals ('Do I want to do this?'), emotions ('How do I feel about doing this?') and personal agency beliefs ('Do I have the skills?' 'Can I trust my environment?').

5 Assuming that the learner wishes to engage with the task, the *executive system* comes into play, with varying degrees of efficiency. This will largely direct and control the learner's behaviour; i.e., the executive system is responsible for the self-monitoring and self-regulation of behaviour.

6 Critical to a successful engagement with the task is the learner's repertoire of *strategies* – both general awareness of the need to be strategic and more specific strategies that are appropriate to particular tasks.

7 Some elements of the task and the information necessary to solve the problem will be held in a *short-term memory* store to enable more sophisticated processing to take place. Learners vary in the carrying capacity of their short-term memory.

8 For tasks of moderate to high complexity the learner will have to 'search' his or her *long-term memory* store to retrieve relevant information. In turn, the learner will also be ensuring that new information, which is deemed to be important, is placed in the long-term memory.

9 To the extent that all of the relevant components described so far are operating at an optimal level, the learner will *retrieve* from his or her memory an appropriate response, or the elements of a response, which will be creatively combined.

10 This response will be encoded into a *performance*, which may be either external (i.e., an observable action) or internal (i.e., a thought).

11 In the case of an external demand, the appropriateness of the learner's response will then be judged and an *external response* (i.e., reinforcement, feedback or punishment) is given. If this response is negative, the whole cycle outlined above may then be repeated.

12 In the case of an internal demand, the learner will determine if the solution works or is satisfying. If not, the cycle may then be repeated.

Although the model is portrayed in a static, linear form, it is important that it be seen as being dynamic and recursive. This is shown in my use of

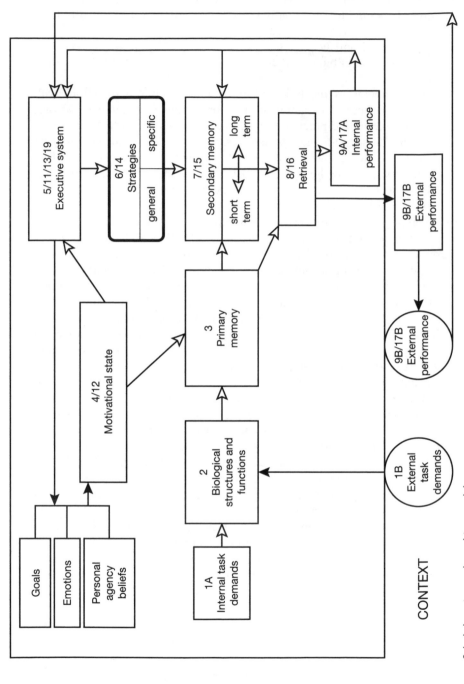

Figure 2.1 A learning and teaching model

more than one number for most elements in the model as they are re-visited during a learner's attempt to solve a problem.

Detailed description of the learning and teaching model

I will now explain the model in more detail. In doing so, I will illustrate each of its components with reference to the task of teaching learners how to write stories. I will also refer to the various strategies outlined in the rest of the book; these will be highlighted in bold.

The context

Input always occurs in a social context: the cultural setting, the family (**Strategy 5**), the peer group (**Strategy 3**), the composition of the class (**Strategy 1**), the grouping arrangements in the class (**Strategy 2**), the various educators with responsibilities for the educational programme (**Strategy 4**), the school environment (**Strategies 6** and **7**) and the classroom environment (**Strategies 8** and **9**).

> In our example, let's assume we are teaching an inclusive class of nine-year-old learners which, for this lesson, is arranged in mixed-ability groups. Let us also assume that in one of the groups there is Joseph, a boy with a learning disability.

Task demands (#1A and #1B)

Task demands come from either external sources (#1B in the model) or internally (#1A). In the case of external sources, the input comes via different *sense modalities*: visual, auditory, olfactory, tactile, kinaesthetic and in various combinations and sequences.

> In our example of story-writing, the task is phrased in the auditory mode ('Today, let's write a story about our visit to the zoo, from the time we left school until we returned', followed by discussion), perhaps with some visual assistance (e.g., photos of the visit displayed on a chart or on computers).

Tasks call upon a *knowledge base and strategies* for attacking the problem.

> In our example, the required knowledge base might include such things as the information about the animals we saw and how we travelled to and from the zoo. The strategies called for would require a method for writing a narrative-type story.

Several strategies in the book refer to the nature of external task demands, in particular **Strategies 17, 18** and **19**.

Biological structures and functions (#2)

In order for learners to respond to task demands they must, of course, be able to (a) *attend to*, (b) *perceive* and (c) *understand* features of the task, while ignoring others. This may be a non-voluntary and effortless process, or it may be an active and voluntary process under the control of the executive system (see later), or a mix of both. Learners vary in the efficiency with which they can selectively attend to stimuli. Some have severe organic impairments, which might affect their hearing, their vision or their capacity to understand tasks. Some have clinically diagnosed attention deficit disorders. As an educator you must ensure that such sensory, physical or intellectual barriers to learning are reduced as far as possible. Failing that, you must accommodate your teaching to take them into account.

> In our example, we would probably have known from the outset that Joseph had normal hearing, vision and perceptual skills and is of average intelligence. As we shall see, his difficulties lie elsewhere.

Primary memory (association) (#3)

When we are confronted with tasks, we typically make associations. Our automatic memory clicks into action. For example, if you hear the question, 'Salt and –?' you would most likely think of 'pepper'. Similarly, when asked, '$7 \times 7 = ?$' without thinking (I hope!) you would answer '49'. This automatic memory is quite important as it frees a learner's processing resources for more important activities. It is a good thing, therefore, to have a store of facts or associations that can be available when called for. For example, learners should be helped to achieve automaticity with the phonological/alphabetic code and the ability to translate letters to sounds and sounds to words in their reading[3] (see **Strategy 15**). This means that learners should be given ample practice with repetition and drills to build up such a store. However, I must emphasize that this does not mean that I am advocating drill and rote learning for all classroom learning. It plays a role, but must not be over-done. See **Strategy 20** for an elaboration of this point.

> In our example, you could call upon primary memory by asking the class to brainstorm all the things they can think of when they hear the word 'zoo'. I would guess the learners would come up with such ideas as 'cages', 'smells' and the names of various animals. Joseph would probably have no difficulty with this task, but might not be very skilled in being able to make associations concerning animals and their habitats.

Motivational states and personal dispositions (#4 and #12)[4]

According to motivation researchers, the extent to which learners' 'motivational headquarters' engage with a task will be influenced by these factors:

a   its relevance to their *personal goals* (e.g., Joseph may not want to undertake the story-writing task because he has difficulty in organizing his ideas and with spelling);

b   their emotional state (e.g., Joseph may be very anxious about being embarrassed in front of his peers when he attempts the story-writing task);

c   their *belief in their own capacity* to deal with such a question (e.g., Joseph may have long labelled himself as 'no good at writing stories');

d   their *trust in the environment* (I would hope that, despite his difficulties, Joseph would feel safe in your class and would have trust in you as his teacher); and

e   their *concept of themselves* (Joseph may well have a low self-image, not only as a story writer, but as a learner, and even as a person).

Let's go into this idea of motivation in a bit more detail. As you can see in my model, we could use another 'formula' to show what makes up motivation:

Motivation = Goals × Emotions × Personal agency beliefs

Goals

Much of our behaviour is governed by our goals, i.e., what we consider to be desired (positive) and undesired (negative) future outcomes.[5] These goals might be conscious or unconscious, vague or precise, general or specific, and short-term or long-term.

An important distinction can be made between task-focused and ability-focused goals, with learners tending to favour one or the other.[6]

In *task-focused goals*, learners focus on mastering tasks, increasing competence, learning for intrinsic reasons, improvement, effort and attempting difficult tasks. They believe that competence is developed through effort. They are, therefore, more likely to:

a   engage in deep cognitive processing such as thinking about how newly learned material relates to previous knowledge;

b   use more adaptive help-seeking strategies;

c   show higher levels of creativity;

d   seek challenges; and

e   show persistence in the face of obstacles.

In a *ability-focused goals*, learners focus on demonstrating their ability, outperforming others, gaining favourable judgements of their competence or avoiding failure. They generally believe that competence is inherited and fixed, especially as they approach adolescence. They are therefore more likely to:

a   use surface-level strategies such as rote memorization;
b   avoid challenge, because of the risks of failure; and
c   show negativity when confronted by obstacles.

Clearly, your aim as an educator should be to help learners to adopt task-focused goals. It is very likely that Joseph is more ability-focused than task-focused, at least in his written story work.

Emotions

Emotions are all part of the mind's ability to process information and regulate our behaviour. I am sure you will agree that we tend to remember events that are charged with emotion and that too much emotion can make us irrational and undiscriminating. I would argue, too, that all teaching elicits emotional responses in learners, whether the emotions are pleasant or unpleasant.

As an educator, your task is to ensure that you take account of the emotional states that learners bring to school each day and ensure that the learning experiences you provide are heavily weighted in favour of eliciting such *positive emotions* as satisfaction, pleasure, joy, excitement, curiosity, interest and affection.

In the case of Joseph, the task of writing a story is possibly going to elicit *negative emotions* such as discouragement, annoyance, anger, anxiety, embarrassment and shame. The way you design the lesson will play a large part in avoiding these negative emotions and replacing them with more positive ones.

Personal agency beliefs

There are two kinds of beliefs: *capability beliefs* ('Do I have the skill to meet the demands of the task?') and *context beliefs* ('Will my teacher help me to perform the task?'). These two sets of beliefs interact with each other, as shown in Table 2.1.

Clearly, your aim as an educator is to help learners have strong capability beliefs and positive context beliefs, so that they become robust learners.

Joseph, for example, is likely to have weak capability beliefs. If these are coupled with the positive context beliefs that you have engendered

Table 2.1 Intersection of context beliefs and capability beliefs

Context beliefs	Capability beliefs		
	Strong	Moderate	Weak
Positive	Robust	Modest	Fragile
Neutral	Tenacious	Vulnerable	Self-doubting
Negative	Accepting or antagonistic	Discouraged	Hopeless

in your classroom, he is still considered to be 'fragile'. Your task, then, is to encourage him to develop stronger capability beliefs, the key to which lies in him achieving success.

For a more detailed discussion of motivational factors, see **Strategy 9**.

Executive system (#5/11/13/19)

As can be seen in the model, the executive system plays a critical role in problem-solving. It is goal-oriented and it controls, edits, plans, directs and monitors our behaviour. In a word, it is responsible for our metacognition. It carries out these functions by receiving messages from our motivational headquarters (#4 and #12). In turn, the executive system can activate our motivations. It also receives information in the form of feedback provided by external sources such as educators (#10 and #18) and from our own evaluations of our behaviours (#9A and #17A). Perhaps most important of all, it directs our selection of strategies (#6/14). It also monitors and regulates our attention (although, as noted in the section on Primary memory (#3 in the model), some of this is under automatic rather than conscious control. The executive system is increasingly important as development proceeds. See **Strategy 12** for how the executive system is responsible for the self-monitoring and self-regulation of behaviour.

Strategies (#6/14)

As we shall see in **Strategy 11**, most learners develop efficient and effective cognitive skills through their life experiences, with minimal teaching of how to go about the process of learning. Others, however, don't appear to use good techniques or strategies to help them learn. They either don't know what strategies to use, or they use the wrong ones, or they don't spontaneously use strategies at all.[7] These deficiencies may compound other disabilities or they may constitute the disability itself.

Essentially, students' learning strategies result from two things:

- the development of their knowledge about their own cognitive abilities, e.g., limitations of their short-term memory, how much practice they need, how many strategies they have available; and
- the development of their ability to consciously regulate cognition by using self-regulatory strategies such as planning, checking, monitoring, testing and changing strategies. These strategies vary from task to task.

There is considerable evidence that students with learning disabilities, such as Joseph, have inefficient cognitive strategies.

Strategies may be divided into two main categories: general and specific.

General strategies

These involve you in helping learners to recognize the need to be strategic. You can do this by developing with them positive 'habits of mind', curbing impulsivity, encouraging reflection, activating and organizing prior knowledge, approaching tasks in an effective and efficient manner, making key cognitive steps more concrete, and helping them to self-regulate these processes **(Strategy 12)**.

Specific strategies

These involve using strategies that are appropriate to the particular subject or task. For detailed explanations of such approaches, see **Strategies 11**, **12** (especially the section on Meichenbaum's six-step process), **13**, **14** and **16**.

In the case of Joseph, I am assuming that this is where his main difficulties lie: he has inadequate strategies at his disposal for responding to the demands of story-writing. As I describe in **Strategy 11**, you could use a narrative story-writing strategy to guide him.[8]

Secondary memory (#7/15)

When learners are confronted with a problem, they must activate their memory to assist them to find a solution. Memory is by far the most important capacity possessed by humans and must be nurtured in all learners.

As we shall see in **Strategy 13**, there are two main kinds of secondary memory: short-term and long-term.

Short-term memory

Our short-term memory, sometimes referred to as our 'working memory', temporarily stores small amounts of information while it is being used. It stores information in either an auditory or visual form, and either in a verbal or a non-verbal form. It has been described as a 'workspace' in which material from the long-term memory (see below) is processed, rehearsed or retained for immediate use.[9] There are limitations as to how much we can hold, and for how long, in our working memory at any one time. Some experts say we are generally limited to a duration of approximately 20 seconds and to a maximum of seven items (for example, remembering a telephone number while you dial it). For some learners with special educational needs these limitations may be even greater. For example, there is evidence that learners with specific language impairment have short-term memory deficits, especially in visuo-spatial short-term memory.[10] The information in our short-term memory is quickly lost if it is not rehearsed or organized in some way.

> It may be that Joseph is even more limited in his short-term memory skills and needs some training to extend them. For example, he may forget the instructions to write about the zoo trip and limit himself to thinking about the animals he saw.

Long-term memory

In order to be used at a later time, knowledge must be stored in the long-term memory. This is sometimes referred to as the 'permanent memory' and its capacity is seemingly infinite. Here, too, as with primary memory, review and practice (**Strategy 20**) play an important role. As will be noted in **Strategy 13**, another important way of ensuring long-term memory storage is to transform input into some form of meaningful mental representation. These representations are usually quite different from the original input (e.g., the difference between remembering the exact conversation and the 'gist' of it).[11]

There is a lot of research that shows students with learning disabilities have problems remembering and therefore have a memory store that is limited in quantity and/or quality.[12] The main reason for this seems to be because they don't process information in a way that can help them to remember it. They don't seem to know how to go about remembering – what strategies to use. And when they do remember, what they recall often appears to be welded to the context in which it was first learned. In other words, 'they do not appear to make spontaneous generalizations across time, material, situations and persons as readily as other children'.[13] Closely related to all of this, the learner's executive system may not ensure that information accessed from the long-term memory meets the task demands.

> Joseph probably has some limitations in his long-term memory of zoo-related facts. For example, he may not have an idea of how animals can be classified into various groups, or if he does have this information he may lack the skills to bring it to bear in the story-writing task.

Retrieval (#8/16) and performance (9A/17A and 9B/17B)

Assuming all has gone well up to this point, the learner then has to retrieve an appropriate response, whether it be an answer to a mathematical problem, a response to a question in social studies, a physical action such as a dance routine or a gymnastic performance or, in the example we are discussing, a story about a trip to the zoo. This process largely involves the learner retrieving information from the network of facts stored in the long-term memory to the working memory. Sometimes this involves recalling particular facts; other times it requires combining facts in creative ways to come up with a response. In the case of many learners with special educational needs, this process might be inefficient and slow. They might be limited by a relatively small store of facts, or a poorly organized store. Also, they might lack a strategy for searching their long-term memory, resorting instead to guessing or to other impulsive behaviour. Or their processing speed might be quite slow.

> Given his limited store of facts about animals, Joseph's story about the zoo is likely to be limited to a simple listing of information and to be lacking in thematic organization.

External response (#10/18)

If the initial task demand was from an external source, such as a teacher, the learner then might expect some feedback (**Strategy 21**) or reinforcement (**Strategy 17**) to acknowledge his or her performance.

> Joseph's story is going to be quite limited and will pose a challenge to his teacher in deciding what feedback to give him. If it is too negative, it will further discourage him; if it is too positive, it provides no basis for improvement. Perhaps the answer is to be neutral and next time recognize the need to help Joseph to be more effective in searching his long-term memory for relevant facts, as well as helping him to build up his long-term memory store.

Internal response (#5/11/13/19)

Whether or not the task was externally or internally set, the learner will, ideally self-monitor his or her response, according to his or her personal criteria (**Strategy 12**). This will take place at the Executive System level.

Conclusion

The learning and teaching model I have outlined in this chapter draws attention to the wide range of individual differences among learners in their:

- biological structures;
- primary memories, or associations;
- goals for learning;
- confidence in themselves as learners;
- trust in their environments;
- executive systems;
- capacity to hold material in their short-term working memories;
- knowledge held in their long-term memories;
- strategies for accessing their long-term memories; and
- strategies for placing material in their long-term memories.

Fortunately, all of these elements of learning are modifiable through effective teaching and the provision of responsive learning environments. That is your challenge – and mine!

Key references

1 The model represents a synthesis of ideas drawn from a range of sources, particularly: Ames, C. (1992). 'Classrooms: goals, structures, and student motivation'. *Journal of Educational Psychology*, 84(3), 261–271; Ashman, A.F. and Conway, R.N.F. (1997). *An introduction to cognitive education: Theory and application*. London: Routledge; Borkowski, J.G., Johnston, M.B. and Reid, M.K. (1986). 'Metacognition, motivation, and the transfer of control processes'. In S.J. Ceci (ed.) *Handbook of cognitive, social, and neuropsychological aspects of learning disabilities*. Hillsdale, NJ: Lawrence Erlbaum Associates; Detterman, D.K. (1979). 'Memory in the mentally retarded'. In N.R. Ellis (ed.) *Handbook of mental deficiency, psychological theory and research* (2nd edn). Hillsdale, NJ: Lawrence Erlbaum Associates; Dockrell, J. and McShane, J. (1993). *Children's learning difficulties: A cognitive approach*. Oxford: Blackwell; and Ford, M.E. (1992). *Motivating humans*. Newbury Park, CA: Sage.
2 Ford, op. cit.
3 Coyne, M.D., Kame'enui, E.J. and Simmons, D.C. (2001). 'Prevention and intervention in beginning reading: Two complex systems'. *Learning Disabilities Research and Practice*, 16(2), 62–73.
4 This section is based mainly on Ford, op. cit. and Ford, M. (1995). 'Motivation and competence development in special and remedial education'. *Intervention in School and Clinics*, 31(2), 70–83; and Hidi, S. and Harackiewicz, J.M. (2000). 'Motivating the academically unmotivated: A critical issue for the 21st century'. *Review of Educational Research*, 70(2), 151–179.
5 Anderman, E.M. and Maehr, M.L. (1996). 'Motivation and schooling in the middle grades'. *Review of Educational Research*, 64(2), 287–309.
6 Ames, op. cit.; Dweck, C.S. (1986). 'Motivational processes affecting learning'. *American Psychologist*, 41(10), 1040–1048; and Blumenfeld, P.C. (1992). 'Classroom learning and motivation: Clarifying and expanding goal theory'. *Journal of Educational Psychology*, 84(3), 272–281.
7 Sugden, D. (1989). 'Skill generalization and children with learning difficulties'. In D. Sugden (ed.) *Cognitive approaches in special education*. London: Falmer Press.
8 Harris, K.R. and Presley, M. (1991). 'The nature of cognitive strategy instruction: Interactive strategy construction'. *Exceptional Children*, 57(5), 392–404.

9 Miyake, A. and Shah, P. (eds) (1999). *Models of working memory: Mechanisms of active maintenance and executive control*. Cambridge: Cambridge University Press.
10 Archibald, L.M.D. and Gathercole, S.E. (2006). 'Short-term and working memory in specific language impairment'. *International Journal of Language and Communication Disorders*, 41(6), 675–693.
11 Dockrell and McShane, op. cit., p. 73.
12 Swanson, H.L. (1988). 'Memory subtypes in learning disabled readers'. *Learning Disability Quarterly*, 11(4), 342–357.
13 Sugden, op. cit., p. 85.

Chapter 3

Strategy 1: Inclusive education

'Adapt the mainstream to suit all learners'

Rating

★★★☆

 ## The strategy

At its most basic, inclusive education means educating learners with special educational needs in regular education settings. As we shall see in this chapter, however, it means much more than mere placement. Rather, it means putting in place a whole suite of provisions, including adapted curriculum, adapted teaching methods, modified assessment techniques and accessibility arrangements, all of which require support for the educator at the classroom level. In short, inclusive education is a multi-component strategy or, perhaps, a mega-strategy.

Inclusive education is to be distinguished from *integration*, which I define as locating learners with special educational needs part-time in regular classes. Inclusive education is sometimes referred to as *mainstreaming*, although this term is falling out of favour.

 ## The underlying idea

The idea of inclusive education reflects two, possibly three, main factors. First, if it is handled appropriately, learners with special educational needs will gain academically and socially and will improve their self-esteem. Further, other learners will gain academically, as well as an appreciation of the diversity of their society, a greater recognition of social justice and equality, and a more caring attitude. Second, it is now generally accepted in most countries that learners with special educational needs have a right to be educated alongside their peers who do not have special needs. A third argument is sometimes put forward: that inclusive education is more economically viable, given the expense involved in transporting and accommodating learners in special schools, especially in rural areas.

There are several significant events in the evolution of the idea of inclusive education. One of the first expressions of the philosophy occurred nearly 40 years ago when Scandinavian countries began referring to the principle of 'normalization'. This was defined as the process of making available to disabled persons 'patterns of life and conditions of everyday living which are as close as possible to the regular circumstances and ways of life of society'.[1]

A second set of events that gave impetus to inclusion occurred in the USA in the 1960s and 1970s, first with the civil rights movement with its focus on racial equality and, second, with the passage of the Education of All Handicapped Children Act in 1975. This Act included the requirement that handicapped children be educated in the 'least restrictive environment'.

The third event took place in June 1994 when representatives of 92 governments and 25 international organizations met in Salamanca, Spain.[2] The resulting agreement, known as the *Salamanca Statement*, demonstrates an international commitment to inclusive education. It included these agreements:

- 'those with special educational needs must have access to regular schools which should accommodate them within a child-centred pedagogy capable of meeting these needs'; and
- 'regular schools with this inclusive orientation are the most effective means of combating discriminatory attitudes, creating welcoming communities, building an inclusive society and achieving an education for all; moreover, they provide an effective education to the majority of children and improve the efficiency and ultimately the cost-effectiveness of the entire education system'.

The Statement called upon all governments to 'adopt as a matter of law or policy the principle of inclusive education, enrolling all children in regular schools, unless there are compelling reasons for doing otherwise'.

More recently, in December 2006, the 61st session of the United Nations General Assembly confirmed a Convention on the Rights of Disabled Persons, which included a significant commitment to inclusive education.[3]

While many countries are moving towards accepting the philosophy of inclusive education, there are major obstacles to its implementation, as I have recently observed in Asia and South Africa, for example.[4] These include such factors as large classes, negative attitudes to disability, examination-oriented education systems, a lack of support services, rigid teaching methods, assessment dominated by a medical model, a lack of parent involvement and, in some countries, a lack of clear national policies.

 The practice

I believe that the success of inclusive education depends upon it being viewed as part of a system that extends from the classroom to the broader society. Its success depends on what goes on day-to-day, minute-by-minute in classrooms and playgrounds. It depends on the skills of educators at the school level who, in turn, depend on the leadership of the educational administrators at the national, state/provincial and district levels. Ultimately, it depends on the vision of legislators to pass the necessary laws and provide the appropriate resources. In this book my focus is on the role of educators.

Although the central feature of inclusive education is the placement of learners with special educational needs in age-appropriate regular classrooms in the learner's neighbourhood school, it goes far beyond this. In my lectures on inclusive education in many countries, I use the following 'formula' to describe what is involved:

Inclusive Education = V + P + 5As + S + R + L
where: V = Vision; P = Placement; 5As = Adapted Curriculum, Adapted Assessment, Adapted Teaching, Acceptance, Access; S = Support; R = Resources; L = Leadership.

For inclusive education to be successful, I believe that all of these elements must be present. I am sure that you will have noticed that these elements define quality education for *all* learners. This is not surprising for, as I noted in the introduction, as well as requiring some specialized strategies, learners with special educational needs simply require good teaching, provided it is adapted to take account of their cognitive, emotional and social capabilities. In a way, inclusive education is like a Trojan horse: it has the potential to change the education not only for learners with disabilities, but also for all learners.

Let us take each of the above elements in turn.

 ## Vision

Inclusive education requires a commitment on the part of educators at all levels of the system to its underlying philosophy and a willingness to implement it.

 ## Placement

As I mentioned earlier, placement in an age-appropriate classroom in the learner's neighbourhood school is a necessary (but not sufficient) requirement for inclusive education. It goes further than that, however, for it is important that learners with special educational needs in regular classrooms are not then placed in ability-based groups for all their activities, thus creating a form of within-class segregation. Rather, I advocate that such learners be involved in a flexible mix of whole-class instruction, mixed-ability groups and ability groups, with some individual attention if possible.

Adapted curriculum

Making appropriate adaptations or modifications to the curriculum is central to inclusive education and is probably the biggest challenge educators face in creating inclusive classrooms.

The curriculum in an inclusive classroom has the following features:

- It is a single curriculum that is, as far as possible, accessible to *all* learners, including those with special educational needs. (Conversely, special educational needs are created when a curriculum is not accessible to all learners.)
- It includes activities that are age-appropriate, but are pitched at a developmentally appropriate level.
- Within your inclusive classroom, it is likely that you will have learners who are functioning at two or three levels of the curriculum. This means that you will have to use multi-level teaching or, at a minimum, make adaptations to take account of the diversity within your classroom.
- To make the curriculum accessible, consider the following alternatives in relation to content, teaching materials and the responses expected from the learners:
  - *modification*: e.g., computer responses instead of oral responses;
  - *substitution*: e.g., braille for written materials;
  - *omission*: e.g., omitting very complex work;
  - *compensation*: e.g., self-care skills, vocational skills.[5]

Let me give you an example of curriculum differentiation that I noted recently in South Africa. There, a 'curriculum ladder' is used to indicate how to adapt work according to the strengths and needs of individual learners. In spelling, for example:

- in step 1 educators ascertain if learners can work at the same level as their peers;
- in step 2 the learners may be able to do the same activity but with adapted expectations (e.g., fewer words);
- in step 3 they may be able to do the same activity but with adapted expectations and materials (e.g., matching words to pictures);
- in step 4 they may be able to do a similar activity but with adapted expectations (e.g., using words that are functional to the learners' environment);
- in step 5 they may be able to do a similar activity but with adapted materials (e.g., using a computer spelling program);
- in step 6 they may be able to do a different, parallel activity (e.g., learning a computer program with a spell check);
- in step 7 they may be able to carry out a practical and functional activity with assistance (e.g., playing with a word puzzle, flash cards etc., possibly assisted by a peer or a teaching assistant).[6]

Adapted assessment

On one side of the coin is the curriculum; on the other side is assessment.

Assessment is not simply a tool for sorting or selecting which learners should have opportunities to continue their education. Nor is it primarily a means of ranking learners by imposing a set of norms over them. When assessment is used for selection or ranking it is inevitable that learners with special educational needs will fare the worst, thus stigmatizing them as 'failures' and de-motivating them. Assessment is increasingly seen as serving educational purposes by promoting learning and guiding teaching (**Strategy 21**). In other words, it should be as much 'assessment *for* learning' as 'assessment *of* learning'. It should provide the best possible account of what a learner knows, can do or has experienced.

In an inclusive classroom, assessment should meet the following criteria:

- It should assist you to adapt the curriculum and your teaching methods to all learners. In other words, when it shows that learners have not mastered a particular task, it should allow you to diagnose why this occurred and then to re-design learning opportunities. This is referred to as the *formative* purpose of assessment (**Strategy 21**).
- It should provide feedback to learners and parents.
- It should focus on identifying what has or has not been achieved (i.e., *criterion-referenced assessment*), rather than putting learners in some sort of order of merit (i.e., *norm-referenced assessment*). In relation to this point, I believe that at various points in their education, all students should have the opportunity to obtain a recognized statement or certificate which clearly describes what they have studied and what they have achieved.
- Methods of assessment of learners with special educational needs should take account of their particular disabilities (e.g., a blind learner might need to be tested orally or in Braille, a deaf learner might need to be tested via sign language and a learner with a learning disability might require more time in an exam).
- Assessment of learners with special educational needs should result in individual education plans (IEPs). These IEPs should be regularly reviewed (e.g., every six months) and should involve the child's parents, educators and specialists. An IEP does not require that a learner be given individual teaching. Rather, it means that an educator is always aware of the individual needs of the learner.

 Adapted teaching

Inclusive education challenges educators to develop a wide repertoire of teaching strategies. These, of course, are the focus of this book and I will not discuss them in any detail at this point, except to emphasize the important role of cooperative group teaching (**Strategy 2**), peer tutoring (**Strategy 3**) and classroom climate (**Strategy 9**). I single out the first two because of the role they can play in enabling you to differentiate the curriculum, and the third because of the importance of creating an atmosphere of respect and challenge for all learners.

In addition to the strategies I present in this book, the literature is replete with suggestions, which I will summarize below. These suggestions are drawn from a range of sources, especially the literature on effective teaching,[7] educational psychology research on 'empirically supported interventions'[8] and inclusive education.[9]

- You consciously *reflect on your teaching* and its classroom outcomes, show a willingness to be self-critical and continuously seek ways to modify your practices where this is indicated.
- You *fully consider learners' cultural and language backgrounds* in planning and delivering your teaching. You look at the ways in which different cultures are (or are not) represented in your curricular materials. You ensure that textbooks avoid such common biases as invisibility (groups either neglected or under-represented), stereotyping (traditional or rigid roles assigned to particular cultures) and linguistic bias (e.g., the use of only names of the dominant culture).
- You are *authoritative* (not authoritarian). You convey authority through your behaviour: what you say, how you say it (through your voice's tone, pitch and volume) and your body language. You manage learners' behaviour with methods that are not too harsh or too weak. You don't take yourself too seriously and have the capacity to see the humorous side of things. Striking the right balance between firmness and permissiveness for individual learners with behavioural difficulties is one of the major challenges in working with such students. Given that their behaviour often fluctuates, it is important that you understand their 'signals', particularly the early warning signs of disruptive behaviour.
- You focus on *managing learning*, rather than on managing behaviour. In other words, you create learning conditions that enable learning to take place, rather than concentrating on controlling students' negative behaviours. This is a very important principle for students with special educational needs, particularly those with behaviour difficulties. With such students, there is a danger of over-emphasizing conformity and control and focusing more on eliminating undesirable behaviours than on them learning behaviours that are more appropriate.
- You require learners to *complete tasks*. In order to achieve the objectives you have set and to engender learners' sense of accomplishment, you ensure they always complete assigned tasks. Students with learning or

behavioural difficulties are particularly at risk for developing a sense of failure and helplessness because they rarely complete tasks. Some even develop sophisticated methods for avoiding doing so. Consequently, they have nothing to show their parents or friends or that they can look at and say, 'I did this!'. You can help by ensuring that tasks are within the capacity of all learners, adjusting the lesson pace and allowing additional time to complete assignments. 'Non-completers' are guided carefully through all stages of the process, particularly the final ones.

• You develop *positive self-beliefs* in your students. You do this by encouraging and ensuring success. You draw learners' attention to evidence of their progress and you recognize their achievements. Students with special educational needs are, almost by definition, at risk for negative self-concepts. It is, therefore, imperative that they be helped to achieve success and to avoid the failure cycle. In general, success rates should be 75–80 per cent.[10] Success should not be narrowly defined as academic accomplishment, but should also include effort, persistence, integrity and relational factors. The best antidote to students developing behaviour disorders is to ensure that they succeed academically and socially.

• You *communicate clearly and accurately* in both your spoken and written language. You adjust to the communication competencies of students with special educational needs, taking particular care to appropriately use available technology (**Strategies 22** and **23**).

• You take account of *learners' prior knowledge*. You recognize that learners are more likely to understand and recall knowledge when they can link it to their prior knowledge. You are aware, however, that some learners' prior knowledge contains significant misconceptions or misunderstandings, which must be taken into account if the learning that takes place in classroom experiences is not to be undermined.

• You *gain and maintain learners' attention*. A rule of thumb is that learners' attention to you or to tasks during seatwork is maintained at 80–85 per cent or higher. Gaining silence before speaking, and maintaining a brisk – but appropriate – pace during a lesson is important for obtaining and maintaining attention (**Strategy 24**). Students with learning or behavioural difficulties may fall a long way below this target. Their actual levels could be ascertained by carrying out systematic observations – perhaps using a colleague or student teacher. You could then evaluate the effectiveness of your teaching and how you might increase these levels. Remember, though, that attention has to be deserved rather than demanded.

• You *actively involve* students in their learning. Students with learning difficulties frequently respond best when they have a chance to learn through all of their senses, with practical activities, as well as 'chalk and talk'.

✴ Acceptance

Inclusive education relies on educators, learners and their parents accepting the right of learners with special educational needs to be educated in general education classrooms and to receive equitable resourcing. In my personal experience in New Zealand and other countries, I have found such acceptance to be widespread, but not universal. I have also found that the main factor that brings about shifts towards positive attitudes is the face-to-face, day-by-day contact with learners with special educational needs. As an educator, you play a very important role in modelling accepting attitudes through your behaviour, particularly as you deal with any challenging events that might arise as your students learn to deal with diversity.

✴ Access

For learners with physical disabilities to be included, adequate access to classrooms must be provided. This means the provision of such features as ramps and lifts, adapted toilets, doorways that are sufficiently wide to take wheelchairs, and adequate space for wheelchairs to be manoeuvred in classrooms.

✴ Support

Inclusive education requires support from a team of professionals. Ideally, this team would consist of: (a) a general educator, receiving advice and guidance from (b) a specialist adviser (referred to as SENCOs in some countries, such as the UK, and as RTLBs in New Zealand, etc.), access to (c) appropriate therapists and other professionals (e.g., psychologists, hearing advisers, social workers, physiotherapists, speech and language therapists, and occupational therapists) and (d) assistant teachers (referred to as paraprofessionals, learning support assistants or teacher aides in some countries). The composition of such teams would vary according to the needs of the particular learners in the inclusive classroom. I realize that, in the case of scarce resources, this ideal might not be possible to accomplish and that you might have to make the best of what can be afforded.

Inclusive education also requires active support from parents/caregivers (**Strategy 5**).

Thus, as an educator working in an inclusive classroom, you will need to acquire teamwork skills. These include respect for the contributions that other people can make, openness to new ways of looking at teaching learners with special educational needs (indeed, *all* learners) and being prepared to explain and justify your own ideas (**Strategy 4**).

Resources

Clearly, inclusive education requires high levels of resourcing. I believe, though, that it requires no more resources than would be available to support a learner with special educational needs in a special school. In other words, what is required is a redistribution of resources, as is taking place in many countries that have developed the policy of 'resources following the learner'.

Leadership

To bring all of the above elements together, leadership is required at all levels: government, national education departments or ministries, provincial or state departments, districts, school principals and classroom teachers. All should be able to explain the underlying philosophy and show by their actions that they are committed to its successful implementation. School principals, along with teachers, have a responsibility to develop an inclusive culture in their schools (see **Strategy 6**).

The evidence

There is a considerable, almost bewildering, body of research that addresses the question of how inclusion impacts on the achievements of learners with and without special educational needs. In interpreting these studies, several cautions must be taken into account. These include the following: (a) some of the earlier studies may not be relevant to current conditions, (b) many of the studies compare placements only and do not 'drill down' into the nature of the educational programmes the learners received, (c) many studies are methodologically flawed and, of course, (d) all studies are specific to the context in which they were conducted.

In general, studies have come up with mixed results, the majority reporting either positive effects or no differences for inclusion. (Some would argue that if there are no differences, this is also an argument for inclusion: why have segregated education programmes when they are no better than placement in regular classes?) The following is a representative sample of research carried out in this area.[11]

Positive findings

✓ In an early meta-analysis, 11 empirical studies carried out between 1975 and 1984 were analysed. It was shown that mainstreamed disabled students **(mentally retarded, learning disabled, hearing impaired** and **mixed exceptionalities)*** consistently outperformed non-mainstreamed students

---

* Please note that throughout this book I use the original terminology employed by the authors.

with comparable special education classifications. Two types of main-streaming were included: part-time with occasional pull-out resource class attendance, and full-time inclusion in general classes. Of the 115 effect sizes calculated, two-thirds indicated an overall positive effect of mainstreaming. The overall effect size was 0.33, which translates into a gain of 13 percentiles for students in mainstreamed settings.[12]

✓   A Canadian study of third-grade learners with 'at-risk' characteristics (e.g., **learning disabilities, behaviour disorders**) compared the impact on achievement of a multi-faceted inclusive education programme. The intervention group (N = 34) received all instruction and support in general education classrooms, while the comparison group (N = 38) received 'pull-out' resource room support. The intervention group also received a programme that included collaborative consultation (**Strategy 4**), cooperative teaching (**Strategy 2**), parent involvement (**Strategy 5**) and adapted instruction in reading, writing and mathematics. The comparison group continued using general education teaching methods characterized by whole-class instruction and minimal cooperation between the general and special teachers. Significant effects were found in the writing scores for the inclusive education group. The **general education learners** were not held back by the presence of the at-risk students in the classroom; on the contrary, their reading and mathematics scores benefited from the additional interventions offered by the programme.[13]

✓   A US study addressed the effects of an inclusive school programme on the academic achievement of learners with **mild or severe learning disabilities** in grades two to six. The experimental group comprised 71 learning-disabled students from three inclusive education classrooms. In these classrooms special education teachers worked collaboratively with general education teachers, each learner's programme was built upon the general education curriculum and instructional assistants were used to support the learners with special educational needs. The control group of 73 learning-disabled students were in classrooms which were to become part of the inclusive programme, but in which the students received traditional resource class programmes. Results showed that the students with mild learning disabilities in the inclusive classrooms made significantly more progress in reading and comparable progress in mathematics, compared with those in the resource classes. Students with severe learning disabilities made comparable progress in reading and mathematics in both settings.[14]

✓   In a study carried out in Hawaii, the effects of placement in general education classrooms or in self-contained special education classrooms on the social relationships of learners with **severe disabilities** were reported. Nine matched learners were studied in each of the two placements. The results showed that the learners who were placed in the general education classrooms had higher levels of contact with non-disabled peers, received and provided higher levels of social support and had much larger friendship networks.[15]

✓ In another US study of the effects of inclusion on learners with **severe disabilities**, 40 students in two groups were assessed across two years of inclusive versus self-contained programmes. The inclusive group were found to have made significant gains on a developmental measure and in social competence compared with the segregated group.[16]

✓ A recent Dutch study reported on the differences in academic and psychosocial development of **at-risk** pupils in special and mainstream education. It was found that pupils in special education classes did less well in academic performances and that these differences increased as the pupils got older. In psychosocial development, variables such as social behaviour and attitudes to work also favoured pupils in regular classes.[17]

✓ A UK study compared the outcomes for adolescents with **Down syndrome** of similar abilities but educated in mainstream or in special schools. The results showed no evidence of educational benefits for those in segregated settings, despite the higher teacher–learner ratios. Those who attended their neighbourhood mainstream schools made significant gains (2–3 years) over their special school peers in expressive language and in academic achievement.[18]

✓ A 2004 study in England showed that the presence of relatively large numbers of learners with special educational needs (not analysed by category) in ordinary schools did not have a negative impact on the achievement of **general education learners** at the local education authority level. Rather, attainment seemed to be largely independent of levels of inclusive education. Other factors, such as socioeconomic status, gender, ethnicity and language, seemed to be much more significant. Furthermore, the researchers found evidence that learners with special educational needs were making good progress academically, personally and socially. They also found some evidence (chiefly in the views of teachers and pupils) that inclusion can have positive effects on the wider achievements of all learners, such as on their social skills and understanding. On the other hand, they also found some indications that having special educational needs might be a risk factor for isolation and for low self-esteem.[19]

✓ A recent English study produced similar results, finding no evidence that the presence of higher proportions of learners with special educational needs (also not analysed by category) in secondary schools lowers the performance of **general education learners**. Indeed, as with the previous study, many educators in those schools believed that the inclusive education strategies used actually contributed to improved overall educational achievement.[20]

✓ The impact of inclusion on the achievement of **general education** elementary school students was also investigated in a US study. Two groups were studied: 35 learners whose classes included five students with learning disabilities, and 108 who had no classmates with special educational needs. Measures of academic achievement were taken over a three-year period at three points: pre-inclusion, inclusion and post-inclusion. The researchers found no significant differences between the two groups of learners on basic skills of language arts, reading and mathematics. Certainly, there was no evidence of any decline in the academic or behavioural performances of learners in the inclusive setting.[21]

✓   A recent South African study used the British *Index for Inclusion* as the basis for implementing inclusion in three schools. Four themes were found to be the critical components: an inclusive school philosophy; democratic leadership, structures, processes and values; addressing learner diversity and behaviour; and resourcing.[22]

Mixed findings

✓   In one of the earliest meta-analyses, 50 studies compared general (i.e., inclusive) and special class placements. It was found that placement in general classes resulted in better outcomes for learners **with mild mental retardation**, but poorer outcomes for students with **learning disabilities** or **behavioural/emotional problems**.[23]

✓   A comprehensive review of inclusion research involving learners with **autism** also reported mixed results. In one set of studies, those who were fully included: (a) displayed higher levels of engagement and social interaction, (b) gave and received higher levels of social support and (c) had larger friendship networks. This was counterbalanced, however, by another study that found that these learners were more frequently on the receiving, rather than the giving, end of social interactions. The review also described a study in which the effect of inclusive education, compared with segregated education, on the language ability of autistic learners was evaluated. The fact that there were no differences between the two placements was interpreted as supporting inclusion, since segregated placements were shown to be of no benefit.[24]

✓   Several studies have found that quality of instruction, rather than placement, is the most important predictor of learner achievement. For example, in one study of mathematics achievement of students with **hearing impairments**, placement in regular or special classes did not seem to impact on achievement. Rather, specific features of quality placement included a supportive teacher, regular and extensive reviews of material, direct instruction and a positive classroom environment.[25]

Negative views

Inclusive education is not without its critics, most of whom argue that: (a) the evidence is insufficient to justify it, (b) it is supported purely on ideological grounds, with accompanying rhetoric, (c) it exaggerates the capacity of regular schools to provide quality education for learners with special educational needs and (d) that it is not feasible for all categories of disabilities all of the time (e.g., learners with **severe learning disabilities, profound deafness**).[26] I do not have the space to examine these arguments in any detail, except to say that while they express legitimate concerns, I believe that inclusive education *that meets the criteria I outline here* is justified both philosophically and empirically.

 ## Addressing risks

There are two risks that should be attended to:

- The major risk associated with inclusive education is that it is implemented only in a partial form. As I emphasized above, for it to succeed, inclusive education goes well beyond placing a learner with special educational needs in a general education classroom and hoping for the best.
- A second risk is that it may be implemented without asking what is the best education that this particular learner with special educational needs can receive at this time and in this place? Ultimately, we must be concerned with providing an education that ensures the best quality of life for all learners. While I believe that inclusive education holds out the best promise in general, I recognize that in some limited circumstances it might not be the best alternative.

 ## Conclusion

Inclusive education is a complex and controversial approach to educating learners with special educational needs. If it is properly implemented, it can bring about academic and social benefits to all learners.

 ## Further reading

Ainscow, M., Booth, T. and Dyson, A. (2006). *Improving schools, developing inclusion.* Abingdon: Routledge.

Andrews, J. and Lupart, J. (2000). *The inclusive classroom: Educating exceptional children.* University of Calgary: Nelson Thomson Learning.

Booth, T., Ainscow, M., Black-Hawkins, K., Vaughan, M. and Shaw, L. (2000). *Index for inclusion.* Bristol: Centre for Studies on Inclusive Education.

Dyson, D.A., Farrell, P., Polat, F. and Hutcheson, G. (2004). *Inclusion and pupil achievement.* Research Report No. RR578. London: DfES.

Karten, T.J. (2005). *Inclusion strategies that work! Research-based methods for the classroom.* Thousand Oaks, CA: Corwin Press.

McGregor, G. and Vogelsberg, T. (1998). *Inclusive schooling practices: Pedagogical and research foundations: A synthesis of the literature that informs best practices about inclusive schooling.* Baltimore, MD: Brookes

Mitchell, D. (ed.) (2005). *Contextualizing inclusive education: Evaluating old and new international perspectives.* Abingdon: Routledge.

Renaissance Group. *Inclusion.* Online. www.uni.edu/coe/inclusion/ (accessed 1 October 2006).

UNESCO (2001a). *Understanding and responding to children's needs in the inclusive classroom: A guide for teachers.* Paris: UNESCO.

UNESCO (2001b). *Open file on inclusive education: Support materials for managers and administrators.* Paris: UNESCO.

Wade, S. (ed.) (2000). *Inclusive education: A casebook and readings for prospective and practicing teachers.* Mahwah, NJ: Lawrence Erlbaum Associates.

Key references

1 Nirje, B. (1969). 'The normalization principle and its human management implications'. In R. Kugel and W. Wolfensberger (eds) *Changing patterns in residential services for the mentally retarded.* Washington, DC: President's Committee on Mental Retardation.

2 UNESCO (1994). *The Salamanca Statement and Framework for Action on Special Needs Education.* Paris: UNESCO.

3 The full text of Article 24 includes the following:
1. States Parties recognize the right of persons with disabilities to education. With a view to realizing this right without discrimination and on the basis of equal opportunity, States Parties shall ensure an inclusive education system at all levels, and life-long learning, directed to:
   (a) The full development of the human potential and sense of dignity and self worth, and the strengthening of respect for human rights, fundamental freedoms and human diversity;
   (b) The development by persons with disabilities of their personality, talents and creativity, as well as their mental and physical abilities, to their fullest potential;
   (c) Enabling persons with disabilities to participate effectively in a free society.
2. In realizing this right, States Parties shall ensure that:
   (a) Persons with disabilities are not excluded from the general education system on the basis of disability, and that children with disabilities are not excluded from free and compulsory primary education, or from secondary education, on the basis of disability;
   (b) Persons with disabilities can access an inclusive, quality, free primary education and secondary education on an equal basis with others in the communities in which they live;
   (c) Reasonable accommodation of the individual's requirements is provided;
   (d) Persons with disabilities receive the support required, within the general education system, to facilitate their effective education;
   (e) Effective individualized support measures are provided in environments that maximize academic and social development, consistent with the goal of full inclusion.

4 Mitchell, D.R. and Chen, Y. (1996). 'Special education in Asia'. In R. Brown, A. Neufeld and D. Baine (eds) *Beyond basic care: Special education and community rehabilitation in low-income countries* (pp. 8–42). North York, ONT: Captus Press.

5 Jönsson, T. (1993). *Toward an inclusive school.* Geneva: UNDP.
6 Department of Education (2005). *Guidelines for inclusive learning programmes.* Pretoria: Education Department, Republic of South Africa.
7 For example, Ramsay, P. and Oliver, D. (1995). 'Capacities and behaviour of quality teachers'. *School Effectiveness and School Improvement,* 6(4), 332–336; Reynolds, D., Bollen, R., Creemers, B., Hopkins, D., Stoll, L. and Lagerweij, N. (eds) *Making good schools: Linking school effectiveness and school improvement.* London: Routledge; Rouse, M. and Florian, L. (1996). 'Effective inclusive schools: A study in two countries'. *Cambridge Journal of Education,* 26(1), 71–85; Scott, B.J., Vitale, M.R. and Mastern, W.G. (1998). 'Implementing instructional adaptations for students with disabilities in inclusive classrooms: A literature review'. *Remedial and Special Education,* 19(2), 106–119; Stanovich, P.J. and Jordan, A. (1998). 'Canadian teachers' and principals' beliefs about inclusive education as predictors of effective teaching in heterogeneous classrooms'. *The Elementary School Journal,* 98(3), 221–238; and Englert, C.S., Tarrant, K.L. and Mariage, T.V. (1992). 'Defining and redefining instructional practices in special education: Perspectives on good teaching'. *Teacher Education and Special Education,* 5(2), 62–86.
8 For example, McIntosh, D.E., Rizza, M.G. and Bliss, L. (2000). 'Implementing empirically supported interventions: Teacher-child interaction therapy'. *Psychology in the Schools,* 37(5), 453–462.
9 For a synthesis, see Mitchell, D. (2000). 'Criteria of effective teaching in inclusive classrooms: A New Zealand study'. Paper presented at Special Education World Congress, Vancouver, Canada; see also Ainscow, M. (1999). *Understanding the development of inclusive schools.* London: Falmer Press.
10 Brophy, J.E. and Good, T.L. (1986). 'Teacher behavior and student achievement'. In M.C. Wittrock (ed.) *Handbook of research on teaching.* 3rd edn. New York: Macmillan.
11 For recent comprehensive reviews of the literature, see Katz, J. and Mirenda, P. (2002). 'Including students with developmental disabilities in general education classrooms: social benefits'. *International Journal of Special Education,* 17(2), 25–35; Katz, J. and Mirenda, P. (2002). 'Including students with developmental disabilities in general education classrooms: educational benefits'. *International Journal of Special Education,* 17(2), 14–24; Nakken, H. and Pijl, S.J. (2002). 'Getting along with classmates in regular schools: a review of the effects of integration on the development of social relationships'. *International Journal of Inclusive Education,* 6(1), 47–61; and Salend, S.J. and Duhaney, L.M.G. (1999). 'The impact of inclusion on students with and without disabilities and their educators'. *Remedial and Special Education,* 20(2), 114–126.
12 Wang, M.C. and Baker, E.T. (1986). 'Mainstreaming programs: Design features and effects'. *Journal of Special Education,* 19, 503–526.
13 Saint-Laurent, L., Dionne, J., Giasson, J., Royer, E., Simard, C. and Pierard, B. (1998). 'Academic achievement effects of an in-class service model on students with and without disabilities'. *Exceptional Children,* 64(2), 239–253.
14 Waldron, N.L. and McLeskey, J. (1998). 'The effects of an inclusive school program on students with mild and severe learning disabilities'. *Exceptional Children,* 64(4), 395–405.
15 Fryxell, D. and Kennedy, C. (1995). 'Placement along a continuum of services and its impact on students' social relationships'. *Journal of the Association for Persons with Severe Handicaps,* 20(4), 259–269.
16 Fisher, M. and Meyer, L.H. (2002). 'Development and social competence after two years for students enrolled in inclusive and self-contained educational

programs'. *Research and Practice for Persons with Severe Disabilities*, 27(3), 165–174.

17 Karsten, S., Peetsma, T., Roeleveld, J. and Vergeer, M. (2001). 'The Dutch policy of integration put to the test: Differences in academic and psychosocial development of pupils in special and mainstream education'. *European Journal of Special Needs Education*, 16(3), 193–205.

18 Buckley, S. (2006). 'Reflections on twenty years of scientific research'. Portsmouth: The Down Syndrome Educational Trust. http://downsed.org/research/history/20 years/ (accessed 20 September 2006).

19 Dyson, D.A., Farrell, P., Polat, F. and Hutcheson, G. (2004). *Inclusion and pupil achievement*. Research Report No. RR578. London: DfES.

20 Rouse, M. and Florian, L. (2006). 'Inclusion and achievement: student achievement in secondary schools with higher and lower proportions of pupils designated as having special educational needs'. *International Journal of Inclusive Education*, 10(6), 481–493.

21 Sharpe, M.N., York, J.L. and Knight, J. (1994). 'Effects of inclusion on the academic performance of classmates without disabilities: A preliminary study'. *Remedial and Special Education*, 15(5), 281–287.

22 Engelbrecht, P., Oswald, M. and Forlin, C. (2006). 'Promoting the implementation of inclusive education in primary schools in South Africa'. *British Journal of Special Education*, 33(3), 121–129.

23 Carlberg, C. and Kavale, K. (1980). 'The efficacy of special versus regular class placement for exceptional children: A meta-analysis'. *Journal of Special Education*, 14(3), 295–309.

24 Harrower, J.K. and Dunlap, G. (2001). 'Including children with autism in general education classrooms: A review of effective strategies'. *Behavior Modification*, 25(5), 762–784.

25 Kluwin, T.N. and Moores, D.F. (1989). 'Mathematics achievement of hearing impaired adolescents in different placements'. *Exceptional Children*, 55(4), 327–335.

26 See, for example, Sasso, G.M. (2001). 'The retreat from inquiry and knowledge in special education'. *The Journal of Special Education*, 34(4), 178–193; and Kavale, K.A. and Mostert, M.P. (2003). 'River of ideology, islands of evidence'. *Exceptionality*, 11(4), 191–208.

Chapter 4

Strategy 2: Cooperative group teaching

'Help learners to learn from each other'

Rating

★★★☆

 The strategy

Effective teachers use a mix of whole-class, group and individual activities. Cooperative group teaching (sometimes referred to as *cooperative learning*) involves learners working together in small learning groups, helping each other to carry out individual and group tasks. It is a particularly effective strategy for teaching learners with special educational needs, especially in mixed-ability groups.

When learners work without your constant direction and support, you can be freed to spend more time with small groups and individuals. However, this does not mean complete freedom for them to do as they wish. Nor does it mean putting learners together and then expecting or allowing them to work as individuals. Rather, it requires you to guide and monitor them on ways of working together. In cooperative group teaching, learners are expected to work *as groups*, not just *in groups*.

Cooperative group teaching is, of course, one of the most cost-effective strategies. If you have large classes (as is the case in many developing countries), it can be a major strategy for helping your students to learn. Using cooperative group teaching is a bit like creating small classes out of big ones and creating many teachers instead of one.

This strategy relates to the context component of the learning and teaching model I describe in Chapter 2.

 The underlying idea

According to leaders in cooperative learning, this strategy has four essential components:

- *interdependence*: all group members seek to achieve a group goal and help each others' achievement;
- *individual accountability*: each member of the group is held responsible for his or her own learning, which in turn contributes to the group goal;
- *cooperation*: the learners discuss, problem-solve and collaborate with each other;
- *evaluation*: members of the group review and evaluate how they worked together and make changes as needed.[1]

Cooperative group teaching is based on two main ideas about learning. First, it recognizes that when learners cooperate, or collaborate, it has a synergistic effect. In other words, by working together they can often achieve a result that is greater than the sum of their individual effects or capabilities. Second, it recognizes that much of our knowledge is socially constructed; that is, we learn from others in our immediate environments – our families, our friendship groups and our workplaces. Thus, cooperative group teaching is a 'natural' way of teaching and learning. Furthermore, it can influence the ethos of your class and school, or your classroom climate by developing the values of helping and caring (**Strategies 6** and **9**). Ultimately, it can contribute to making your community more cohesive and respectful of diversity.[2]

Although the strategy became widespread in education from the 1980s, it is by no means a modern idea. In Western countries it dates back at least to the time of Joseph Lancaster in his school in England in the late 1700s (see **Strategy 3: Peer Tutoring** – a close relative to cooperative group teaching – for more details).

 The practice

By far the most common form of group work that I have observed across many countries is what I refer to as *mutual assistance groups*. Essentially, this involves the more able members of a group providing support or assistance to less able learners, either in a planned way or spontaneously. Assignments are structured for completion by individual learners, who may seek or give assistance to others in the group, but there is little or no sense of a shared task or of being members of a group. While I believe that this approach has some legitimacy, you could take it further, as I will now explain.

True *cooperative group teaching* is something different. Let me explain it by using the analogy of a jigsaw puzzle, where every member has a distinct piece necessary for the completion of the puzzle. In other words, all members of the group have to participate to achieve a group goal. It requires interdependence, which can take one or more forms:

- *goal interdependence*: the group has a single goal (e.g., complete the puzzle);

- *reward interdependence*: the whole group receives acknowledgement for achieving the goal (this may be intrinsic, e.g., when the puzzle is completed, and/or extrinsic, e.g., when you praise the group for completing the puzzle);
- *resource interdependence*: each group member has different resources (knowledge or materials) that must be combined to complete a task (e.g., each member has a piece of the puzzle that fits with other members' pieces to make a whole);
- *role interdependence*: each group member is assigned a different role (e.g, leader, reporter, time-keeper).[3]

To take another example, you might be teaching a unit on the animals of Kruger Park. Here you could set groups the task of completing a mural to display on the classroom wall. Each learner, including those with special educational needs, could be assigned an animal to paint, with the group negotiating the placement of the animals and the scenery.

To summarize, cooperative group learning assumes that all learners, including those with special educational needs, have something unique to contribute. The group sinks or swims on the basis of *all* members of the group making their individual contributions.

Typically, cooperative group teaching takes place in groups of six to eight learners. In deciding on the composition of groups in your classroom, you have a choice between ability grouping and mixed-ability grouping. As I explain later in this chapter, my preference is for a combination of both types, with mixed-ability groups on most occasions. If you use ability grouping too much this runs the risk of negating inclusive education.

Your role in cooperative group teaching

To bring about successful cooperative group learning, you should attend to three main issues:

1 *Develop appropriate group tasks*. Designing activities that are suitable for all members of the group, especially those with special educational needs, is critical (see my comments on adapted curriculum in **Strategy 1**). In the case of mutual assistance groups, since you will be relying on peers to give assistance to learners with special needs, you should explain to the group how that assistance should be given. Brief 'coaching cards' would be helpful here. In the case of jigsaw activities, your challenge is to select activities that are within the competence of all members of the group.

2 *Teach group process skills*. These include such things as listening, making eye contact, communicating clearly, asking questions, providing leadership, building trust, making decisions, managing conflict, giving encouragement,

recognizing contributions, understanding other learners' points of view, and (importantly) respecting individual differences. Here role-playing can be an important way of developing group skills, giving learners various scenarios to work on.

3   *Deal effectively with any problems that arise.* Perhaps the most difficult problems that can occur in groups are the challenges of dealing with 'loners', 'dominators', aggressive or disruptive learners and passive learners. The way you deal with these behaviours in your general interactions with the class will act as a model for the other learners. Role-playing scenarios with such behaviours being the focus could be helpful, as could be the appointment of 'buddies' to work alongside particular students in the groups. Also, you should take particular care in selecting members of groups to ensure that learners with challenging behaviours can be accommodated. It is essential that you closely monitor groups where learners show behavioural difficulties and give feedback and positive reinforcement for appropriate behaviours. Explicit training in social skills may also be necessary (**Strategy 7**).

 Ability grouping vs mixed-ability grouping

There are two aspects to placing learners in ability groups: (a) ability grouping *between* classes, sometimes referred to as 'tracking' or 'streaming', and (b) ability grouping *within* classes. As you will see in the Evidence section, reliance on ability grouping is not recommended in either case for learners with special educational needs (except, perhaps, for high-achieving learners).

The literature provides a range of arguments as to why ability grouping is detrimental to low-achieving learners:

• being assigned to low-ability groups communicates low expectations to learners, which might be self-fulfilling;
• because ability groups often parallel social class and ethnic groupings, they may increase divisions along class and ethnic lines;
• between-class ability grouping reduces learners' opportunities to move between groups;
• low-achieving learners tend to receive less instruction when placed in ability groups than when placed in mixed-ability groups;
• ability groups composed of low-achieving learners do not provide a stimulating learning environment and lack positive role models.[4]

In a similar vein, another study pointed out that in US research there is evidence that low-track classes are much more likely to receive course content that focuses on below-grade level knowledge and skills than high-track classes.[5]

In reporting the results of two meta-analyses that examined the impact of ability grouping and mixed-ability grouping on student learning at the elementary and secondary school levels, a researcher summarized his findings as follows:

- use mixed-ability groups for most content areas;
- encourage learners' identification with mixed-ability groups in order to promote acceptance of diversity; and
- use ability grouping only when it will increase the efficacy of instruction or provide more time for instruction on a specific skill.[6]

 The evidence

There is a huge literature on the effects of cooperative learning on achievement and social interactions in general education, as well as in classrooms including learners with special educational needs. In the following selection of research only studies involving the latter are referred to. The evidence is divided into two sections: (a) cooperative learning and (b) ability grouping versus mixed-ability grouping.

Cooperative learning

✓ In an extensive, early study of learners with **educable mental retardation**, one of the factors associated with better outcomes was the use of cooperative learning approaches. It was found that this strategy promoted these learners' interactions with their peers.[7]

✓ A comprehensive study researched the effects of cooperative learning on the reading achievement of upper elementary students with **learning disabilities**. A total of 22 classes with 450 third- and fourth-grade learners, including those with learning disabilities, were involved in the study. Teachers in nine of the classes used an approach called Cooperative Reading and Composition (CIRC) to foster comprehension and metacognitive strategies (see **Strategy II: Cognitive Strategy Instruction**). The other 13 classes formed the controls. In the CIRC classes learners worked in heterogeneous groups on activities including partner reading, examining story structures, learning new vocabulary and re-telling stories. Significant results were reported in favour of those in CIRC classes on standardized reading and writing tests.[8]

✓ Several studies with **deaf and hard of hearing learners** have found that well-structured joint activities increase positive social interactions.[9] For example, in a US study of 30 **deaf** and 30 hearing third graders, cooperative and competitive instructional strategies were compared. The results showed that cooperation was associated with increased interactions and greater interpersonal attraction to each other for both groups of learners.[10]

✓   A US study looked at the impact of learners with **special educational needs** in cooperative learning groups on the mathematics progress of other students in elementary classrooms. The two groups that were compared on pre-tests and post-tests differed only in terms of the presence of students with special educational needs in one of the groups. The results showed that both groups significantly increased their mastery of the targeted mathematics objectives. In other words, the presence of learners with special educational needs in one of the groups made no difference to the achievement of the other learners.[11]

✓   In an interesting variation, a study investigated the effects of computer-assisted cooperative learning in mathematics instruction in classrooms for students with and without **learning disabilities**. A total of 118 third-grade elementary school learners, 25 of whom had learning disabilities, participated in the study. In the cooperative arrangement, commercial software packages were used and the learners worked at the computer in pairs and in teams. Their results were compared with learners who received whole-class instruction and worked at the computer individually. Results showed that learners in the cooperative learning groups had higher mathematics achievement scores than those in the whole-class arrangement. The outcome was an effect size of 0.34 – a good, but moderate, score.[12]

✓   An Australian study investigated the learning outcomes for 22 third-grade students with **learning difficulties** who participated in structured and unstructured group activities in a social studies unit. Those in the structured groups were taught small-group and interpersonal behaviours to promote group cooperation. Activities to be completed were broken down into smaller parts with each learner taking responsibility for completing a part as well as sharing resources and information; those in the unstructured groups did not receive this training. The results showed that the structured group provided more directions and help to other group members and obtained significantly higher performances in comprehension than the unstructured group. This was true both for learners with and without learning difficulties.[13]

Ability grouping versus mixed-ability grouping

✓   A 1993 meta-analysis of six studies reported on the impact on learners' achievement of within-class ability grouping and between-class ability grouping. The results showed a negligible overall effect size of less than 0.10, and a range of –0.03 to 0.22. In other words, ability grouping had no significant impact on learner achievement. Unfortunately, separate results were not reported for learners with special educational needs.[14]

✓   A recent Dutch review of the literature, however, did differentiate between high- and **low-achieving** learners.[15] It concluded that although the mean results of studies show higher achievement in ability groups than in mixed-ability groups, this is mainly due to the fact that high-achieving learners benefit more than low-achieving learners. The authors cite several studies where low-achieving learners performed more poorly in between-class ability groups than in mixed-ability groups.[16]

✓ Ability grouping is not an all-or-nothing idea, for it is possible to have ability groups for some subjects and mixed-ability groups for others. This arrangement is sometimes referred to as 'setting'. A UK study investigated the effects of setting in English, mathematics and science on the academic self-concepts of secondary school learners. The results showed that learners' self-concepts were higher in schools with moderate levels of setting. It was also found that the degree of setting in mathematics and science had no effect on academic self-concepts, but setting in English tended to lower the self-concepts of the higher attaining learners and raise the self-concepts of **lower attaining learners**.[17]

 Addressing risks

As far as learners with special educational needs are concerned, cooperative group teaching carries with it three main risks: within the group these learners can be ignored, actively rejected or given too much assistance. To deal with these risks, you should consider these points:

1   Take care in selecting members of groups that include learners with special educational needs (a point I also make in **Strategy 3**). You should take particular care when including learners with emotional and behaviour disorders in cooperative group learning situations. Its effectiveness with such learners is uncertain at this stage of our knowledge. Indeed, there is some evidence that many teachers who report using this strategy are not implementing it fully.[18]

2   You cannot expect that all learners in a group will respect each other or take a full part in cooperative activities. Therefore, it is important that you teach group process skills and closely monitor their use, especially in the early stages and especially with the learners with special educational needs (see above). But beware that you don't interfere too much lest you negate the idea that learners are expected to help each other. I also think that if cooperative group learning is new to you, you should gradually introduce it with easy tasks, moving to more complex tasks as groups develop skills in working cooperatively.

3   A further risk is that you may place too much reliance on cooperative group learning, at the expense of using other teaching strategies. It is but one of several strategies you should use, albeit a very important one. A

recent meta-analysis supports this point when it noted that a trio of strategies working in concert with students with learning disabilities produced the largest degree of student learning in all subjects. The three strategies were control of task difficulty, directed response questioning and the use of small interactive groups.[19]

4   Finally, you may be living in a community that expects education to be a passive activity where teachers control all learning from the front of the class and where students work silently and independently. For some schools, cooperative group learning represents a major shift in approach to education. If that is the case, you as an educator should discuss its underlying philosophy with your supervisor and your students' parents to allay any anxieties and to gain their support. Of course, you should also discuss it with your students.

 Conclusion

With some exceptions, the research evidence clearly supports the use of cooperative group learning to promote academic achievement and social development, not only for learners with special educational needs, but for all learners. It means that your work as an educator is supplemented by the skills and enthusiasms of all the learners in your class.

 Further reading

Dunne, E. and Bennett, N. (1990). *Talking and learning in groups*. London: Macmillan Educational.
Johnson, D.W. and Johnson, R.T. (1991). *Learning together and alone (3rd edition)*. Englewood Cliffs, NJ: Allyn and Bacon.

Key references

1   Johnson, D.W. and Johnson, R.T. (1991). *Learning together and alone (3rd edition)*. Englewood Cliffs, NJ: Allyn and Bacon.
2   Topping, K.J. (2005). 'Trends in peer learning'. *Educational Psychology*, 25(6), 631–645.
3   Johnson, D.W., Johnson, R.T. and Stanne, M.B. (2000). 'Cooperative learning methods: A meta-analysis'. URL: www.co-operation.org/pages/cl-methods.html (accessed 3 October 2006).
4   Houtveen, T. and Van de Grift, W. (2001). 'Inclusion and adaptive instruction in elementary education'. *Journal of Education for Students Placed at Risk*, 6(4), 389–409.
5   MacIver, D.J., Reuman, D.A. and Main, S.R. (1995). 'Social structuring of the school: Studying what is, illuminating what could be'. *Annual Review of Psychology*, 46, 375–400.
6   Slavin, R.E. (1996). *Education for all: Contexts of learning*. Lisse, France: Swets and Keitlinger.

7   Kaufman, M., Agard, T.A. and Semmel, M.I. (1985). *Mainstreaming: Learners and their environment*. Cambridge, MA: Brookline Books.
8   Stevens, R., Madden, N., Slavin, R. and Farnish, A. (1987). 'Cooperative integrated reading and composition'. *Reading Research Quarterly*, 22(4), 433–454.
9   Antia, S.D., Stinson, M.S. and Gaustad, M.G. (2002). 'Developing membership in the education of deaf and hard of hearing students in inclusive settings'. *Journal of Deaf Studies and Deaf Education*, 7(3), 214–229.
10 Johnson, D. and Johnson, R. (1986). 'Mainstreaming hearing impaired students: The effects of effort in communicating on cooperation and interpersonal attraction'. *Journal of Psychology*, 119(1), 31–44.
11 Hunt, P., Staub, D., Alwell, M. and Goetz, L. (1994). 'Achievement by all students within the context of cooperative learning groups'. *Journal of the Association for Persons with Severe Handicaps*, 19(4), 290–301.
12 Xin, J.F. (1999). 'Computer-assisted cooperative learning in integrated classrooms for students with and without disabilities'. *Information Technology in Childhood Education*, 1(1), 61–78.
13 Gillies, R.M. and Ashman, A.F. (2000). 'The effects of cooperative learning on students with learning difficulties in the lower elementary school'. *The Journal of Special Education*, 34(1), 19–27.
14 Lipsey, M.W. and Wilson, D.B. (1993). 'The efficacy of psychological, educational, and behavioral treatment: Confirmation from meta-analysis'. *American Psychologist*, 48(12), 1181–1209.
15 Houtveen and Van de Grift, op. cit.
16 For example, Gamoran, A. (1992). 'Is ability grouping equitable?: Synthesis of research'. *Educational Leadership*, 50(1), 11–17; and Hallam, S. and Touttounji, I. (1996). *What do we know about the ability grouping of pupils by ability? A research review*. London: University of London, Institute of Education.
17 Ireson, J., Hallam, S. and Plewis, I. (2001). 'Ability grouping in secondary schools: Effects on pupils' self concepts'. *British Journal of Educational Psychology*, 71(2), 315–326.
18 For a review, see Sutherland, K.S., Wehby, J.H. and Gunter, P.L. (2000). 'The effectiveness of cooperative learning with students with emotional and behavioral disorders'. *Behavioral Disorders*, 25(3), 225–238.
19 Swanson, H.L. and Hoskyn, M. (1998). 'Experimental intervention research on students with learning disabilities: A meta-analysis of treatment outcomes'. *Review of Educational Research*, 68(3), 277–321.

Chapter 5

Strategy 3: Peer tutoring

'Utilize peers to teach each other'

Rating

★★★☆

 The strategy

Peer tutoring refers to situations in which one learner (the 'tutor') provides a learning experience for another learner (the 'tutee'), under your supervision. It is sometimes referred to as *peer-mediated instruction, peer-assisted learning strategies (PALS), class-wide peer tutoring, buddying programmes, paired reading* and *peer support*. As a strategy, it is closely related to **Strategy 2: Cooperative Group Teaching**.

This strategy relates to the context component of the learning and teaching model I describe in Chapter 2.

Peer tutoring is a powerful tool for increasing the overall effectiveness of teaching in inclusive classrooms. It can be used across subject areas, not only in reading, but also in maths, science, social studies, physical education – indeed, in all curriculum areas.

Peer tutoring is best used to promote fluency through practicing or reviewing skills or knowledge, rather than as a means of initially teaching skills or knowledge. In other words, it is used as a supplement to other methods.

It can take many forms, with pairs comprising different combinations according to age and ability level. A common pattern is for a more able learner to tutor a less able learner of roughly the same age. A variant of it, which occurs when an older learner tutors a younger learner, is sometimes referred to as *cross-age tutoring*. Another variant is *class-wide peer tutoring*, in which all learners in your class would be paired and undertake the roles of both tutors and tutees. There are also differences in terms of the degree of structure involved in the tutoring.

You should also note that learners with special educational needs (usually those with mild disabilities) could gain academically and in self-esteem by acting as tutors, especially with younger learners.

The underlying idea

Peer tutoring is based on the idea that children learn a great deal from each other. It often occurs spontaneously in schools, neighbourhoods and in homes. Much human activity centres on the reciprocal relationship of giving and receiving. Also, as you will know from your own experience as an educator, and perhaps as a parent, you learn through teaching.

Peer tutoring is by no means a modern idea. For example, in the late 1700s Joseph Lancaster used it in his school in Southwark, England, when he was confronted with the task of single-handedly teaching some 350 children. Since most of his learners came from poor families that could not afford to pay fees, Lancaster introduced a 'monitorial' system, in which one teacher taught a select group of older pupils, the monitors, who, in turn, taught the rest. Also in the late eighteenth century, Andrew Bell promoted this system. He had the idea of using half of the class as tutors to the other half, with the teachers and teaching assistants being responsible for making sure the system was working.

The modern form of peer tutoring re-appeared in the USA in the 1960s when educators there recognized that it offered an economical way of providing individual attention to underachieving learners. One of the most widely researched approaches is 'class-wide peer tutoring', which was developed at the Juniper Gardens Children's Project in Kansas City, USA.[1]

Properly handled, peer tutoring brings benefits to:

- *the tutees*, by being provided with increased individual attention, work pitched at their instructional level, repeated practice, immediate feedback, peer support and additional time engaged with tasks;
- *the tutors*, who can make gains by having their own skills reinforced and expanded, as well by having their self-confidence and sensitivity to others enhanced;
- you, *the educator*, by enabling you to increase the level of cooperation in your class and by giving you more time to spend with other learners;
- *the education system*, given its cost-effectiveness.[2]

 The practice

Peer tutoring means much more than simply asking an able learner to 'Help Johnny with his reading, please'. Rather, to be successful it has to be carefully planned and sensitively supervised.

 Putting peer tutoring into practice

Here are some suggestions for putting peer tutoring into practice with a learner who has reading difficulties:

- Use a structured lesson format, with clear goals and a systematic step-by-step approach.
- Carefully select the reading material so that it is within the tutee's level of understanding.
- Train the tutor (or tutors if you are using several) in approaches to presenting the material through modelling, supporting correct answers, responding to errors and giving constructive feedback (**Strategy 21**) etc. I suggest that you demonstrate these skills to the tutors and that you provide them with cards that summarize the approach you want followed. The teaching strategy outlined in Pause, Prompt, Praise (**Strategy 24**) could be very helpful, too. In this approach, the tutor listens to the tutee as he or she reads a passage of continuous prose. When the latter makes an error, the tutor pauses for five seconds to encourage self-correction. If this does not occur, the tutor provides an appropriate prompt and then praises the tutee's correct response.[3]
- Set up tutoring sessions for a limited time period. For example: 10-minute sessions, three times per week for two weeks.
- Actively supervise the tutoring.
- Regularly assess the tutee's progress and recognize this with a certificate at the end of the tutoring.
- Recognize the tutor's help, perhaps also with a certificate at the end of the activity.

✳ *Ideas for class-wide peer tutoring*

In class-wide peer tutoring, you could try these ideas:

- Randomly assign learners into pairs, and ask them to alternate the roles of tutors and tutees. Reassign the pairs weekly.
- Arrange for the tutoring to take place in 15–20-minute sessions on three to five days per week, for, say, two weeks.
- Select self-correcting materials (e.g., flash cards with the answers available, as you might use in drill and practice activities (**Strategy 20**).
- Train and carefully supervise the learners (especially in the initial stages of implementation) to play the roles of tutors and tutees. This requires training in:
  - asking questions,
  - presenting instructional cues,
  - providing positive feedback,
  - correcting errors, and
  - keeping a record of the session.

Note: you could add an observer to each pair, with each of the three roles being rotated. The observer could assist either of the other partners to perform their roles.

- Monitor the learners' progress. In some versions of class-wide peer tutoring the pairs compete with each other, with daily point earning and public posting of performances (if you use this approach, make sure all students can experience being in a winning team).

 ## The evidence

Evidence (mainly from the USA) points to peer tutoring bringing a variety of benefits, depending on the particular approach being used:

✓ Tutees have been shown to benefit most from being tutored by older and more able tutors rather than same-age tutors.[4]

✓ A major survey conducted over 20 years ago still holds good today. After surveying 52 well-designed studies of peer tutoring (not necessarily involving learners with special needs), it was concluded it has a moderately beneficial effect on tutees' achievement, and a smaller but still significant effect on their attitudes towards subject matter. For tutors, peer tutoring had a small, but significant, effect on academic outcomes, self-concepts and attitudes towards subject matter.[5]

✓ Similarly encouraging results were reported in an analysis of ten peer-tutored paired reading projects involving learners ranging from eight to 18 years of age. On average, the tutees gained in reading age at 3.8 times the normal rate and tutors at 4.3 times.[6]

✓ In a study of the effects of peer-assisted learning strategies (PALS) on students' reading achievement in 22 US elementary and middle schools, 20 teachers implemented the programme for 15 weeks and 20 control teachers did not. It was found that all three groups of learners (**low achievers** in the PALS teaching with and without disabilities and average achievers) demonstrated greater reading progress.[7]

✓ A peer tutoring and a 'special friends' programme in a high school involved learners with **severe mental retardation, moderate mental retardation, autism and deaf/blindness.** Learners without disabilities who participated in the programme increased their social interactions with the learners with disabilities, compared with a control group who were not involved in the programme.[8]

✓ In a class-wide peer tutoring programme in a regular elementary school classroom, learners with **autism** (*and* their tutors) showed improvements in reading fluency and comprehension. As well, both groups showed increased social interactions during their free time.[9]

✓ In another class-wide peer tutoring programme carried out in 39 regular education classrooms, students with **learning disabilities, behaviour disorders** and **mild mental retardation** showed improved social skills, compared with learners who did not have access to the programme.[10]

✓   Another study reported on how learners with **moderate and severe disabilities** were supported in junior high school general education classes. Class-wide peer tutoring was combined with a multi-element curriculum and accommodations (e.g., reducing the difficulty level of tasks). The results were that both the learners with disabilities and those without disabilities showed improved levels of academic responding and decreased levels of competing behaviours.[11]

✓   In a recent study of elementary school cross-age tutoring, seven 10–11-year-old learners peer tutored seven six-year-old **learners in need of writing assistance** over a ten-week period. Tutoring took place over 20-minute sessions four times a week. The tutors gave responsive feedback to the tutees and used a problem-solving approach, rather than following a fixed sequence of assistance. The results were that both the tutees and the tutors made gains in writing rate, accuracy and audience ratings of their writing.[12]

✓   Class-wide peer tutoring has received a great deal of research support.[13] For example, a 12-year longitudinal experimental study of **at-risk learners** who received this tutoring, compared with those who did not, found: (a) more active engagement during lessons in grades one to three; (b) improved achievement at grades two, three, four and six; (c) reduced numbers requiring special education services by grade seven; and (d) fewer drop-outs from school by the end of grade 11.[14]

✓   Learners with disabilities can also be effectively employed as peer tutors. For example, elementary school learners with **learning disabilities** were trained to teach their peers using a time delay procedure for teaching spelling. In this approach, the tutors used a 'describe–model–guided practice–feedback' sequence. The tutors asked the tutees to spell a word and if the latter made no response within three seconds, they provided a prompt. The learners alternated in acting as tutors and tutees. The results showed that peer tutors were able to reliably implement the time delay procedure and that this procedure was effective in teaching spelling.[15]

✓   In a recent meta-analysis involving 19 studies, a good effect size of 0.56 was obtained.[16] Another meta-analysis of 11 studies yielded a somewhat lower, but still robust, effect size of 0.36 for reading.[17] The authors of the latter study, however, were at pains to point out that peer tutoring was not more effective when contrasted to other, teacher-led interventions such as one-to-one teaching, teacher-led small group instruction or to direct instruction.

 Addressing risks

I would like to make four points here:

1   There is a risk that tutees can become overly dependent on their tutors. You can avoid this by training tutors to work with their peers with

special educational needs, with an emphasis on encouraging reciprocal interactions (e.g., opportunities to ask as well as answer questions). They should be carefully supervised and their work should be acknowledged. Be careful, though, not to negate the idea that peers can be trusted to help each other.

2   There is also a risk that learners who are willing and/or successful in peer tutoring are asked to undertake an unreasonable load of tutoring, to the point where gains to their own development are jeopardized. Time-limited tutoring (e.g., for a period of six weeks) and rotating this role among a range of learners in your class can help guard against this risk.

3   You should also recognize that not all learners are suitable to undertake peer-tutoring responsibilities. For example, some might express reluctance to work with learners with special educational needs or they might be inappropriate role models. Some might see tutoring as an opportunity to set up a power relationship in which they can control the behaviour of another, less competent learner. This requires you to exercise sensitivity and judgement in approaching learners to take on this role. Take care to ensure that the partners are socially compatible.

4   Finally, let me emphasize that peer tutoring is a supplement, not a substitute, for good teaching, a point I noted earlier. It should not be seen as a cheap substitute for teachers (as it was in Lancaster's and Bell's days), but rather as a way of deepening students' learning.

 ## Conclusion

Peer tutoring has many advantages to all concerned, provided it is carefully planned and sensitively monitored. It has proven to be an effective strategy in increasing the academic achievement and social interactions of learners with and without disabilities. It is very appropriate as an alternative method of reviewing material, but not as a method for introducing new content.

 ## Further reading

Fulk, K. and King, K. (2001). 'Classwide peer tutoring at work'. *Teaching Exceptional Children*, 34(2), 49–53.

Jones, K. and Charlton, T. (eds) (1996). *Overcoming learning and behaviour difficulties: Partnership with pupils*. London: Routledge.

Kalkowski, P. 'Peer and cross-age tutoring'. In *School Improvement Research Series (SIRS)*. NW Regional Education Laboratory. URL: www.nwrel.org/scpd/sirs/9/c018. html (accessed 12 December 2006).

Northwest Regional Education Laboratory School Improvement Research Series. URL: www.nwrel.org/scpd/sirs/9/c018.html (accessed 1 February 2007).

Topping, K. and Ehly, S. (eds) (1998). *Peer assisted learning*. Mahwah, NJ: Lawrence Erlbaum Associates.

Key references

1 Greenwood, C.R., Maheady, L. and Delquadri, J. (2002). 'Class-wide peer tutoring'. In G. Stoner, M.R. Shinn and H. Walker (eds) *Intervention for achievement and behavior problems* (2nd edn) (pp. 611–649). Washington, DC: National Association of School Psychologists.

2 For a theoretical model of how peer learning works, see Topping, K.J. (2005). 'Trends in peer learning'. *Educational Psychology*, 25(6), 631–645.

3 Wheldall, K. and Colmar, S. (1990). 'Peer tutoring for low progress readers using "pause, prompt and praise"'. In H.C. Foot, M.J. Morgan and R.H. Shute (eds) *Children helping children* (pp. 117–134). London: John Wiley.

4 Hornby, G., Atkinson, M. and Howard, J. (1997). 'Peer/parent tutoring – Is it effective?' In *Controversial issues in special education* (pp. 134–148). London: David Fulton.

5 Cohen, P.A., Kulik, J.A. and Kulik, C.C. (1982). 'Educational outcomes of tutoring: A meta-analysis of findings'. *American Educational Research Journal*, 19(2), 237–248.

6 Topping, K. (1987). 'Peer tutored paired reading: Outcome data from ten projects'. *Educational Psychology*, 7(2), 133–145.

7 Fuchs, D., Fuchs, L., Mathes, P.G. and Simmons, D.C. (1997) 'Peer-assisted learning strategies: making classrooms more responsive to diversity'. *American Educational Research Journal*, 34(1), 174–206.

8 Haring, T.G., Breen, C., Pitts-Conway, V., Lee, M. and Gaylord-Ross, R. (1987). 'Adolescent peer tutoring and special friend experiences'. *Journal of the Association for Persons with Severe Handicaps*, 12, 280–286.

9 Kamps, D.M., Barbetta, P.M., Leonard, B.R. and Delquadri, J. (1994). 'Classwide peer tutoring: An integration strategy to improve reading skills and promote peer interactions among learners with autism and general education peers'. *Journal of Applied Behavior Analysis*, 27(1), 49–61.

10 Fuchs, D., Fuchs, L., Mathes, P.G. and Martinez, E.A. (2002). 'Preliminary evidence on the social standing of learners with learning disabilities in PALS and No-PALS classrooms'. *Learning Disabilities Research and Practice*, 17(4), 205–215.

11 McDonnell, J., Mathot-Buckner, C., Thorson, N. and Fister, S. (2001). 'Supporting the inclusion of learners with moderate and severe disabilities in junior high school general education classes: The effects of classwide peer tutoring, multi-element curriculum, and accommodations'. *Education and Treatment of Children*, 24(2), 141–160.

12 Medcalf, J., Glynn, T. and Moore, D. (2004). 'Peer tutoring in writing: A school systems approach'. *Educational Psychology in Practice*, 20(2), 157–178.

13 For reviews, see Maheady, G.F., Harper, G.F. and Mallette, B. (2003). 'Class wide peer tutoring: Go for it'. *Current Practice Alerts*, Issue 8; and Hall, T. and Stegila, A. (2003). *Peer mediated instruction and intervention*. Wakefield, MA: National Center on Accessing the General Curriculum. URL: www.cast.org/publications/ncac/ncac_peermii.html (accessed 13 September 2006).

14 Greenwood, Maheady and Delquadri, op. cit.

15 Telecsan, B.L., Slaton, D.B. and Stevens, K.B. (1999). 'Peer tutoring: Teaching learners with learning disabilities to deliver time delay instruction'. *Journal of Behavioral Education*, 9(2), 133–154.

16 Kavale, K.A. and Forness, S.R. (2000). 'Policy decisions in special education: the role of meta-analysis'. In R. Gersten, E. P. Schiller and S. Vaughn (eds)

Contemporary special education research: Syntheses of knowledge base on critical instructional issues (pp. 281–326). Mahwah, NJ: Lawrence Erlbaum Associates.

17 Mathes, P. and Fuchs, L. (1994). 'The efficacy of peer tutoring in reading for students with disabilities: A best-evidence synthesis'. *School Psychology Review*, 23(1), 59–80.

Chapter 6

Strategy 4: Collaborative teaching

'Become an effective team player'

Rating

★★★☆

 The strategy

Collaboration can be defined as a process that enables groups of people with diverse expertise to combine their resources to generate solutions to problems over a period of time.[1] Collaborative teaching is sometimes referred to as *collaborative consultation, cooperative teaching, co-teaching, team-based services* or *community of practice*.

This strategy relates to the context component of the learning and teaching model outlined in Chapter 2.

Educating learners with special educational needs requires collaboration with many people – fellow professionals and parents in particular. Indeed, there are few areas of education that call upon so much collaboration and teamwork. This is particularly true in inclusive education (**Strategy 1**) where, ideally, general classroom teachers may work with specialist teachers, therapists, medical specialists, paraprofessionals/teacher aides and, of course, parents.[2] Instead of being a soloist, you now become a member of an orchestra. As an educator, though, you should be a leader of the orchestra.

Collaborative approaches are increasingly being emphasized, even required, in such countries as the UK and the USA.[3]

In special and inclusive education patterns of collaboration vary. They range from the consultations general classroom teachers might have with special education advisers/special education needs coordinators (referred to as SENCOs in the UK) and with multi-disciplinary teams, through co-teaching arrangements, to supervising the work of a teacher aide/teaching assistant or other paraprofessionals.

The underlying idea

Along with collaborative teaching, three other related strategies are explained in this book: **2: Cooperative Group Teaching**, **3: Peer Tutoring** and **5: Parent Involvement**. These are all based on the principle that much of our knowledge is socially constructed; that is, we learn from others in our immediate environments. Another way of expressing it is to quote what a Maori king in New Zealand once said:

> *Kotahi te kohao*
> *O te ngira*
> *E Kahuna ai*
> *Te miro ma*
> *Te Miro pango*
> *Te miro Whero*

> There is but one eye
> of the needle
> Through which passes
> The white thread
> The black thread
> The red thread

Collaborative teaching has three main benefits:

1   It has potential to create synergy – where 'the whole is greater than the sum of the parts'.
2   It has the potential to provide opportunities for you to learn new ways of addressing barriers to learning – and for colleagues to learn from you. It thus reduces the professional isolation that can often occur in teaching.
3   It increases the coordination of services for learners with special educational needs. One of the things that parents often find frustrating is the 'maze' of services and individual personalities with whom they are expected to negotiate.

To release this potential, you have to learn the skills of working as a team member for at least part of your teaching. If you have been used to working alone as a sole professional, it is a big step to develop new ways of working in which you share responsibility and expertise with other professionals in other disciplines. The 'private' now becomes the 'public'; what was once implicit and unexpressed in your professional practice now has to become explicit and explained to others. Your autonomy may even seem to be lessened as you adapt to other people's ideas and personalities. Ultimately, though, collaborative teaching will benefit you and your learners with special educational needs.

The practice

 General principles of collaboration[4]

Here is a summary of the most important things to take into account if you are to develop successful collaborative arrangements:

*   Establish clear common goals for the collaboration.
*   Define your respective roles and who is accountable for what, but accept joint responsibility for the decisions and their outcomes.
*   Take a problem-solving approach – with a sense that all those in the collaborative arrangement share ownership of the problem and its solution.
*   Establish an atmosphere of trust and mutual respect for each others' expertise.
*   Be willing to learn from others.
*   Aim for consensus decision-making.
*   Ask for and give immediate and objective feedback to others in a non-threatening and non-judgemental manner.
*   Give credit to others for their ideas and accomplishments.
*   Develop procedures for resolving conflicts and manage these processes skilfully. Better still, anticipate possible conflicts and take steps to avoid them as far as possible. This is not to say that disagreements can, or even should, be avoided.
*   Arrange periodic meetings to review progress in the collaborative arrangements.

 Forms of collaboration

There are six main forms of collaboration in which you may become involved:

1   *Co-teaching.*[5] Sometimes known as *cooperative teaching*, this occurs in inclusive education settings when a general education teacher and a special education teacher combine their expertise to meet the needs of all learners in the class. Both assume the roles of equal collaborators. It does not normally mean that the special education teacher takes exclusive responsibility for learners with special educational needs and the general teacher the rest of the class. Rather, it means respecting each other's expertise in order to benefit all learners in the class. In addition to the points outlined above, to make co-teaching work, there needs to be:

*   active support from your school's leadership;
*   adequate, regular joint planning time;
*   agreement on procedures for handling learners' disruptive or off-task behaviours;

- agreement on lesson objectives and structures, including teaching strategies and assessment methods;
- clear communication with parents about the co-teaching arrangement.

2 *Consultation.*[6] This is an indirect service delivery model, in that the consultant does not work directly with learners, except to occasionally demonstrate a teaching strategy. The essence of this approach is that a special education teacher/adviser (or some other specialist) provides advice and guidance to the general classroom teacher on the programme to be followed by any learners with special educational needs. Both teachers meet outside classroom teaching time (admittedly, a logistical problem, which has to be solved by the school leadership[7]) and discuss any curricular, teaching and assessment adaptations required for such learners. As well, the special education teacher might provide additional instructional materials and help to modify the classroom environment. In all of this the classroom teacher carries the main responsibility.

To make this consultation model work, the special education teacher must be thoroughly familiar with the curriculum being followed in the classroom and the classroom teacher must assume chief responsibility for educating all learners in his or her class.

3 *Partnerships with teacher aides/paraprofessionals.*[8] Here I am assuming that the teacher aide or paraprofessional has more limited training, and therefore responsibility, than a teacher. Thus, in making decisions on their roles, the overriding consideration is that, although many of them might be well qualified and very experienced, they should not be permitted to take on the full role of a teacher. Responsibility for the design of their work and for its supervision rests ultimately with the teacher. Of course, planning should be a joint activity in which the general points I outline above are followed as far as possible.

Although the prime purpose of teacher aides is usually to provide support to the learner(s) with special educational needs, this does not necessarily mean that they must work exclusively with such learners. In my experience in New Zealand I have observed teacher aides frequently taking on broader roles, working with groups of learners that might or might not include those with special educational needs. Most importantly, teacher aides should avoid making such learners overly dependent on their support (reflected, for example, in them taking up excessively close proximity to learners with special educational needs); rather, they should help them to become increasingly independent.

4 *Partnerships with specialists.* In addition to educators, many other professionals have an interest in learners with special educational needs.

Depending on the specific nature of their needs, you might have contact with a range of government departments (e.g., Health, Welfare, Justice) and advocacy groups/organizations representing different disability groups. These contacts might involve you interacting with such professionals as psychologists, doctors, speech-language therapists, occupational therapists, physiotherapists, police officers, social workers, advocates and community representatives.

Working with people with professional backgrounds (and sometimes world views) that are markedly different from your own poses a major challenge.

5   *Partnerships with parents.* See **Strategy 5**.

6   *School-wide teams.* In South Africa I was impressed by the idea of institution-level support teams – an idea that many other countries have adopted in various forms.[9] In the South African model, the primary function of these teams is to put in place 'properly co-ordinated learner and educator support services that will support the learning and teaching process by identifying and addressing learner, educator and institutional needs'.[10] A key to the success of such teams is the support and encouragement offered by the school principal and other senior leaders. The chief function of school-wide teams is to develop a school-wide supportive culture and policies on learners with special educational needs, as well as focusing on identifying and supporting individual learners. The teams need a dedicated leader/facilitator and a recorder of decisions and plans, utilizing advanced technology where available to facilitate communication.[11]

 The evidence

✓   In an extensive review of outcome research on consultation carried out between 1985 and 1995, the authors found that nearly 67 per cent of the studies reported some positive findings, while 28 per cent reported neutral findings and only 5 per cent noted negative results. These were similar findings to those reported in previous reviews of the research. However, they also recognized that although the impetus for setting up consultation models is widely encouraged, research-based support has been accumulating only slowly – hence the cautious rating I give to this strategy.[12]

✓   An early meta-analysis concluded that consultation participants (consultants, consultees and clients) were substantially 'better off' (not defined) than those who did not participate in consultation.[13]

✓   A study examined the impact of collaborative consultation on the accuracy of **referrals to special education**. Referral accuracy was determined by taking a ratio of the number of students assessed to the number of students verified. The results indicated a significant increase in referral accuracy when a collaborative consultation model was implemented.[14]

✓ Another US study asked whether a consultant-driven pre-referral inter-vention could be shortened in duration without reducing its effectiveness. The participants were 60 general educators and their 60 most **difficult-to-teach pupils**, from 17 elementary schools. The teachers were assigned randomly to a short (N = 24) and long version (N = 24) of the pre-referral intervention and to a control group (N = 12). Both the long and the short variants of the pre-referral intervention improved teacher percep-tions of their difficult-to-teach students and decreased referrals for testing and possible special education placement.[15]

✓ A review of the literature from 1985 to 1995 on school-based **mental health services** for children found that of the 5,046 references initially identified, 228 were programme evaluations. Three inclusion criteria were applied to those studies: use of random assignment to the intervention, inclusion of a control group and use of standardized outcome measures. Although some of the evidence was mixed, 16 studies met these criteria. Three types of interventions were found to have empirical support for their effectiveness. These were: cognitive behavioural therapy (**Strategy 16**), social skills training (**Strategy 10**) and teacher consultation, the focus of the present strategy.[16]

✓ An article reported on a study from the School Consultation Research Project, a cooperative group of school psychologists from four US universities interested in exploring relationships among processes and outcomes in consultation. The results showed that the more that consultant and consultee see the process in a similar way, understand their roles and work together as a team, the more favourable are consultee perceptions of: (a) the benefits of consultation, (b) consultee competence, (c) client improvement and (d) consultant effectiveness.[17]

✓ A small-scale qualitative study examined the impact of co-teaching in regular classrooms that included **deaf and hard of hearing** learners. Each class had a general education teacher and a teacher of the deaf learners. It was found that the co-teaching model permitted both categories of teachers to combine their expertise to meet the needs of all learners, and provided them with a sense of shared responsibility and collegial support.[18]

 Addressing risks

The main risks to the successful implementation of collaborative teaching can be summarized as follows:

• difficulties in assembling the key participants, particularly when teachers are involved (as they should be) and have to juggle competing demands on their time;

• difficulties in communicating across disciplines and in accommodating to a range of philosophies and personalities;

- a lack of clear goals for collaboration;
- a lack of support from administrators;
- a lack of training.

All of these potential barriers can be addressed.

 Conclusion

Collaborative approaches to educating learners with special educational needs are becoming increasingly embedded in education systems around the world. Although many aspects of collaboration are still to be researched, there is sufficient empirical evidence in support of its underlying philosophy to justify its implementation.

 Further reading

Idol, L., Nevin, A. and Paolucci-Whitcomb, P. (1994). *Collaborative consultation.* 2nd edn. Austin, TX: Pro-ed.
Journal of Educational and Psychological Consultation

Key references

1 Idol, L., Nevin, A. and Paolucci-Whitcomb, P. (1994). 'The collaborative consulta-tion model'. *Collaborative consultation.* 2nd edn (pp. 1–15). Austin, TX: Pro-ed.
2 Rainforth, B. and England, J. (1997). 'Collaboration for inclusion'. *Education and Treatment of Children,* 20(1), 85–105.
3 For UK, see DfEE (1998). *Meeting special educational needs: A programme of action.* London: DfEE.
4 See also Friend, M. and Cook, L. (1992*). Interactions: Collaborative skills for school professionals.* White Plains, NY: Longmans; and Idol *et al.,* op. cit.
5 See Dieker, L.A. and Barnett, C.A. (1996). 'Effective co-teaching'. *TEACHING Exceptional Children,* 29(1), 5–7; Reeve, P.T. and Hallahan, D.P. (1996). 'Practical questions about collaboration between general and special educators'. In E.L. Meyen, G.A. Vergason and R.J. Whelan (eds) *Strategies for teaching exceptional children in inclusive settings* (pp. 401–418). Denver, CO: Love Publishing; and Walter-Thomas, C., Bryant, M. and Land, S. (1996). 'Planning for effective co-teaching: The key to successful inclusion'. *Remedial and Special Education,* 17(4), 255.
6 See Elliott, D. and McKenney, M. (1998). Four inclusion models that work. *TEACHING Exceptional Children,* 30(4), 54–58.
7 For a summary of strategies for increasing teachers' consultation time, see Idol, L. (1997). 'Key questions related to building collaborative and inclusive schools'. *Journal of Learning Disabilities,* 30(4), 384–394.
8 See Freschi, D.F. (1999). 'Guidelines for working with one-to-one aides'. *TEACHING Exceptional Children,* 31(4), 42–45; Marks, S.U., Schrader, C. and Levine, M. (1999). 'Paraeducator experiences in inclusive settings: Helping, hovering, or holding their own?' *Exceptional Children,* 65(3), 315–328; and French, N.K. (1998). 'Working together: Resource teachers and paraeducators'.

Remedial and Special Education, 19(6), 357–368.
9 For a description of a US example, see Adelman, H.S. and Taylor, L. (1998). 'Involving teachers in collaborative efforts to better address the barriers to student learning'. *Preventing School Failure*, 42(2), 55–60.
10 Department of Education (2001). *Education White Paper 6: Special Needs Education*. Pretoria: Department of Education.
11 Adelman, H.S. and Taylor, L. (1998), op. cit. 'Involving teachers in collaborative efforts to better address the barriers to student learning'. *Preventing School Failure*, 42(2), 55–60.
12 Sheridan, S.M. and Welch, M. (1996). 'Is consultation effective?' *Remedial and Special Education*, 17(6), 341–355.
13 Medway, F.J. and Updyke, J.F. (1985). 'Meta-analysis of consultation outcome studies'. *American Journal of Community Psychology*, 13(5), 489–505.
14 Yocom, D.J. and Staebler, B. (1996). 'The impact of collaborative consultation on special education referral accuracy'. *Journal of Educational and Psychological Consultation*, 7(2), 179–192.
15 Fuchs, D., Fuchs, L.S. and Bahr, M.W. (1990). 'Mainstream assistance teams: A scientific basis for the art of consultation'. *Exceptional Child*, 57(2), 128–139.
16 Hoagwood, K. and Erwin, H.D. (1997). 'Effectiveness of school-based mental health services for children: A 10-year research review'. *Journal of Child and Family Studies*, 6(4), 435–451.
17 Erchul, W.P., Hughes, J.N., Meyers, J., Hickman, J.A. and Braden, J.P. (1992). 'Dyadic agreement concerning the consultation process and its relationship to outcome'. *Journal of Educational and Psychological Consultation*, 3(2), 119–132.
18 Luckner, J.L. (1999). 'An examination of two coteaching classrooms'. *American Annals of the Deaf*, 144(1), 24–34.

Strategy 5: Parent involvement

'Respect families' rights, skills and needs'

Rating
★★★☆

 The strategy

Parents[1] play important, if not critical, roles in educating and supporting learners with special educational needs. They are first and foremost parents, with all the rights and responsibilities of that role, but they are also sources of information, partners in designing and implementing programmes for their children, and 'consumers' of the education you provide.

This strategy relates to the following components of the learning and teaching model: context, external task demands and external responses.

 The underlying idea

Why develop partnerships with parents?[2]

There are many good reasons why you as an educator should seek to develop effective relationships with the parents of the children you teach, particularly those with special educational needs. Several stand out:

* Parents are most probably the only people who are involved with their child's education throughout their entire school years. They are thus likely to have great interest in their child's learning overall and be the most affected by the outcomes of any schooling decisions.
* Parents know their child's development and the factors that might be responsible for their special educational needs. They can generally tell you what motivates their child and which teaching and management strategies are most effective.
* They will help you to gain a greater understanding of some aspects of their child's behaviour. However, it is very important that you maintain

a delicate balance between recognizing the significant role played by parents in influencing a child's behaviour and blaming them. There is rarely a simple cause-and-effect explanation for a child's behaviour and certainly it would be counterproductive for you to take a critical stance. On the same note, you should avoid falling into the trap of only involving parents when there is a problem.

- Working with parents increases the likelihood of consistency in expectations of behaviour at home and at school. It also increases the opportunities for reinforcing appropriate behaviours and increasing the range of reinforcers that are available to do this.
- By being closely involved, parents will gain a greater understanding of their children's schooling and the school's vision and goals.
- Regular contact with parents will heighten your own sense of accountability.
- Children will obtain positive messages about the importance of their education if they see their parents and educators working together.

Why might some parents need support?

- Children with special educational needs can be a source of both joy and emotional distress. As well as accepting their children, some parents might also reject them or be over-protective as they experience feelings of shock, denial, disbelief, anger, guilt, depression and shame at various times. These feelings might be triggered throughout the child's life, particularly at significant occasions such as birthdays and during transitions associated with schooling.[3]
- Parents of children who have special educational needs have extra demands on them. Some of them take on the role of advocates for their and other children, acting as agents of change for the education system as a whole. They might have to instigate inclusive school practices and manage transitions associated with schooling. They, of course, provide care for their child for a prolonged period and must ensure that other people relate to their child in a way that helps their child acquire and maintain adaptive behaviour. They must also access and maintain specialist services for their child. In many societies, responsibility for meeting these demands very often falls to the mother.
- Parents might also have to learn specialized skills. Since their children might not learn important skills as naturally or independently as their siblings, parents might need to learn systematic teaching techniques. In the case of those who must deal with severe behaviour patterns, they may have to learn systematic behaviour management techniques (**Strategy 17**). They might also need to learn to use, or teach their children how to use, special equipment and assistive devices (**Strategies 22 and 23**).

- Parents of children with special educational needs might be concerned about things that do not usually trouble other parents. They may be more worried about their child's safety in the playground, whether other children will be kind or cruel and whether parents of other children will complain about their child. As a consequence, they might pressure the school to separate their child from their classmates.

- Having a child with special educational needs often affects the family itself. Parents might find it hard to get babysitters and to remain part of their church or other community organizations. Friends and family might start avoiding them, or suggest that behaviour problems are the result of poor parental discipline. In some societies parents are made to feel ashamed or guilty for giving birth to a child with a disability. The financial costs associated with their child's needs might strain the family's budget.

- Although siblings may learn to love and accept others in their family unconditionally and to develop a sense of responsibility, they might also become embarrassed about their brother or sister with special educational needs, feel left out or resent the time that parents give him or her.

- Caring for their family can be emotionally taxing for parents who have a child with special educational needs. The extent to which this occurs can be affected by:

  - The amount of change imposed on the family and the seriousness of those changes. For some families, a child with special needs will require a number of adjustments to their daily routines or dramatic changes in earning power and lifestyle. Others might be required to make only a few minor adjustments.

  - The family's adaptability, a factor which is, in turn, influenced by the personal resources of each family member, particularly their level of education, their health, their self-esteem and the quality of the informal and formal social supports available to them.

  - The family's internal resources, for example, the size of the family, the number of parents in a family and their religious commitment.[4]

 The practice

 What do we mean by parent involvement?

Five different levels of parent involvement have been identified:[5]

Level 1 *Being informed.* At this most basic level, the school informs parents about its programmes and, in turn, is asked for information.

Level 2 *Taking part in activities.* At this level, parents are involved in activities, but to a limited extent. For example, they might be invited to attend various functions.

Level 3 *Dialogue and exchange of views.* Here, parents are invited to examine school or classroom goals and needs.

Level 4 *Taking part in decision-making.* At this level, parents are asked about their views when decisions affecting their child are being made. A clear case of this level of involvement is the Individual Education Plan conference.

Level 5 *Having responsibility to act.* This is the highest level, with parents making decisions in partnership with the school and being involved in both planning and evaluating parts of the school programme. A good example of this would be involving the parents of children with special educational needs in formulating and evaluating school policies. Another example of involvement at this level is the role that parents may play as tutors for their own children.

 What helps the development of effective partnerships?

In addition to the suggestions I outline in **Strategy 4: Collaborative Teaching**, several things can help you to establish good working relationships with parents:

- Regular contact with parents helps to establish relationships within which even the smallest successes can be celebrated and any difficulties more easily anticipated and more quickly resolved. Regular contact can be facilitated through daily report cards, home–school notebooks and invitations written by the children to view their displayed work.
- Parents might be more able to contribute in meetings if they are explicitly encouraged to do so, are clear about the nature of their contribution and are provided guidelines to do this.
- Meetings with parents might be more effective if they are well structured. Individualized educational planning meetings, for instance, could include a time for building rapport, obtaining information from parents, giving information to them, summarizing the information exchanged and planning a time for follow-up.
- Conflict arises in any partnership and should be dealt with in a positive, non-threatening manner.

 How can parents be supported?

You might not be able to solve all or any of the specific concerns that parents may want to talk about with you. However, giving them a few minutes of your time can go a long way to helping them resolve those concerns for themselves. Listening actively is helpful because it allows people to clarify their thoughts and feelings. Active listening involves responding to issues that are important, inviting people to explain their concerns through comments such as 'tell me more' and helping people reflect on their feelings and ideas by tentatively suggesting what you think they feel and say. It is important here, however, that you do not go beyond your capabilities and that you refer more complex problems to appropriate professionals.

In brief, parents have much knowledge and experience that they might be more willing to share within the context of a partnership relationship. They might be able to help you anticipate, tackle and overcome barriers to learning. But parents may also need your support as well. Sometimes an understanding ear might be all that is needed.

The above directly involves educators. In the following, I will outline three parent training programmes that would normally be designed and delivered by specialists such as psychologists. I include them as I think it is important that you be aware of the strategies if any learners in your classes are involved in them or if you want to refer parents for help. You could well work in collaboration with parents and professionals involved in any training programme, by describing any child behaviours that concern you. In addition, it is vital that your classroom strategies are consistent with those that parents may be using at home. It could well be, too, that in reading about them you might pick up some tips to use in your classroom management strategies.

 ### Behavioural parent training

In behavioural parent training (sometimes referred to as *parent management training*), parents are typically helped to use effective behavioural management strategies in their homes. This strategy is often based on the assumption that children's conduct problems result from maladaptive parent–child interactions, such as paying attention to deviant behaviour, ineffective use of commands, and harsh punishments. Thus, parents are trained to define and monitor their child's behaviour, avoid coercive interchanges and positively reinforce acceptable behaviour by implementing developmentally appropriate consequences for their child's defiance. Such parent training is typically conducted in the context of group or individual therapy. It includes a mixture of didactic instruction, live or videotaped modelling, and role-plays. As its name implies, an important element of behavioural parent training is the effective administration of reinforcement (**Strategy 17**). This involves reinforcement to be administered contingently (i.e., after the target behaviour), immediately, frequently and with a variety of high-quality reinforcers that are meaningful to the child. As well, such techniques as shaping and prompting will be used.[6]

 ### Parent–child interaction therapy

This strategy is closely related to behavioural parent training, but without the close adherence to behavioural principles. It is usually a short-term intervention programme aimed at parents of children with a broad range of behavioural, emotional or developmental problems. Its main aim is to help parents develop warm and responsive relationships with their children and develop acceptable behaviours. It includes non-directive play, along with more directive guidance on interactions, sometimes using an ear microphone.[7]

Triple P – Positive Parenting Programme

This is a multi-level parenting and family support strategy aimed at reducing children's behavioural and emotional problems. It includes five levels of intervention of increasing strength:

1   a universal media information campaign targeting all parents: e.g., promoting the use of positive parenting practices in the community, destigmatizing the process of seeking help for children with behaviour problems and countering parent-blaming messages in the media;
2   two levels of brief primary care consultations targeting mild behaviour problems: (a) delivering selective intervention through primary care services such as maternal and child health agencies and schools, using videotaped training programmes to train staff; and (b) targeting parents who have mild, specific concerns about their child's behaviour or development and providing four 20-minute information-based sessions with active skills training;
3   two more intensive parent training programmes for children at risk for more severe behaviour problems: (a) running a 10-session programme that includes sessions on children's behaviour problems, strategies for encouraging children's development and managing misbehaviour; and (b) carrying out intervention with families with additional risk factors that have not changed after lower levels of intervention.[8]

The evidence

✓   A 1998 review of treatments of children and adolescents with **conduct disorders**, covering the period from 1966 to 1995, found 29 well-designed studies. Parent training was one of two treatments that were identified as being 'well-established'.[9]
✓   A 1996 meta-analysis of the effects of behavioural parent training on **antisocial behaviours** of children yielded a significant effect size of 0.86 for behaviours in the home. There was also evidence that the effects generalized to classroom behaviour and to parents' personal adjustment. It was noted, however, that these studies compared parent management training with no training, and not with other strategies.[10]
✓   However, a recent meta-analysis did compare the effectiveness of two different strategies: behavioural parent training (30 studies) and cognitive

behavioural therapy (see **Strategy 12**) (41 studies) for children and adolescents with **antisocial behaviour** problems. The effect size for behavioural parent training was 0.46 for child outcomes (and 0.33 for parent adjustment) compared with 0.35 for child outcomes with cognitive behavioural therapy. Age was found to influence the outcomes of the two interventions, with behavioural parent training having a stronger effect for pre-school and elementary school-aged children, while cognitive behavioural training had a stronger effect for adolescents.[11]

✓ Another study combined parent involvement and cognitive behavioural therapy. Three groups were compared: (a) those receiving cognitive behavioural therapy with parent involvement (N = 17), (b) those receiving cognitive behavioural therapy without parent involvement (N = 19) and (c) a waiting list control group (N = 14). The children involved in the study were aged from seven to 14 years and all were diagnosed with **school phobia**. Both treatment conditions resulted in reductions in the children's social and general anxiety at the end of the treatment and on follow-up after six and 12 months, with no corresponding improvements for the waiting list group. These results do appear, however, to favour cognitive behavioural therapy, as the parental involvement had no additional positive effect.[12]

✓ A US study examined changes in parent functioning as a result of participating in a behavioural parent training programme designed for children aged six to 11 with **attention-deficit hyperactivity disorder (ADHD)**. The programme comprised nine sessions conducted over a two-month period. The content included: (a) an overview of ADHD, (b) a review of a model for understanding child behaviour problems, (c) positive reinforcement skills (e.g., positive attending, ignoring, compliance with requests, and a home token/point system), (d) the use of punishment strategies (e.g., response cost and time out), (e) modifying strategies for use in public places and (f) working cooperatively with school personnel, including setting up daily report card systems. Compared with equivalent families on the waiting list for the treatment, those receiving the behavioural parent training showed significant changes in their children's psychosocial functioning, including improvements in their ADHD symptoms. As well, the parents showed less stress and enhanced self-esteem.[13]

✓ A review of outcomes of parent–child interaction therapy (see above) concluded that it was generally effective in decreasing a range of children's **disruptive and oppositional behaviours**, increasing child compliance with parental requests, improving parenting skills, reducing parents' stress levels and improving parent–child relationships.[14]

✓ A US study investigated the long-term maintenance of changes following parent–child interaction therapy for young children with **oppositional defiant behaviour**. This study involved interviewing 23 mothers of children aged from six to 12 years. Changes that had occurred at the end of the intervention were maintained three to six years later.[15]

✓ An Australian paper reports on studies of the Triple P – Positive Parenting Programme (outlined above), administered to parents in groups. One of these involved 1,673 families in Perth, Western Australia. Parents who received the intervention reported significantly greater reductions on measures of **child disruptive behaviours** than parents in the non-intervention comparison group. Prior to the intervention, 42 per cent of the children had disruptive behaviour, this figure reducing to 20 per cent after intervention.[16]

✓ In a summary of parent-mediated interventions involving children with **autism**, an overview paper concluded that parents learnt behavioural techniques to increase and decrease selected target behaviours in their children.[17] Among the studies cited was one in which parents were taught to help their children follow photographic schedules depicting activities such as leisure, self-care and housekeeping tasks. The results showed increases in social engagement and decreases in disruptive behaviour among the children with autism.[18]

 ## Addressing risks

The main risks to parental involvement in their children's education centre on their ability or willingness to avail themselves of opportunities. Some do not have the time, some have extremely negative attitudes towards the school, some are going through personal crises, some are quite content to 'leave it to the experts', some lack transport, some face ostracism or rejection in their communities and some think they have nothing to say or to offer. This is not to let you off the hook, but to recognize the reality that not all parents can be, or want to be, closely involved in their children's schooling. Certainly, you should take whatever steps you can to break down barriers and you should persevere with providing opportunities for involvement, even if these are not taken up.

 ## Conclusion

Parents are key partners in their children's education. They have a fundamental right to be involved in major decisions affecting their children. Parents of children with special educational needs often require support and guidance in managing their children's challenging behaviour. There is clear evidence that when this is provided both children and parents can benefit.

 ## Further reading

Ballard, K. (ed.) (1994). *Disability, family, whanau and society*. Palmerston North, New Zealand: The Dunmore Press.

Dunst, C.J. (2002). 'Family-centered practices: Birth through high school'. *The Journal of Special Education*, 36(3), 139–147.
Hornby, G. (1994). *Counselling in child disability: Skills for working with parents.* London: Cassell.
Hornby, G. (2000). *Improving parental involvement.* London: Cassell.
Turnbull, A.P. and Turnbull, H.R. (2001). *Families, professionals and exceptionality: Collaborating for empowerment* (4th edn). Upper Saddle River, NJ: Prentice Hall.

Key references

1 The term 'parent' encompasses a range of people, including natural parents, adoptive or foster parents, guardians, extended family and caregivers. Here I will use 'parent' to cover all categories of such relationships.
2 See, for example, Kauffman, J.M., Mostert, M.P., Trent, S.C. and Hallahan, D.P. (1998). Chapter 7 in *Managing classroom behavior: A reflective case-based approach.* 2nd edn. Needham Heights, MA: Allyn and Bacon.
3 Mitchell, D. (1986). 'A developmental systems approach to planning and evaluating services for persons with handicaps'. In R.I. Brown (ed.) *Rehabilitation Education, Volume 2* (pp. 126–156). Beckenham: Croom Helm.
4 Mitchell, op. cit.
5 Department of Education (1988). *Getting started on consultation.* Wellington: Curriculum Review Action Unit, Department of Education.
6 For reviews of some of the vast literature on parent management training, see, for example, Kazdin, A.E. and Weisz, J.R. (1998). 'Identifying and developing empirically supported child and adolescent treatments'. *Journal of Consulting and Clinical Psychology*, 66(1), 19–36; and McCart, M.R., Priester, P.E., Davies, W.H. and Azen, R. (2006). 'Differential effectiveness of behavioral parent training and cognitive behavioural therapy for antisocial youth'. *Journal of Abnormal Child Psychology*, 34(4), 525–541.
7 Eyberg, S.M., Boggs, S.R. and Algina, J. (1995). 'Parent-child interaction therapy: A psychosocial model for the treatment of young children with conduct problem behavior and their families'. *Psychopharmacology Bulletin*, 31(1), 83–92.
8 Sanders, M. (1999). 'Triple P-positive parenting program: Towards an empirically validated multilevel parenting and family support strategy for the prevention of behavior and emotional problems in children'. *Clinical Child and Family Psychology Review*, 2(2), 71–90.
9 Brestan, E.V. and Eyberg, S.M. (1998). 'Effective psychosocial treatments of conduct disordered children and adolescents: 29 years, 82 studies, and 5,272 kids'. *Journal of Clinical Child Psychology*, 27(2), 180–189.
10 Serketich, W.J. and Dumas, J.E. (1996). 'The effectiveness of behavioural parent training to modify antisocial behavior in children: a meta-analysis'. *Behavior Therapy*, 27(2), 171–186.
11 McCart *et al.*, op. cit.
12 Spence, S.H., Donovan, C. and Breechman-Toussaint, M. (2000). 'Social skills, social outcomes and cognitive features of childhood social phobias'. *Journal of Child Psychology and Psychiatry*, 41(6), 713–726.
13 Anastopolous, A.D., Shelton, T.L., DuPaul, G.J. and Guevremont, D.C. (1993). 'Parent training for attention-deficit hyperactivity disorder: its impact on parent functioning'. *Journal of Abnormal Child Psychology*, 21(5), 581–597.
14 McIntosh, D.E., Rizza, M.G. and Bliss, L. (2000). 'Implementing empirically supported interventions: Teacher-child interaction therapy'. *Psychology in the Schools*, 37(5), 453–462.

15 Hood, K.K. and Eyberg, S.M. (2003). 'Outcomes of parent-child interaction therapy: Mothers' reports of maintenance three to six years after treatment'. *Journal of Clinical Child and Adolescent Psychology*, 32(3), 419–429.
16 Sanders, op. cit.
17 Matson, J.L., Benavidez, D.A., Compton, L.S., Paclawskyj, T. and Baglio, C. (1996). 'Behavioral treatment of autistic persons: A review of research from 1980 to the present'. *Research in Developmental Disabilities*, 17(6), 433–465.
18 Krantz, P.J., Macduff, M.T. and McClannahan, L.E. (1993). 'Programming participation in family activities for children with autism: Parents' use of photographic activity schedules'. *Journal of Applied Behavior Analysis*, 26, 137–138.

Chapter 8

Strategy 6: School culture

'Create an atmosphere of respect and challenge for all learners'

Rating

★★★★

 The strategy

Creating a positive school culture, or *ethos*, involves developing and implementing goals for the school. These goals will reflect the shared values, beliefs, attitudes, traditions and behavioural norms of its members, particularly those who are in leadership positions. In terms of inclusive schools, this means developing: (a) a strong commitment to accepting and celebrating diversity, (b) a sensitivity to cultural issues, (c) setting high, but realistic, standards.

You will see that most of the studies relate to inclusive education (see also **Strategy 1**) and that they are predominantly qualitative in nature. This strategy will be of most interest to school leaders, especially principals. It is closely linked with **Strategy 9: Classroom Climate**. It relates most closely to the context component of the learning and teaching model outlined in Chapter 2.

 The underlying idea

The idea that individual schools have unique cultures is a relatively recent arrival on the educational scene. Drawn from anthropological and organizational research, and the social psychology of schooling, it provides a powerful tool for understanding and influencing many of the behaviours that take place in schools.

A school's culture both determines and reflects how its members behave towards each other: educators with educators, educators with learners, learners with learners, parents with educators, parents with learners . . . .

Sometimes, a school's culture is expressed in a formal vision statement, in other school documents or in pronouncements of school leaders. Mostly, however, it is unspoken and is shown in the interactions that take place in classrooms, in the playground during breaks, in the staffroom and even in the community – anywhere where members of the school community meet each other. In general, a school's culture is a characteristic of the school as an organization and not of individuals, although all members of the school community contribute to forming its culture.[1]

 ## The practice

 ### Developing a positive school culture

Developing a positive school culture for learners with special educational needs requires the exercise of leadership. As we shall see below in the evidence section, while the principal has the critical leadership role in most schools, it can be carried out by many different individuals in a school, some playing different roles, others playing similar roles.

 ### Leadership roles

Here are some of the important leadership roles[2] that need to be exercised in a school in order to bring about an inclusive culture:

1 *Provide and sell a vision*: this involves defining the philosophy and goals of inclusion and promulgating them wherever possible, e.g., in school publications, talks to parents and the community, and in casual conversations.
2 *Provide encouragement and recognition*: this can be formal and informal, public or private, but it has the common feature of recognizing those who are promoting inclusion.
3 *Obtain resources*: as I point out in **Strategy 1**, since one of the key barriers to the successful implementation of inclusion in many countries is the lack of appropriate resources, leadership has to advocate for adequate resources to be brought into the school. Once these are in the school, leaders should ensure that they are equitably distributed.
4 *Adapt standard operating procedures*: this involves recognizing that since rules, regulations and requirements may have evolved without the significant presence of learners with special educational needs in the school, they might have to change; examples here include curriculum, textbooks and examinations that might be inappropriate for these learners.
5 *Monitor improvement*: increasingly, it is not acceptable for leaders just to 'do good', but to show that what they are doing is having a positive impact on learners' achievements and social behaviour.
6 *Handle disturbances*: since inclusive education is rarely a settled and universally agreed policy in any school, it is inevitable that there will be overt and covert resistance that has to be handled.[3]

Class size

Class size needs to be given very careful consideration. It is a complex matter. Evidence points to benefits being obtained when the class size is reduced to 15 or so. Although I am unable to locate any research involving the impact of reducing very large classes (i.e., 50 plus), common sense would suggest that these make for difficulties in teaching and learning, especially in the case of learners with special educational needs. As one group of researchers put it:

> at the extremes (e.g., very large and very small) the size of the class will have discernible and meaningful effects on students' learning. With the more usual class sizes, however, the findings are less consistent but seem to favor – at least slightly – smaller classes.[4]

 Further practices

As with other strategies, further practices are outlined in the following section on evidence.

 The evidence

✓ A recent British study investigated the ways in which schools in a local education authority addressed **underachievement** in boys, focusing on three groups causing most concern: black Caribbean, black African and white British boys. Three primary and three secondary schools that were producing results above expectation were studied. The results showed that these successful schools stressed: (a) an inclusive ethos; (b) overall school effectiveness; (c) a broad, diverse curriculum; (d) monitoring of individual performances; (e) high, but realistic expectations; and (f) strong connections with parents.[5]

✓ Another British study presented a case study of an inclusive comprehensive school catering for 11–18-year-old learners, some of whom had **special educational needs** and were educated in regular classrooms. The study looked at the school as an organization, which was continually facing up to 'dilemmas' as it attempted to resolve educational issues – a situation that is common to most schools. In spite of displaying many characteristics common to 'effective schools' (such as a commitment to the values of inclusion, a committed leadership and opportunities for staff to collaborate in problem-solving), there were tensions within the school as it attempted to resolve how learners with special educational needs should be educated.[6]

✓ In a qualitative study of a US elementary school, the relationship between school culture and inclusion was analysed. The researchers found three underlying characteristics of the school's culture to be related to the success of its inclusion programme: (a) an inclusive leader, who employed a democratic approach and had a clear set of values; (b) a broad vision of the school community, shown by including families as well as the wider community in every aspect of the school; and (c) shared language and values, shown, for example, in widespread use of the phrase, 'a school for everyone'.[7]

✓ In another qualitative study, three US schools were studied over a school year, with the aim of examining leadership in inclusive education for a range of **learners with severe disabilities**. The study looked at who carried out six leadership functions: (a) providing and selling a vision, (b) providing encouragement and recognition, (c) obtaining resources, (d) adapting standard operating procedures, (e) monitoring improvement and (f) handling disturbances. The results showed that multiple individuals, including those who did not have formal authority in the schools, carried out these leadership roles.[8]

✓ A Canadian study investigated the extent to which teachers' and principals' beliefs about inclusive education led to effective teaching. In the 12 schools in the study, the students ranged from second to eighth grades and 8 per cent had been identified as **exceptional** (but not gifted). The strongest finding in the study was the direct connection between the 'school norm', as reflected in the principals' beliefs, and teachers' teaching behaviours.[9]

✓ According to a recent review of class size, the evidence points to the following conclusions:

  • Achievement, attitude, teacher morale and student satisfaction gains are greater in small classes, i.e., classes with 10–15 learners. Differences between class sizes of 40 and 20 are negligible. (The writer makes no mention of the effects of reducing class sizes of 50, 60 or more learners, common in many developing countries.)

  • The above holds true for primary and secondary schools, across all subjects and across **various ability levels**.

  • There is little evidence that instructional methods change when class size is reduced, although there is some evidence that a large part of any improvements can be explained by higher levels of learners' engagement with tasks.[10]

 Addressing risks

There are probably three risks to consider:

• The key risk is that the principal perceives himself/herself, and is perceived by others, to be solely responsible for forming and expressing a school's culture. Rather, this should be seen as a shared responsibility.

- A second risk is to assume that once a school culture has been formed, it is seen to be permanent. This is not the case, as it is constantly changing and needs continuous tending.
- A third risk is that it is rare to have a unanimously agreed school culture. Usually, there will be those who overtly or covertly do not subscribe to the dominant culture. Their views have to be accommodated without threatening the broader culture.

 Conclusion

A school's culture both determines and reflects how its members behave towards each other. It behoves all those in the school community – especially those in leadership positions – to do all they can to create an atmosphere of respect for all learners and to provide them with challenging educational environments.

 Further reading

Clark, C., Dyson, A. and Millward, A. (eds) (1995). *Towards inclusive schools?* London: David Fulton.

Key references

1 Lindsay, G. and Muijs, D. (2006). 'Challenging underachievement in boys'. *Educational Research*, 43(3), 313–332.
2 Based on Heller, M.F. and Firestone, W.A. (1995). 'Who's in charge here? Sources of leadership for change in eight schools'. *Elementary School Journal*, 96(1), 65–86.
3 Mayrowetz, D. and Weinstein, C.S. (1999). 'Sources of leadership for inclusive education: Creating schools for all children'. *Educational Administration Quarterly*, 35(3), 423–449.
4 Wolery, M. and Jones, K.B. (1998). 'Class size reduction: Do the politicians' statements match research findings?' *Journal of Behavioral Education*, 8(4), 393–395.
5 Lindsay and Muijs, op. cit.
6 Clarke, C., Dyson, A., Millward, A. and Robson, S. (1999). 'Inclusive education and schools as organizations'. *International Journal of Inclusive Education*, 3(1), 37–51.
7 Zollers, N.J., Ramanathan, A.K. and Yu, M. (1999). 'The relationship between school culture and inclusion: How an inclusive culture supports inclusive education'. *Qualitative Studies in Education*, 12(2), 157–174.
8 Mayrowetz and Weinstein, op. cit.
9 Stanovich, P.J. and Jordan, A. (1998). 'Canadian teachers' and principals' beliefs about inclusive education as predictors of effective teaching in heterogeneous classrooms'. *The Elementary School Journal*, 98(3), 221–238.
10 Hattie, J. (1999). *Influences on student learning*. Inaugural lecture, University of Auckland, New Zealand.

Chapter 9

Strategy 7: School-wide positive behaviour support

'Create a multi-tiered system to prevent or minimize problem behaviours'

Rating

★★★☆

 The strategy

School-wide positive behaviour support (SW-PBS) is a behaviour-based proactive approach to building a school's capacity to deal with the wide array of behavioural challenges. It emphasizes: (a) the prevention and reduction of chronic problem behaviour, (b) active instruction of adaptive skills, (c) a continuum of consequences for problem behaviours and (d) interventions for learners with the most intractable problem behaviours.[1] As such, it is a cluster of effective strategies, centring on the school as an organization, and aimed at enhancing the quality of life of all its members.[2]

SW-PBS is sometimes referred to as *positive behavioural support, positive behavioural intervention and support, school-wide behavioural management systems, effective behavioural support* and *school-wide discipline plans.* Although these terms are not exact synonyms, they refer to strategies that have much in common.

This strategy relates to the context, external task demands and external responses in the learning and teaching model outlined in Chapter 2.

 The underlying idea

The emergence of the SW-PBS strategy reflects a range of factors.[3] While these have mostly been expressed by US writers and reflect US conditions, I am confident that they also apply to other developed countries, and probably to most developing countries. The following is a summary of the factors on the *negative* side that have been advanced as a rationale for SW-PBS:

- Learners who display or are at risk of antisocial behaviours are an increasing concern and unless these behaviours are appropriately dealt with they could lead to severe difficulties in adulthood.[4]

- Such behaviours disrupt the learning of peers and make teaching an unattractive profession.
- Families, schools and communities contribute to the development of challenging behaviours by failing to provide learners with acceptable social skills and by modelling inappropriate social interactions through, for example:
  - harsh behaviour management practices;
  - reactive, crisis-driven, punitive disciplinary practices such as exclusions/expulsions, suspensions and inflexible 'zero tolerance' policies;
  - lack of clarity about rules, expectations and consequences;
  - failure to enforce rules; and
  - failure to accommodate to individual differences among learners.

On the *positive* side, SW-PBS has been justified on such grounds as:

- There is evidence that schools can be successful in reducing challenging behaviours through such strategies as:
  - social skills training (**Strategy 10**);
  - curricular adaptations (**Strategy 1**);
  - proactive classroom management (**Strategies 7** and **17**);
  - individual behavioural interventions (**Strategy 17**);
  - parent training (**Strategy 5**);
  - providing maximum opportunities to learn (**Strategy 24**); and
  - early intervention.
- There is a growing body of evidence that by developing a proactive, school-wide system that incorporates these strategies, SW-PBS can be effective in decreasing the level of problem behaviour. Such an approach recognizes that a school has its own unique culture (**Strategy 6**) and is a complex organization comprising: (a) people of varying ages, abilities and authority, (b) environments ranging from classrooms to cafeterias, (c) policies, (d) routines and (e) procedures, all of which must function as a coordinated whole.[5]

 The practice

SW-PBS has four main elements:[6]

 Team-based systems approach

A core feature of SW-PBS is that it is a team-based systems approach, with a school-wide plan. It is as much concerned with fixing problem contexts as with dealing with problem behaviours. This requires all members of the school staff (including bus drivers, caretakers/janitors, etc.) to work together on a common agenda of goals and approaches to learners' behaviour. To achieve this, several factors are very important: school leadership, administrative support, on-site professional development for staff and consistency across all staff members. It is a good idea to set up a school-wide support team to guide and direct the process.

Proactive focus on prevention

It is essential that the main role of SW-PBS be seen as preventing problem behaviours from occurring or from becoming more serious, chronic conditions. In this sense it has a proactive focus, although I do recognize that existing problem behaviours must also be responded to.

Within this prevention theme a three-tiered approach is typically taken.[7] Derived from models of delivering health services in the community, this involves setting up a continuum of behaviour support practices in a school, with three levels: primary, secondary and tertiary prevention. *Primary prevention* has the goal of creating a positive social culture and preventing new cases of problem behaviour from occurring. It does this by involving all learners and adults within a school. It does not require individual learners to be identified. *Secondary prevention* recognizes that primary prevention does not work for all learners. It is aimed at identifying and supporting individual learners who are at risk of engaging in more serious problem behaviour before they reach that stage. *Tertiary prevention* focuses on the smaller number of learners who engage in serious and chronic problem behaviour and who require intensive, individualized intervention.[8] Put another way, the three levels equate with universal support, group support and individual support, respectively. It should be noted that in SW-PBS learners who receive group or individual support also participate in universal support programmes.[9]

One study estimated that, on the basis of 'office referrals' for disciplinary infractions, 76 per cent of learners in 'typical' US schools were without serious problem behaviours and therefore would benefit from universal support, 15 per cent were at risk for problem behaviours and needed group support, while 9 per cent needed individual support.[10]

Evidence-based intervention

There are two aspects to this. First, it is important that intervention strategies be based on the best available research evidence (such as contained in this book). Second, it is important that decisions made on the implementation of SW-PBS, and any adjustments to it, be based on data obtained from observations and interviews/discussions within the school.

Social skills instruction

There are four main procedures for teaching pro-social behaviour (see also **Strategy 10**).

1   *Convey clear expectations.* Here you should clearly define and explain what constitutes unacceptable behaviour and its consequences, as well as explain and teach about the school's expectations for positive social behaviours. Unfortunately, educators seem to be better at the former than the latter!

2   *Reinforce appropriate behaviour.* This requires educators to identify appropriate behaviours when they occur in various locations in the school, to identify suitable rewards and to ensure they are delivered.

3   *Provide corrective consequences for inappropriate behaviour.* Learners who perform inappropriate behaviour should receive a consequence, which could include a verbal reprimand, a detention or referral to a senior staff member with responsibility for school discipline.

These procedures are illustrated in a US study of a middle school with 530 students where SW-PBS was introduced.[11] At the beginning of the school year, the staff defined 'The High Five' expected behaviours: (a) be respectful, (b) be responsible, (c) be there – be ready, (d) follow directions and (e) hands and feet to self. These expectations were translated into specific behaviours appropriate to each of six school locations (e.g., classrooms, gym and cafeteria). For example, being respectful in the classroom meant listening to others without interrupting, while in the gym it meant sharing equipment and space. Features of the instruction included:

a   teaching of The High Five expectations in the location where the target behaviours were to occur;
b   teaching learners to discriminate between acceptable and unacceptable behaviours;
c   distributing rewards contingent upon performing the expected behaviours (each staff member had a supply of The High Five tickets to give out when they spotted appropriate behaviours and these could be 'spent' on such rewards as food and access to the gym);
d   giving frequent reminders of expectations in each of the main locations.

4   *Regular supervision.* Once SW-PBS has been introduced, it is essential that there is regular supervision of behaviours in the main areas of the school: classrooms, playgrounds, hallways and facilities such as gyms and cafeterias.

As with the other strategies I describe in this book, further examples of practice are contained in the next section on Evidence.

The evidence

A range of research has been carried out into outcomes of SW-PBS. All of the following studies were conducted in the USA.

✓ A study carried out in a rural middle school catering for sixth, seventh and eighth-grade learners evaluated an SW-PBS programme designed to define, teach and reward appropriate learner behaviour. In the beginning of the first year of the programme learners were taught school expectations (see previous section on 'social skills instruction'). Throughout the year, the learners received rewards for appropriate behaviour and office referrals for infractions. Results showed a 42 per cent reduction in **office referrals** compared with the previous year when no interventions were carried out.[12]

✓ Another study reported on a project aimed at assisting elementary and middle schools to implement a school-wide discipline plan based on the Effective Behaviour Support model[13] and the Second Step violence prevention curriculum[14] with all students in the school. Nine treatment and six comparison schools were studied. The results showed greatly reduced **office referrals for unacceptable behaviour** and improved social skills knowledge for learners in the treatment schools.[15]

✓ On the assumption that the SW-PBS approach to discipline is effective in supporting 80–85 per cent of the student population, a study designed complementary individually targeted interventions for those who do not respond to SW-PBS approaches at the primary prevention level. The study used a 'Behavior Education Program' where learners 'checked-in' and 'checked-out' with teachers throughout the day on targeted social behaviours. The results showed a reduction in the variability of **problem behaviour**, as well as some decrease in the level of problem behaviour.[16]

✓ Hallway behaviours in a middle school were the focus of the next study. The purpose was to determine whether an SW-PBS intervention that included positive practice, verbal praise, correction of inappropriate behaviour, active supervision and discussion of behaviour with learners would improve **problematic hallway behaviours**. The five-week intervention with 950 learners led to a reduction of 42.4 per cent in such behaviours.[17]

✓ Another study investigated the effects of SW-PBS on **discipline problems** and academic outcomes of learners in an elementary school. The approach emphasized such factors as: improving instructional methods, formulating behavioural expectations, increasing classroom active engagement, reinforcing positive performances and monitoring performances. The intervention led to decreased discipline problems and improved academic performances.[18]

✓ SW-PBS was implemented over a two-year period in an elementary
  school. As a result of decreased student **behaviour problems**, instructional time increased across the school by 72.7 learner-days in the first
  year and 86.2 learner-days over baseline in the second year.[19]

✓ The purpose of another study was to explore the effects of a proactive
  school-wide discipline approach on the frequency of **problem behaviour**
  exhibited by elementary students. Specifically, the study was designed
  to explore the impact of a social skill instruction programme, combined
  with active supervision and direct intervention on problem behaviours,
  across three specific school settings: cafeteria, break and a hallway
  transition. Results showed that educators reduced the rate of problem
  behaviours across each targeted setting.[20]

✓ In a meta-analysis of Positive Behaviour Support outcomes reported in
  109 published articles, the authors concluded that PBS interventions:

  • are increasingly addressing **severe challenging behaviours**;
  • produce small to significant changes in adaptive, positive behaviours;
  • produce 90 per cent or more reductions in challenging behaviours
    from baseline levels in 52 per cent of interventions, and 80 per cent
    or more in 68 per cent of interventions;
  • do not vary significantly in outcome according to whether antecedent-
    based or reinforcement-based interventions are used alone or in
    combination;
  • show successful maintenance over periods from between one and
    24 months in about two-thirds of interventions;
  • are likely to generalize across new settings and intervention agents
    in about two-thirds of cases using the 90 per cent criterion – but
    evidence of generalization across different forms of challenging
    behaviour is weak; and
  • are twice as likely to be successful if intervention is based on
    functional analysis.[21]

 Addressing risks

There are three main risks in implementing SW-PBS:

1 There is insufficient 'buy-in' to the approach. There should be a
   commitment from at least 80 per cent of staff.[22]
2 There is inadequate monitoring of the approach. This is a vital component
   of SW-PBS. It is necessary for the planning process as well as helping
   to convince the participants that it is working and, if not, that problems
   with its implementation must be addressed.
3 Perhaps the major risk is that some staff members are reluctant to shift
   their focus from a reactive and punitive approach to a proactive and

preventative one. Changing these habits of mind requires skilled leadership and convincing data.

 Conclusion

SW-PBS is a promising strategy for reducing the occurrence of problem behaviours in learners by taking a proactive, multi-tiered, preventative, team-based systems approach.

 Further reading

Journal of Positive Behavioral Interventions
Lewis, T.J. and Newcomer, L.L. (2005). 'Reducing problem behavior through school-wide systems of positive behavior support'. In P. Clough, P. Garner, J.T. Pardeck and F. Yuen (eds) *Handbook of emotional and behavioural difficulties* (pp. 261–272). London: Sage.
National Technical Assistance Center on Positive Behavioral Interventions and Supports (PBIS): URL: www.pbis.org/main.htm (accessed 19 January 2007).
Sugai, G. and Pruitt, R. (1993). *Phases, steps and guidelines for building school-wide behavior management programs: A practitioner's handbook.* Eugene, OR: Behavior Disorders Program.

Key references

1 Horner, R.H., Sugai, G., Todd, A.W. and Lewis-Palmer, T. (2005). 'School-wide positive behavior support: An alternative approach to discipline in schools In L. Bambara and L. Kern (eds) *Individualized supports for students with problem behavior: Designing positive behavior plans.* New York: Guilford Press, pp. 359–390.
2 Carr, E.G., Dunlap, G., Horner, R.H., Koegel, R.L., Turnbull, A.P., Sailor, W., Anderson, J., Albin, R.W., Koegel, L.K. and Fox, L. (2002). 'Positive behavior support: Evolution of an applied science'. *Journal of Positive Behavior Interventions,* 4(1), 4–16.
3 This section is based on the following sources: Hawken, L.S. and Horner, R.H. (2003). 'Evaluation of a targeted intervention within a schoolwide system of behavior support'. *Journal of Behavioral Education,* 12(3), 225–240; Lewis, T.J. and Newcomer, L.L. (2005). 'Reducing problem behavior through school-wide systems of positive behavior support'. In P. Clough, P. Garner, J.T. Pardeck and F. Yuen (eds) *Handbook of emotional and behavioural difficulties* (pp. 261–272). London: Sage; Lewis, T.J. and Sugai, G. (1999). 'Effective behavior support: A systems approach to proactive schoolwide management'. *Focus on Exceptional Children,* 31(6), 1–24; Lewis, T.J., Sugai, G. and Colvin, G. (1998). 'Reducing problem behavior through a school-wide system of effective behavioral support: Investigation of a school-wide social skills training program and contextual interventions'. *School Psychology Review,* 27(3), 446–459; OSEP Center on Positive Behavioral Interventions and Supports (2004). *School-wide positive behavior support: Implementers' blueprint and self-assessment.* Eugene, OR: Center on Positive Behavioral Interventions and Supports, University of Oregon. URL: www.osepideasthatwork.org/toolkit/pdf/SchoolwideBehaviorSupport.pdf

(accessed 20 January 2007); and Sprague, J., Walker, H., Golly, A., White, A., Myers, D.R. and Shannon, T. (2001). 'Translating research into effective practice: The effects of a universal staff and student intervention on indicators of discipline and school safety'. *Education and Treatment of Children*, 24(4), 495–511.

4 In a summary of research into negative outcomes, points such as these were made in relation to US schools:

- problem behaviour is the single most common reason why students are removed from regular school and home settings;
- only half of American school children report feeling safe in their schools;
- 82 per cent of crimes are committed by people who have dropped out of school;
- school discipline is one of the top concerns of American educators.

Source: Lewis and Sugai, op. cit.

5 Sprague *et al.*, op. cit.
6 See note 2 for sources.
7 Freeman, R., Eber, L., Anderson, C., Irvin, L., Horner, R., Bounds, M. and Dunlap, G. (2006). 'Building inclusive school cultures using school-wide PBS: Designing effective individual support systems for students with significant disabilities'. *Research and Practice for Persons with Severe Disabilities*, 31(1), 4–17; OSEP Technical Assistance Center on Positive Behavioral Interventions and Support. URL: www.pbis.org/schoolwide.htm (accessed 21 January 2007); and Lewis and Sugai, op. cit.
8 This group of learners could well have intervention plans that are guided by functional behavioural assessment (**Strategy 18**), which identify the events that predict and maintain problem behaviours.
9 Turnbull, A., Edmonson, H., Griggs, P., Wickham, D., Sailor, W., Freeman, R., Guess, D., Lassen, S., McCart, A., Park, J., Riffel, L., Turnbull, R. and Warren, J. (2002). 'A blueprint for schoolwide positive behavior support: Implementation of three components'. *Exceptional Children*, 88(3), 377–402.
10 Turnbull *et al.*, op. cit.
11 Taylor-Greene, S., Brown, D., Nelson, L., Longton, J., Gassman, T., Cohen, J., Swartz, J., Horner, R.H., Sugai, G.M. and Hall, S. (1997). 'School-wide behavioral support: Starting the year off right'. *Journal of Behavioral Education*, 7(1), 99–112.
12 Taylor-Greene *et al.*, op. cit.
13 Sugai, G. and Horner, R. (1994). 'Including students with severe behavior problems in general education settings: Assumptions, challenges, and solutions'. *Oregon Conference Monograph*, 6, 102–120.
14 Grossman, D.C., Neckerman, H.J., Koepsell, T.D., Liu, P., Asher, K.N., Bedland, K., Frey, K. and Rivara, F.P. (1997). 'Effectiveness of a violence prevention curriculum among children in elementary school: A randomised controlled trial'. *The Journal of the American Medical Association*, 277(20), 1605–1612.
15 Sprague *et al.*, op. cit.
16 Hawken, L.S. and Horner, R.H. (2003). 'Evaluation of a targeted intervention within a schoolwide system of behavior support'. *Journal of Behavioral Education*, 12(3), 225–240.
17 Oswald, K., Safran, S. and Johanson, G. (2005). 'Preventing trouble: Making schools safer using positive behavior supports'. *Education and Treatment of Children*, 28(3), 265–278.

18 Luiselli, J.K., Putnam, R.F., Handler, M.W. and Feinberg, A.B. (2005). 'Whole-school positive behavior support: Effects on student discipline problems and academic performance'. *Educational Psychology*, 25(2/3), 183–198.
19 Scott, T.M. and Barrett, S.B. (2004). 'Using staff and student time engaged in disciplinary procedures to evaluate the impact of school-wide PBS'. *Journal of Positive Behavior Interventions*, 61(1), 21–27.
20 Lewis, Sugai and Colvin, op. cit.
21 Carr, E.G., Horner R.H., Turnbull A.P. *et al.* (1999) *Positive Behavior Support for people with developmental disabilities: A research synthesis*. Washington, DC: AAMR.
22 OSEP Technical Assistance Center on Positive Behavioral Interventions and Support, op. cit.

Chapter 10

Strategy 8: Indoor environmental quality

'Provide a physical environment that enables learning'

Rating
★★★★

  The strategy

As Winston Churchill so memorably stated, 'We shape our buildings, and afterwards our buildings shape us.'

This strategy is aimed at ensuring that all the elements of the physical environment that may affect students' ability to learn are optimal. It involves attending to such matters as the design and arrangement of furniture, acoustics, lighting, temperature and ventilation. It relates to the context component of the learning and teaching model described in Chapter 2.

I recognize that some of the points I make in this chapter may be outside of your personal control because of decisions made by those responsible for school building policies, architects and builders. I also recognize, sadly, that in some countries even a physical entity of a classroom may not be affordable. Even in developed countries, not all learners are educated in schools that meet minimum standards.[1]

 The underlying idea

Simply put, learners who spend time in well-designed, well-maintained classrooms that are comfortable, well-lit, reasonably quiet and properly ventilated with healthy air will learn more efficiently and enjoy their educational experiences.

 The practice

Here I will outline five major aspects of the physical environment that you should attend to:

- physical space and equipment;
- temperature, humidity and ventilation;
- lighting;
- acoustics; and
- stimulating and safe classrooms.

 Arrange physical space and equipment to facilitate learning

Learning in a school takes place in a physical space we call a classroom. As an educator you can do little to alter the dimensions of this space and to deal with overcrowding, but you can do a great deal to ensure that its use is conducive to effective teaching and learning. For example, you can:

- Arrange furniture and equipment in such a way as to manage inappropriate behaviour and to disrupt undesirable 'traffic' patterns and movement around the classroom.[2]
- Ensure the physical environment is accessible to students with mobility difficulties.
- Where necessary, ensure that all equipment and apparatus is specifically adapted for use by learners with special educational needs.
- Ensure that furniture is arranged to minimize the chance of 'clumsy' learners bumping into other learners' workspaces.
- Ensure that learners who need to be near the front of the classroom, because of hearing or vision impairments or for behaviour management purposes, are placed in those locations.
- Place linked centres close together so that the space and materials can be shared. For example, the reading and writing areas could be combined to create a language corner.
- Arrange movable room dividers to create corners in the classroom.[3]
- Store frequently used equipment and materials in stackable drawers and crates on wheels. This allows learners to move the units to where they are needed and keeps busy areas clear. They can also more easily be brought to learners who might not have the mobility to get them by themselves.
- Label everything that has been put in containers. An effective way of doing this is to label boxes with a simple symbol, or picture, indicating what is inside.[4]
- Make special adaptations for learners with physical disabilities who need wider doors, ramps, tables and chairs at the correct height for a wheelchair, aisles sufficiently wide to navigate, and individual workspaces.

Control temperature, humidity and ventilation

School and classroom temperature, humidity, ventilation and the presence of mould, fungi, dust and mildew are important factors that need to be controlled. For children with multiple sclerosis, excessive heat can affect them and create classroom problems, while for learners with asthma, excessive humidity and poor air quality can restrict their participation.[5]

 Control lighting

Lighting needs to enable learners to see the details of given tasks easily and accurately in lighting conditions that pertain during the day and throughout the year. A major difference between classrooms and most other environments is that learners must constantly adjust their vision between 'heads-up' and 'heads-down' reading conditions.[6] Lighting should take account of this range of demands on learners' vision.

Here are some suggestions:

- Try to use a combination of direct and indirect lighting to reduce glare and reflections as much as possible.
- Maximize the use of day-lighting, but supplement it by electric lighting, which can, if possible, be automatically dimmed in response to daylight levels.
- Place mirrors on walls opposite windows.
- Be quick to replace burnt-out lights.
- About 20 per cent of a classroom's wall space should consist of windows.[7]
- Ensure that the contrast between a task object and its immediate background is sufficient to enable learners to clearly view the task.
- Use convex whiteboards to reduce glare.
- Check that fluorescent lighting is in good working order as excessive flickering could trigger a seizure in learners with photosensitive epilepsy.[8]
- The lighting level for computer use should be about half as bright as that normally found in a classroom.
- Strictly enforce the amount of time that learners continuously use computers. A ten-minute break every hour will minimize focusing problems and eye irritation.
- Develop the '20/20/20 rule': every 20 minutes, take 20 seconds and look 20 feet (6 metres) away.
- Carefully check the height and angle of the computer screen (just below eye level and about 20 degrees angle), and the distance from the eyes (18–26 inches or 45–66 centimetres).
- Ensure that there is no glare on the screen (use a mirror to check sources of glare).[9]

Provide optimal acoustics

Since much classroom learning takes place through listening and speaking (estimates vary from 50–90 per cent[10]), it is essential that learners can hear educators' speech clearly. Unfortunately, this is not always the case, with typical classrooms in many developed countries providing inadequate acoustical environments in terms of three interrelated factors:[11]

- *Poor signal-to-noise ratio* (i.e., an educator's voice compared with background noise). For example, if your voice arrives at a learner's desk at 50 decibels[12] (50 dB) and the background noise is 55 dB, the resulting signal-to-noise ratio (SNR) is –5. This compares unfavourably with an optimum SNR of +15 dB for learners with normal hearing and very unfavourably with the requirements of learners with special educational needs.
- *Excessive sound reverberation* (i.e., sound bounce, or echo). Technically, this is measured by 'reverberation time', which is the time between the cessation of a sound source and a measured decay of 60 dB. Ideally, this should be no longer than 0.4–0.6 of a second.
- *High levels of ambient noise* (i.e., the noises consistently present in an empty classroom). These should be no louder than 30–35 dB.

In order to require, or at least encourage, education systems to provide optimal acoustical environments, the World Health Organization and several countries have adopted standards or are in the process of formulating them.[13]

In a New Zealand study of 106 classrooms, for example, it was found that only 4 per cent had acceptable noise levels for instruction.[14] This situation, which is by no means limited to New Zealand, has a major impact on the students' opportunities to learn, especially for those with mild or fluctuating hearing loss, learning disabilities, attention disorders, language disabilities and learners of English as a second language.

Here, there are two main interrelated strategies for removing acoustical barriers to learning: first, increasing 'good' sounds and, second, reducing 'bad' sounds.

Increasing good sounds

As we shall see in the Evidence section, many learners with special educational needs – indeed, learners in general – benefit from what is referred to as *sound-field amplification*. Simply, this is done by means of a small high-fidelity wireless public address system located in a single classroom with a microphone for the educator and speakers located around the classroom. This enables the educator's voice to be increased by about 10 dB. This method of voice amplification has advantages over hearing aids since the latter magnify both voices and background noise (although I recognize that they are necessary for learners with major hearing loss). Incidentally, sound-field amplification can benefit you, the educator, too, by counteracting any voice fatigue and hoarseness you might be prone to.[15] By the standard of developed countries, they are moderately priced at around £1,000–£1,500 (US$2,000–US$3,000) per system. Care must be taken in placing speakers where teaching takes place and you will need some training in how the system works. I have personally observed a school in my hometown in New Zealand where all classrooms have been fitted with sound-field amplification systems.[16]

Reducing bad sounds

In a classroom, several things can be done to decrease noise levels:

- Use sound-absorbing materials such as large cork bulletin boards, carpets under noisy equipment and felt under chairs to reduce annoying scraping sounds (a creative way is to put half tennis balls on the tips of the legs of the chairs).
- Insulate walls and ceilings and use dividers covered with thick felt or material to absorb noise within and between classrooms. (Note, however, that there is a risk that materials such as felt might gather dust and jeopardize the health of asthmatic learners.)
- Separate noisy and quiet areas. For example, locate the reading corner and the play area at opposite ends of the room.
- Model appropriate voice levels (for example, ask the learners to distinguish between 'inside' and 'outside' voices).
- Encourage learners to speak quietly in group activities and when moving furniture.
- Use music to calm the class (but take care that this does not itself become 'noise' and force learners to speak even louder to make themselves heard).[17]
- Keep doors and windows closed, provided there is adequate ventilation.
- Check the noise levels of any heating, ventilation and air conditioning system in your classroom.
- Involve an audiologist and/or a speech and language therapist in working out ways to make your classroom acoustically satisfactory.
- For further ideas, see these Web sites: www.classroomacoustics.com and http://asa.aip.org.

 Set up classroom environments that are attractive, stimulating and safe

Learners – and educators – spend many hours in classrooms. This learning space should, therefore, be made as attractive, stimulating and safe as possible, not just for aesthetic reasons, but also to provide an environment that is conducive to learning. Here are some suggestions for you to consider:

- regularly display examples of learners' work around the classroom (while it is tempting – and appropriate – to display the 'best' work to recognize high performance, all learners should have their work recognized);
- place visual learning cues and challenging materials on the walls of your classroom;[18]
- identify and eliminate potentially hazardous elements in the classroom.

 ## The evidence

Physical space

✓ A study conducted in New York City showed that students in overcrowded schools scored significantly lower in both mathematics and reading than similar students in less crowded conditions.[19]

Ventilation

✓ In a 1999 US study, ventilation was rated as unsatisfactory by 26 per cent of schools, a rating that caused more concern to schools than any other environmental condition. A related statistic was that 24 per cent of schools stated that air conditioning was needed but not available.[20]

✓ A recent Danish study in two classes of ten-year-old learners investigated the effects of classroom temperatures and the supply of outdoor air on schoolwork. Average air temperatures were reduced from 23.6 °C to 20.0 °C and the supply of outdoor air was increased from 5.2 to 9.6 litres per person. Singly and in combination, the experiment resulted in improved performances in reading and mathematics. Unfortunately, no separate data were reported for learners with special educational needs.[21]

Lighting

✓ A recent UK review of the effects of lighting in classrooms made the following points:
- the visual environment affects learners' ability to perceive visual stimuli and affects their mental attitudes and, therefore, their performances;
- day-lighting has the most positive effects on learners' achievement;
- since day-lighting as a sole source of lighting is not feasible, it must be supplemented by automatically controlled electric lighting that dims in response to daylight levels;

- • lighting should be as glare-free and flicker-free as possible, especially when computers are being used.[22]
- ✓ While many building codes call for uniform brightness of 55 foot candles,[23] some lighting specialists argue for differential brightness according to the usage of learning spaces (e.g., 55 foot candles for the centre of a classroom, with lower illumination in bays that serve as 'break-out' space and higher on display walls).[24]
- ✓ In 1999 a study to determine the impact of day-lighting on student performance was commissioned by the California Board of Energy Efficiency. The study involved 21,000 students in California, Colorado and Washington states. The results of the study indicated that test scores could improve by as much as 26 per cent in reading and 20 per cent in mathematics.[25]
- ✓ The American Optometric Association has recently described a Computer Vision Syndrome as 'the complex of eye and vision problems related to near work which are experienced during or related to computer use'. The symptoms include: eye strain, headaches, blurred vision, dry or red eyes, neck pain and/or backache, double vision and light sensitivity.[26]

Classroom acoustics

- ✓ A New Zealand study examined the effects of sound-field amplification for four learners with **Down syndrome** aged six to seven years. The results showed that the learners perceived significantly more speech when a sound amplification system that amplified the investigator's voice by 10 dB was used.[27]
- ✓ Also using a sound amplification system that increased the intensity of a teacher's voice by 10 dB, a US study found that nine elementary school learners **with developmental disabilities** made significantly fewer errors on a word identification task than they made without amplification.[28]
- ✓ A second New Zealand study examined the effects of sound-field amplification on learners with and without **hearing impairments**. Even though the amplification increased the signal-to-noise ratio by only 5–10 dB (which was still below the international standard of 15 dB), the study found improved on-task behaviours and phonological awareness for both groups of learners.[29]
- ✓ In a large-scale US study, a special project was designed to determine if young learners' listening and learning behaviours improved as a result of sound-field amplification. The three-year project compared the results of learners in 64 experimental classrooms (i.e., amplified) with those in 30 control classrooms (unamplified). The results showed that those in amplified classrooms (where teachers' voices had an average increase of 6.94 dB) showed significant improvement in listening and learning behaviours and progressed at a faster rate than those in the unamplified

classrooms, with younger learners showing the greatest improvement. Unfortunately, no separate data were reported for learners with special educational needs.[30]

✓ A recent UK study that examined the effects of classroom noise on learners' performances found that noise negatively impacted on all learners, especially those with **special educational needs**.[31] In a study of 142 London primary schools, the same authors also found that 65 per cent were exposed to noise levels in excess of World Health Organization standards and that there was a significant negative relationship between noise levels and scores on nationally standardized tests. In other words, the higher the noise levels, the less well the school performed in the tests.[32]

✓ An early US study reported similar results in a school located close to an elevated urban train track. The reading scores of learners in classrooms facing the tracks were compared with those of learners on the other side of the building facing away from the tracks. It was found that the scores of learners in lower grades exposed to the noisy side were three to four months behind relative to the learners in the quieter side, and as much as 11 months behind for higher grades.[33]

 Addressing risks

While I have attempted in this chapter to provide a series of guidelines for providing a high-quality indoor environment, in some cases the steps to be taken are technically complex and require the guidance of specialists in the various fields.

 Conclusion

Although often overlooked, the quality of the classroom indoor environment plays a critical role in learners' achievement and comfort, as well as providing an optimal working environment for you, an educator.

 Further reading

Higgins, S., Hall, E., Wall, K., Woolner, P. and McCaughey, C. (2005). *The impact of school environments: A literature review*. Produced for the Design Council by Centre for Learning and Teaching, University of Newcastle, UK.

National Clearing House for Educational Facilities: URL: www.edfacilities.org/rl/impact_learning.cfm (accessed 28 December 2006).

Key references

1 For example, in 1999 in the USA, 50 per cent of schools reported that at least one of nine critical building features at their school was in less than adequate

condition and three-quarters of those schools had more than one building feature in less than adequate condition. Schools with the highest concentration of poverty were more likely to report that at least one building feature was in less than adequate condition. Source: National Center for Educational Statistics, *Conditions of America's public school facilities*. URL: http://nces.ed.gov/pubs99/1999048.pdf (accessed 28 December 2006). URL: http://nces.ed.gov/surveys/frss/publications/2000032/index.asp?sectionID=2 (accessed 10 December 2006).

2 Council for Exceptional Children (1997). *CEC Code of Ethics and Standards of Practice*. Reston, VA: CEC.

3 Lang, D. (1996). *Essential criteria for an ideal learning environment*. New Horizons for Learning. URL: www.newhorizons.org/strategies/learning_environments/lang.htm (accessed 28 December 2006).

4 Lang, op. cit.

5 Crowther, I. (2003). *Creating effective learning environments*. Scarborough: Thompson Canada; and www.devon.gov.uk/eal/dgfl/docs/accessibilitystrategy.doc (accessed 28 December 2006).

6 The Collaborative for High Performance Schools. *Best Practices Manual, 2002 Edition*. III: Criteria. 2002. URL: www.chps.net/manual/documents/2002_updates/CHPSvIII.pdf (accessed 28 December 2006).

7 Lang, op. cit.

8 www.epilepsy.org.uk/info/photo_other.html (accessed 2 February 2007).

9 Anshel, J.R. (2000). *Kids and computers: Eyes and visual systems*. The RSI Network, Issue 42. URL: www.tifaq.org/articles/kids&computers-jan00-jeffrey_anshel.html (accessed 2 January 2007).

10 Schmidt, C., Andrews, M. and McCutcheon, J. (1998). 'An acoustical and perceptual analysis of the vocal behaviour of classroom teachers'. *Journal of Voice*, 12(4), 434–443.

11 ASHA Working Group on Classroom Acoustics (2005). *Acoustics in educational settings: Technical report*. URL: www.asha.org/NR/rdonlyres/066CDD53-6052-405F-8CB7-3D603D5CCD0F/0/V2TRAcoustics.pdf (accessed 30 December 2006); and ASHA Special Interest Division 16, and Educational Audiology Association (2002). 'Appropriate school facilities for students with speech-language-hearing disorders'. Technical Report, *ASHA Supplement* 23.

12 A decibel is a

unit of measurement of the loudness or strength of a signal. One decibel is considered the smallest difference in sound level that the human ear can discern. . . . A whisper is about 20 dB. A normal conversation is typically from 60 to 70 dB, and a noisy factory from 90 to 100 dB. Loud thunder is approximately 110 dB, and 120 dB borders on the threshold of pain.

(www.answers.com, accessed 28 December 2006)

13 The World Health Organization recommends that to be able to hear and understand spoken messages in classrooms, the *background sound level* should not exceed 35 dB during teaching sessions; for hearing impaired children, a still lower sound level may be needed. For outdoor playgrounds the sound level of the noise from external sources should not exceed 55 dB, the same value given for outdoor residential areas in daytime. It further recommends that the *reverberation time* in classrooms should be about 0.6 second, and preferably lower for hearing impaired children; for assembly halls and cafeterias in school buildings, it should be less than 1 second (World Health Organization (1999). *Guidelines for community noise*. Geneva: WHO).

In a similar vein, US regulations state that *background noise* should not exceed 35 dB for core (classroom) learning spaces, 40 dB for ancillary learning spaces such as cafeterias and gyms, and 45 dB for other ancillary learning spaces, such as corridors if no formal instruction takes place. *Reverberation times* for unoccupied, furnished core learning spaces is 0.6 s or 0.7 s, depending on the size of the room (ANSI S12.60-200X, *Acoustical Performance Criteria, Design Requirements and Guidelines for Schools*, Final draft submitted to ASA/S12 in September 2001 for second ballot).

For the UK, refer to the DfES *Building Bulletin 93* (2003), which specifies acoustic design for schools under the following headings: indoor ambient noise levels, airborne sound insulation, reverberation time, sound absorption in corridors and stairwells, and speech intelligibility in open-plan spaces.

14 Blake, P. and Busby, S. (1994). 'Noise levels in New Zealand junior classrooms: Their impact on hearing and teaching'. *New Zealand Medical Journal*, 107(985), 357–358.

15 Bennetts, L.K. and Flynn, M.C. (2002). 'Improving the classroom listening skills of children with Down syndrome by using sound-field amplification'. *Down Syndrome Research and Practice*, 8(1), 19–24.

16 See also a news item about a US district installing an audio enhancement system. URL: http://staugustine.com/stories/012307/news_new0123.shtml (accessed 27 January 2007).

17 Crowther, op. cit.

18 Florian, L. and Rouse, M. (2000). *Investigating effective classroom practice in inclusive secondary schools in England.* Paper presented at the Special Education World Congress, Vancouver, Canada, April 2000.

19 Rivera-Batiz, F.L. and Marti, L. (1995). *A school system at risk: A study of the consequences of overcrowding in New York City public schools.* New York: Institute for Urban and Minority Education, Teachers College, Columbia University.

20 National Center for Educational Statistics (1999). *Condition of America's public school facilities.* URL: http://nces.ed.gov/surveys/frss/publications/2000032/index. asp?sectionID=5 (accessed 2 January 2007).

21 Wargocki, P., Wyon, D.P., Matysiak, B. and Irgens, S. (2005). *The effects of classroom air temperature and outdoor supply rate on the performance of school work by children.* URL: www.ie.dtu.dk/ (accessed 2 January 2007).

22 Higgins, S., Hall, E., Wall, K., Woolner, P. and McCaughey, C. (2005). *The impact of school environments: A literature review.* Produced for the Design Council. Newcastle, UK: The Centre for Learning and Teaching, University of Newcastle.

23 A foot candle is a 'unit of measure of the intensity of light falling on a surface, equal to one lumen per square foot and originally defined with reference to a standardized candle burning at one foot from a given surface'. URL: www.answers. com (accessed 28 December 2006).

24 Fielding, R. (2006). *Lighting and design for schools and universities in the 21st century.* URL: http://designshare.com (accessed 20 December 2006).

25 Heschong Mahone Group. URL: www.chps.net_schools/heschong.htm (accessed 2 January 2007).

26 See URL: www.aoa.org/x5374.xml (accessed 2 January 2007).

27 Bennetts and Flynn, op. cit.

28 Flexer, C., Millin, J.P. and Brown, L. (1990). 'Children with developmental disabilities: The effects of sound field amplification on word identification'. *Language, Speech, and Hearing Services in Schools*, 21, 177–182.

29 Allcock, J. (1997). *Report of FM Soundfield study, Paremata School 1997*. Oticon. URL: www.oticon.org.nz/pdf/OTICONParemataresearchreport.pdf (accessed 30 December 2006).
30 Rosenberg, G.G., Blake-Rahter, P., Heavner, J., Allen, L., Redmond, B.M., Phillips, J. and Stigers, K. (1999). 'Improving classroom acoustics (ICA): A three-year FM sound field classroom amplification study'. *Journal of Educational Audiology*, 7, 8–28.
31 Shield, B., Dockrell, J., Jeffrey, R. and Tatchmatzidis, I. (2002). *The effects of noise on the attainments and cognitive performance of primary children: Report to the DoH and DEFRA*. London: South Bank University.
32 Shield, B. and Dockrell, J. (2005). *Environmental noise and children's academic attainments*. Paper presented at ASA/CAA 05 Meeting, Vancouver, Canada, May 2005.
33 Bronzaft, A.I. and McCarthy, D.P. (1975). 'The effect of elevated train noise on reading ability'. *Environmental Behavior*, 7(4), 517–528.

Strategy 9: Classroom climate

'Create a positive, motivating classroom environment'

Rating
★★★☆

 The strategy

The classroom climate is a multi-component strategy comprising the psychological features of the classroom, as distinct from the physical features I discussed in **Strategy 8**. It reflects, but is not limited to, features of the school culture outlined in **Strategy 6**.

Classroom climate is sometimes referred to as *classroom environment, psychosocial environment, atmosphere, ambience, ecology* or *milieu*.[1]

In a word, we are dealing with a major component of the *context* of learning, as well as motivation, referred to in my learning and teaching model in Chapter 2.

 The underlying idea

According to a review in the inaugural issue of the journal *Learning Environments Research*, in the time since the pioneering use of classroom environment assessments in the 1960s, the field has undergone remarkable growth, diversification and internationalization.[2]

As we shall see, there is clear evidence that the quality of the classroom climate is a significant determinant of learners' achievement. They learn better when they have positive perceptions of the classroom environment, particularly of you, the educator.

The key principle of classroom climate is to create a psychological environment that facilitates learning. It draws our attention to three main factors:

- *relationships*: the extent to which people in the classroom support and help each other;

- *personal development*: the extent to which personal growth and self-enhancement is facilitated; and
- *system maintenance*: the extent to which the classroom is orderly, and educators are clear in their expectations, maintain control and are responsive to change.[3]

These three factors provide the framework for the ideas that follow.

 ## The practice

 ## Relationships

Create an emotionally safe environment that learners can trust

Learners with special educational needs often experience the emotions associated with failure. All too often, such learners have been the recipients of rejection and even hostility from others. Many have learned not to trust either their learning environment or their own ability to survive in it. Educators should recognize that these learners are at risk for lowered self-concepts, depression, anger, anxiety and fear. In turn, these emotions negatively affect their learning . . . and so on. You can arrest this vicious cycle if you:

- understand learners' emotions and how they facilitate or hinder their motivation to learn;[4]
- set up learning environments that emphasize positive emotions and reduce negative ones as far as possible;[5]
- recognize that learners come to school each day with different emotions, and that these will confuse some of them;
- seek to harness the power of positive emotions in the learning process;
- provide environments characterized by stability and repetition, security, warmth, empathy, affirmation, support, a sense of community, and justice and peace;[6]
- convey to all students that they are worthwhile and are accepted fully as individuals, despite any difficulties they may have in learning;
- develop 'authentic relationships' in which learners can expect unconditional and non-manipulative acceptance, caring, respect and warmth and, where appropriate, compassion from you;[7]
- be supportive and give learners a sense of belonging: 'My teachers like to see me when I get to school', 'I hate it when I get sick and can't go to school';
- give valued roles to all learners in the class to create a 'community of learners';[8]
- make use of humour, when appropriate, to defuse tension, as well as making learning fun.[9]

✳ *Personal development*

Help learners to set goals

Some learners with special educational needs might so devalue their abilities that they do not set goals; others might set goals that are far beyond their capacity; still others might set goals that are socially inappropriate. Research tells us that learners commit themselves to achieving goals when they are seen as reachable rather than impossible, and when there are clear payoffs such as special recognition when the goals are achieved.[10] For a discussion of how goals contribute to motivation, see the learning and teaching model in Chapter 2, especially my comments on the importance of helping learners to develop task-focused goals.

In brief, you should:

- help learners to set goals for their learning and their behaviour;[11]
- often talk about goals, show how lessons fit in with them and help learners to reflect on their progress towards these goals;
- emphasize the goal of developing understanding rather than simply demonstrating ability or outperforming peers;
- convert vague, general goals into specific intentions and commitments by representing them in terms of specific concrete 'targets' or by defining relevant sub-goals;
- use direct, frequent, targeted feedback to maintain commitment to goals;
- help learners to be goal oriented; often talk about goals and show how lessons fit in with them: 'If you want to be able to work with computers, Ruslan, you will need to understand . . .'; 'Seng, when you fill in a tax form you will need to be able to do this sort of maths'; 'If you want to be a good farmer, you will need to understand erosion';
- assist learners to form specific short-term goals: 'I want to get an A grade for this essay'; 'I want to read this book in one week, so I can get onto the next one';
- encourage learners to form general long-term goals: 'I want to complete high school with a qualification'; 'I want to be a good business person when I leave university';
- encourage learners to have a range of goals: 'I want to be good at my academic work, my sporting activities and at the same time have close friends';
- help learners to prioritize goals and to choose between conflicting goals: 'I will try to achieve a balance between my sporting and my academic goals, but I realize that doing well at my schoolwork is going to be the most important for my future.'

Provide a motivating learning environment

Here are a few suggestions on motivation in general:

- Recognize that there are limits to how far you can motivate others and that, in the end, learners become responsible for their own learning: 'Dave, I can help you learn and point you in the right direction, but I can't do your learning for you!'
- Proceed cautiously when faced with chronic motivational problems. Dramatic changes are possible but hard to engineer; patience is a virtue.
- Recognize that a learner's goals, emotions and personal agency beliefs are intrinsically valid to that person, and must be respected as the reality to be dealt with, regardless of what you think they *should* be.
- Be patient, but firm, with learners who have chronic low motivation: 'I can see that your mind isn't on the lesson today, Haidah, but let's get as much as possible done today and we'll really work on your maths over the next few weeks. I think you will be able to do quite well eventually.'
- Spend some time one-to-one with every learner in your class, at least once a week.

 System maintenance

Convey high, but realistic, expectations

Learners with special educational needs have often, through prolonged failure, rejected the notion that they are capable of learning. They can be at further risk if their educators and parents have low expectations for their performances. Therefore, you should:

- Believe that all students can learn, and convey to them that they have the ability to master essential learning outcomes in the curriculum.[12]
- Constantly strive to raise the expectations of learners and their parents.[13]
- Help learners accept that achievement results from effort, as much as from ability.[14]
- Be challenging, but not impossibly demanding: 'My teacher in maths really makes me think!'; 'When I finished the class on volcanoes, I really wanted to go away and learn more about them.'
- Help learners develop strong beliefs in their own ability: 'I can do most things well when I really try'; 'If I can understand maths, I should be able to do well in science'; 'If I study hard, I usually get there.' As Henry Ford once stated, 'Whether you think you can or you can't, you're right.'
- Make sure you give learners time to respond to questions or requests and contribute to discussions.

Establish clear and essential rules and boundaries

Some learners with special educational needs might have difficulty in comprehending and acting on social rules. Some may even focus many of their behaviours on flagrantly breaking rules. As an educator you should pay particular attention to setting up essential rules. For example, you should:

- recognize that classroom routines, rules and expectations make a significant contribution to the quality of learning environments;[15]
- keep such rules and expectations to the minimum essential to ensure an orderly learning environment;
- state rules positively (e.g., 'walk considerately between activities'), rather than negatively (e.g., 'running is prohibited');[16]
- make sure rules are consistent across different educators in the school;
- ideally, arrive at rules through a process of negotiation that involves the learners as well as educators and see that their enforcement is the responsibility of learners as well as educators;[17]
- plan and rehearse transitions from one activity to another to make them efficient and to avoid opportunities for disruptive behaviour (use picture cues to help learners with special educational needs to recall routines: see **Strategy 23**);
- teach learners what acceptable and unacceptable behaviours look like, what consequences are likely to follow each and provide opportunities for them to practise correct responses;[18]
- be authoritative, not authoritarian, in your behaviour and remember that while classroom management strategies are necessary conditions, they are not sufficient to ensure that learning takes place.

Take up appropriate positions in the classroom

In modern classrooms, educators no longer occupy the front of the room with learners sitting in serried rows. Instead, with cooperative group learning (**Strategy 2**) and other developments, educators are increasingly seen as learning 'managers'. While they will spend some time in whole-class instruction, they will also spend a lot of time moving around their students, supervising and giving assistance when required. So where should you position yourself? My suggestions:

- position yourself so that you have a high degree of visibility;[19]
- make frequent eye contact with all learners and regularly scan the class to detect early warning signs of inappropriate behaviour;
- enter learners' 'territory', rather than confining yourself to a static teacher's 'position'; by moving around you will be more likely to detect potential problem behaviours and to reinforce appropriate behaviours;[20]

- ensure that there are no 'hiding places' where learners who wish to opt out of a lesson can do so without fear of being detected by your 'roving eye';
- since learners with behaviour difficulties frequently proceed through a series of phases before they engage in the most extreme behaviours, be alert to the first signs of tension or trouble and act quickly to defuse them; sometimes all that might be required is a non-verbal signal to show that you are noticing what is happening.

 ## The evidence

There is a substantial body of research on various aspects of classroom climate and how they impact on academic achievement and affective learning. Unfortunately, I have not been able to find any research that focuses on learners with special educational needs, although I am confident that the findings are relevant to that group of learners.

✓ In a 1994 analysis of 40 studies, associations were found between a range of classroom environment measures and a variety of cognitive and affective outcome measures across grade levels in several countries.[21]

✓ An early meta-analysis looked at 12 studies carried out in four countries. Higher achievement on a range of outcome measures was found among learners in classes rated as having greater cohesiveness, satisfaction and goal direction and less disorganization and friction.[22]

✓ Another, more recent, meta-analysis found that classroom climate was one of the most important factors to affect pupil achievement.[23]

✓ An OECD study of teaching in 11 countries found that creating a positive classroom climate was a prime characteristic of quality teachers.[24]

✓ A Dutch study found that educators who were perceived to be understanding, helpful and friendly and show leadership without being too strict, enhanced learners' achievement and affective outcomes. Those who were seen as being uncertain, dissatisfied with their students and admonishing were associated with lower cognitive and affective outcomes.[25]

✓ An Australian study investigated the effects of classroom environments on academic efficacy, i.e., learners' judgements of their capabilities to organize and carry out courses of action to attain designated educational goals. A sample of 1,055 secondary school learners in mathematics classes responded to a scale that measured ten dimensions of their mathematics classroom environment. These included student cohesiveness, teacher support, task orientation, cooperation, shared control and student negotiation. The results showed that classroom environments related positively with academic efficacy.[26]

✓ A New Zealand study looked at the relationship between classroom climate and motivated behaviour in learners in secondary school English classes. Five scales measured classroom climate: competition (how learners compete with each other for grades), order and organization (emphasis on learners behaving in an orderly and polite manner), rule clarity (establishing and following a clear set of rules), teacher control (enforcement of rules) and affiliation (level of friendship learners feel for each other). These scales sampled all three of the dimensions described in The Underlying Idea section of this chapter. Motivation was assessed in terms of three classroom behaviours: participation, engagement and task completion. The results showed that classroom climate was significantly related to all of these motivation measures. The most important factor was affiliation, which measured the level of friendship that students feel for each other.[27]

✓ There is evidence that educators tend to have a more positive perception of their classrooms' climate than learners. This suggests that the latter should be involved by giving regular feedback on their perceptions of both the actual and preferred classroom climate.[28]

✓ In a classic study published in 1970, findings from 80 US elementary classrooms formed the basis of a book, *Discipline and group management in classrooms*.[29] In this study effective managers were defined as educators whose classrooms were orderly, had a minimum of student misbehaviour and where students had high levels of on-task behaviour. It was found that effective and ineffective educators did not differ significantly in the ways they dealt with **disruptive behaviour**. Where they did differ, however, was in ways they prevented disruptions from occurring in the first place. These included:

- 'withitness': educators communicate to the learners by their behaviour that they know what the learners are up to;
- overlapping: educators attend to several different events simultaneously, without being totally diverted by disruptions;
- smoothness and momentum in lesson: educators employ smooth and brisk pacing;
- group alerting: educators involve all learners in the task at hand; and
- stimulating seatwork: educators provide learners with a variety of challenging tasks.[30]

✓ An ongoing New Zealand research project, entitled *Kotahitanga* (unity) investigated Maori secondary school students' perceptions of what was involved in improving their educational achievement. The most important influence to emerge centred on the quality of the in-class face-to-face relationships and interactions between them and their teachers. These findings led to the development of an Effective Teaching Profile, which then formed the basis of a professional development intervention. When implemented with a group of 11 teachers in four schools, this was associated with improved learning, behaviour and attendance outcomes for Maori students. It was noted that deficit theorizing by teachers is the major impediment to Maori students' educational achievement for it results in teachers having low expectations, which creates a self-fulfilling prophecy of school failure. Unfortunately, the study did not specifically identify learners with special educational needs although, as a group, Maori students' overall academic achievement levels are low, their rate of suspension from school is three times that of non-Maori and they tend to leave school with fewer formal qualifications than do their non-Maori peers (38 per cent compared to 19 per cent, respectively).[31]

 Addressing risks

The main risk here is to focus exclusively on the content of learning and the strategies for teaching it at the expense of ignoring the evidence that points to the important role played by the context in which learning takes place.

 Conclusion

The quality of the classroom's psychological climate is a significant determinant of learners' achievement. They learn better when they have an emotionally safe and predictable environment that is motivating and promotes positive goal-setting.

 Further reading

Fraser, B.J. and Walberg, H.J. (eds) (1991). *Educational environments: Evaluation, antecedents and consequences.* Oxford: Pergamon Press.
Freiberg, H.J. (ed.) (1999). *School climate: Measuring, improving and sustaining healthy learning environments.* London: Falmer Press.

Journals

Learning Environments Research
School Effectiveness and School Improvement

Key references

1 Adelman, H.S. and Taylor, L. (2005). 'Classroom climate'. In S.W. Lee, P.A. Lowe and E. Robinson (eds) *Encyclopedia of school psychology.* Thousand Oaks, CA: Sage.
2 Fraser, B.J. (1998). 'Classroom environment instruments: development, validity and applications'. *Learning Environments Research*, 1(1), 7–33.
3 Moos, R.H. (1979). *Evaluating educational environments.* San Francisco, CA: Jossey-Bass.

4 Ford, M.E. (1995). 'Motivation and competence development in special and remedial education'. *Intervention in School and Clinic*, 31(2), 70–83.

5 Okano, K. and Tsuchiya, M. (1999). *Education in contemporary Japan: Inequality and diversity*. Cambridge: Cambridge University Press.

6 OECD (1994). *Quality in teaching*. Paris: OECD; and Garbarino, J. (1995). *Raising children in a socially toxic environment*. San Francisco, CA: Jossey-Bass.

7 Ramsay, P. and Oliver, D. (1995). 'Capacities and behaviour of quality teachers'. *School Effectiveness and School Improvement*, 6(4), 332–336.

8 Jackson, L., Ryndak, D.L. and Billingsley, F. (2000). 'Useful practices in inclusive education: A preliminary view of what experts in moderate to severe disabilities are saying'. *The Journal of the Association for Persons with Severe Handicaps*, 25(3), 129–141.

9 Cotton, K. (1990). *Schoolwide and classroom discipline*. Washington, DC: School Improvement Research Series (SIRS), Office of Educational Research and Improvement. URL: www.nwel.org/scpd/sirs/5/cu9.html (accessed 20 December 2006).

10 MacIver, D.J., Reuman, D.A. and Main, S.R. (1995). 'Social structuring of the school: Studying what is, illuminating what could be'. *Annual Review of Psychology*, 46, 375–400.

11 Ford, op. cit.

12 Sipert, D.J. (1996). 'Motivation and instruction'. In D.C. Berliner and R.C. Calfee (eds) *Handbook of educational psychology* (pp. 85–113). New York: Macmillan Library Reference.

13 Teacher Training Agency (1996). Teaching as a research-based profession: Promoting excellence in teaching. London: Teacher Training Agency.

14 Ames, R. and Ames, C. (1991). 'Motivation and effective teaching'. In L. Idol and B.F. Jones (eds) *Educational values and cognitive instruction: Implications for education* (pp. 247–271). Hillsdale, NJ: Lawrence Erlbaum Associates.

15 Englert, C.S., Tarrant, K.L. and Mariage, T.V. (1992). 'Defining and redefining instructional practices in special education: Perspectives on good teaching'. *Teacher Education and Special Education*, 5(2), 62–86; and Reynolds, A. (1992). 'What is competent beginning teaching? A review of the literature'. *Review of Educational Research*, 62(1), 349–359.

16 Kehle, T.J., Bray, M.A., Theodore, L.A., Jenson, W.R. and Clark, E. (2000). 'A multi-component intervention designed to reduce disruptive classroom behavior'. *Psychology in the Schools*, 37(5), 475–481.

17 West, M., Hopkins, D. and Beresford, J. (1995*). Conditions for school and classroom development*. Paper presented at British Educational Research Association Annual Meeting and European Conference on Educational Research, Bath, UK, September 1995.

18 Lewis, T.J. and Sugai, G. (1999). 'Effective behavior support: A systems approach to proactive schoolwide management'. *Focus on Exceptional Children*, 31(6), 1–24.

19 Englert, Tarrant and Mariage, op. cit.

20 Kehle *et al.*, op. cit.

21 Fraser, B.J. (1994). 'Research on classroom and school climate'. In D. Gabel (ed.) *Handbook of research on science teaching and learning* (pp. 493–541). New York: Macmillan.

22 Haertel, G.D., Walberg, H.J. and Haertel, E.H. (1981). 'Socio-psychological environments and learning: a quantitative synthesis'. *British Educational Research Journal*, 7(1), 27–36.

23 Wang, M.C., Haertel, G.D. and Walberg, H.J. (1997). 'Learning influences'. In H.J. Walberg and G.D. Haertel (eds) *Psychology and educational practice*. Berkeley, CA: McCuthan.
24 Organisation for Economic Co-operation and Development (OECD) (1994). *Teacher quality: Synthesis of country studies*. Paris: OECD.
25 Wubbels, T., Breckelmans, M. and Hooymayers, H. (1991). 'Interpersonal teacher behaviour in the classroom'. In B.J. Fraser and H.J. Walberg (eds) *Educational environments: Evaluation, antecedents and consequences*. Oxford: Pergamon Press.
26 Dorman, J. (2001). 'Associations between classroom environment and academic efficacy'. *Learning Environments Research*, 4(3), 243–257.
27 Anderson, A., Hamilton, R.J. and Hattie, J. (2004). 'Classroom climate and motivated behaviour in secondary schools'. *Learning Environments Research*, 7(3), 211–225.
28 Fraser, B.J. (1999). 'Using learning environment assessments to improve classroom and school climate'. In H.J. Freiberg (ed.) *School climate: Measuring, improving and sustaining healthy learning environments*. London: Falmer Press.
29 Kounin, J.S. (1970). *Discipline and group management in classrooms*. New York: Holt, Rinehart and Winston.
30 For a review of other, similar, research see Cotton, op. cit.
31 Bishop, R., Berryman, M., Tiakiwai, S. and Richardson, C. (2003). *Te Kotahitanga: The experiences of Year 9 and 10 Maori students in mainstream classrooms*. Wellington: Ministry of Education. URL: www.minedu.govt.nz/ goto/tekotahitanga (accessed 9 January 2006). A more recent analysis of results from this project found that gains in numeracy achievement yielded effect sizes of 0.76 for learners whose teachers participated in the Kotahitanga Project, compared with 0.52 for those whose teachers were not involved in the project (Bishop, R., Berryman, M., Cavanagh, T., Teddy, L. and Clapham, S. (2006). *Te Kotahitanga Phase 3 whanaungatanga: Establishing a culturally responsive pedagogy of relations in mainstream secondary school classrooms. Final report*. Wellington: Ministry of Education).

Chapter 12

Strategy 10: Social skills training

'Teach learners how to positively interact with others'

Rating

★★✭☆

 The strategy

Social skills training is a set of strategies aimed at helping learners to establish and maintain positive interactions with others. It relates to the context and motivation components of the learning and teaching model described in Chapter 2.

 The underlying idea

What do we mean by social skills?

Socially competent people are capable of managing their social environments by understanding and responding to social situations effectively.[1] They have the following characteristics:[2]

- *Social sensitivity*: accurately making sense of the meaning of a social event, i.e., decoding social cues.
- *Role-taking*: 'reading' people and understanding how they are experiencing the world.
- *Social insight*: accurately reading social situations and comprehending what is happening in a social gathering.
- *Social comprehension*: understanding social institutions and processes, such as friendships and social reciprocity.
- *Psychological insight*: understanding the personal characteristics and motivations of others.
- *Moral judgement*: evaluating social situations in relation to moral codes and ethical principles.
- *Social communication*: understanding how to intervene effectively and influence the behaviour of others, a skill that involves self-monitoring.

- *Communication*: conveying accurately to others what one is thinking or feeling.
- *Social problem-solving*: resolving conflicts and understanding how to influence the behaviour of others to achieve desired goals.

Why is social skills training needed?

Most children quite easily acquire the social skills that are appropriate to their culture, but some do not and must be explicitly taught them. Some have poor social perception and consequently lack social skills; this is particularly true of those with autism and emotional and behavioural disorders.[3] It is also true of learners with severe disabilities, many of whom have difficulty in forming friendships.[4]

What are possible goals for social skills training?

The goal of social skills training should be to establish a range of behaviours so that learners can select what is appropriate for them in various social contexts.

It is unrealistic to expect that social skills training programmes will always lead to close friendships between all members of the class. Such relationships are based on a whole host of other factors, including mutual interests, compatibility, contacts in the neighbourhood, family connections and so on. This point is intended to remind you that your goals for social skills training should be realistic and be commensurate with the relationships that are likely to ensue.

 The practice

 What are the steps in social skills training?

In general, social skills training involves teaching learners how to:

- formulate goals for social interaction;
- decode or interpret the most important cues in a social context;
- decide on behaviours that would best meet the social goals for the situation;
- perform the behaviour; and
- judge if the behaviour was effective in meeting the goals.[5]

 What social skills should be taught?

The skills most widely associated with social competence are:

- *Conversation skills* (including 'small talk'): greetings, saying 'please' or 'thank you', learning and using names, selecting appropriate topics, keeping conversations alive, making and maintaining eye contact (but note cultural differences here), employing appropriate facial expressions, using an appropriate tone of voice, standing in appropriate positions relative to others, inhibiting impulsive behaviour and active listening.

- *Coping with conflict*: saying 'No', dealing with aggressive persons, responding to teasing, apologizing, gaining attention, asking for help, problem-solving skills, dealing with criticism, negotiating, persuading, responding to others' needs, respecting individual differences.
- *Friendship skills*: making friends, giving and accepting thanks, initiating and responding to humour, taking turns, having acceptable grooming and hygiene, being in tune with the peer group culture (e.g., knowing about fashion, music, films, tv . . .), appreciating the place of rules in everyday life.
- *Group skills*: as I emphasized in **Strategy 2**, it is important to teach group process skills.

Problems that can arise, and possible solutions, include the following:[6]

- *Domination by one or more group members*: assign incompatible but relevant roles (e.g., observer or recorder), set rules (with the group) as to how often individuals can speak, and praise individuals for not being bossy.
- *Non-participation*: establish participation rules (e.g., everyone must speak at least once, speakers must not be interrupted), assign non-threatening roles (e.g., timekeeper) and model ways of participating.
- *Conflict*: teach conflict resolution skills (e.g., compromises and win-win strategies) and inform the group that you are available to mediate as a last resort.
- *Continued inappropriate behaviour*: temporarily exclude individuals from the group in a non-punitive way and develop simple behavioural contracts (**Strategy 17**).

Some social behaviours (e.g., greeting a teacher) involve a number of social skills. These may include making eye contact, smiling and saying hello. It may be necessary to teach each skill in turn, but generally it is better to focus on a set of behaviours.

The opportunities to use some of the above skills might be relatively limited (e.g., introducing someone) and the learner might gain little from it in social terms. On the other hand, some skills might be used often and across a wide range of situations (e.g., greeting a classmate) and it might be more beneficial to focus on them.

Above all, look for ways to assist children to transfer skills from one setting to another. Without practice in generalizing social skills, these will often be only narrowly applied in different settings. Social skills training should not be viewed as a process in which initial instruction is sufficient. Rather, you should provide on-going instruction and supervision.

These skills (or the lack of them) can be assessed by such means as observations, parent and teacher interviews, and the use of checklists.[7]

 How can social skills be taught?

Social skills can be taught through such methods as:

- encouraging learners to analyse for themselves what makes up social skills;
- giving direct instruction on social skills;
- explaining and modelling the performance of social skills: for example, you could demonstrate a skill by:
  - using live models,
  - role playing,
  - miming,
  - using videos (e.g., local television soap operas), stopping the action at critical times to discuss behaviours and appropriate responses;
- reinforcing appropriate behaviours (not just focusing on getting rid of 'bad' behaviour);
- prompting to remind learners about the relevance of certain behaviours in certain contexts ('John, what do you say when someone asks you if you want to play a game?');
- using literature to represent real-life social situations and problems relating to social skills;
- designing classroom tasks to increase trust, acceptance, sharing and mutual support between learners and to enable the valuing of diverse knowledge and skills;[8]
- asking learners to verbally rehearse the steps involved in a skill;
- giving explicit feedback (**Strategy 21**): indicating which steps of the skill were performed successfully and which require further improvement (e.g., 'Good, Roger, you played well with the group this time; I saw you sharing very nicely. Next time you could try talking to two people in the group').

A possible sequence of steps for teaching a set of social skills follows:

- Describe and discuss the set of skills with the learner so that he/she understands why the skills are important and how they would help them to get on with others.

- Identify the separate skills that make up the set and break each skill down into its component parts so that the learner can focus on manageable parts. Demonstrate each part or have the learner copy you so that you can gauge their mastery of the skill. Give cues or prompts when necessary. Focus the learner's attention on the specific parts of the skill that have been mastered, or that require more attention, by giving specific feedback on the performance.
- In order to maximize success with the skill, have the learner try it out in a structured situation. Again, give specific feedback on the performance.
- Provide opportunities for the skills to be practised and provide descriptive praise.
- Watch out for times when the learner practises the skill without your prompting and give less frequent praise to allow classmates to positively reinforce the skills.
- Recognize the important role played by support staff in encouraging social interactions among learners with special educational needs and their peers.[9]

 A word about 'theory of mind'

In recent years, a good deal has been written about the notion of 'theory of mind' (sometimes referred to as 'mindblindness'), particularly in relation to teaching social skills to learners with autistic spectrum disorders, and sometimes in relation to deaf learners. Briefly, this refers to the ability to understand that other people have beliefs, desires and intentions that are distinct from one's own and to form hypotheses as to what these are.[10] If learners do not understand that other people have different thoughts to themselves they will experience problems in relating and communicating with them. In other words, there are deficits in social cognition, or empathy, relative to mental age.[11] This has led to the development of intervention programmes to assist learners with theory of mind problems to 'mind-read', i.e., to recognize emotions and other people's perspectives.[12]

 Understand your own reactions

It is very important that you understand and learn to deal with your personal reactions to learners with behaviour disorders, lest you become part of the problem rather than part of the solution. Undoubtedly, many educators find poor social skills very aversive. You may well experience fear, anger, anxiety, lowered self-esteem, frustration, despair, even sadness, when confronted with them. It is important that you ask yourself, 'Why do I feel this way? And if I feel this way – and it is my job to deal with these sorts of behaviours – how do others feel?'

The evidence

✓ A US study reviewed the results of 64 single-subject studies that examined the effects of social skills interventions with learners who had **emotional or behavioural disorders**. The average age of the participants was 9.8 years and 72 per cent were boys. In the studies surveyed, social skills training usually focused on direct instruction of specific skills and included modelling, role-playing, reinforcement and self-control strategies. The authors concluded that although the effects of social skills training were positive, they were modest. **Delinquent** students seemed to benefit more than those with autism or emotional/behaviour disorders.[13]

✓ In a second review, the same team carried out a meta-analysis of social skills training for learners with **emotional or behavioural disorders**, this time carrying out a meta-analysis of 35 studies. A mean effect size of 0.2 was produced, which means that the average learner would be expected to gain only a modest eight percentile points after participating in a social skills training programme. Slightly greater effect sizes were found for interventions that focused on specific social skills such as cooperating or social problem-solving, compared with more general interventions.[14]

✓ In a review of several meta-analyses involving social skills training, effect sizes ranged from 0.2 (see the previous item) to 0.87, with an average of 0.44. At least in part, this range was attributed to the 'resistance to intervention' shown by some groups of learners with special educational needs.[15]

✓ A recent UK study found that two social skills training interventions directed at primary school learners at risk for social exclusion had positive effects on their social skills and social inclusion.[16]

✓ A meta-analysis of 43 studies showed that social skills training produced significant effects on learners' social interactions and cognitive problem-solving.[17]

✓ A very comprehensive review of research into interventions to facilitate social interactions for young children with **autism** included the following conclusions:
  • *Ecological interventions.* These involved changing the general features of the physical or social environment (e.g., the composition of the learner's peer group). They produced weak to moderate improvements in the social interactions of young children with autism.
  • *Collateral skills interventions.* These involved training learners with autism in social interaction (e.g., teaching generalized play skills and socio-dramatic skills). These activities seem to increase social interactions by bringing learners with autism into contact with typically developing peers.

- *Learner-specific interventions.* These are procedures, such as reinforcement, designed specifically to increase social skills. They include: (a) interventions to increase social knowledge (e.g., social stories, which describe specific social situations along with appropriate social responses in clear, concrete terms), (b) intensive reinforcement to 'prime' social responding (**Strategy 17**), (c) social skills training and (d) self-monitoring (**Strategy 12**). These were found to increase social interactions, but were mainly limited to social initiations, rather than sustained interactions, by learners with autism.
- *Peer-mediated interventions.* These included interventions to increase peers' social initiations and interactions and structured peer tutoring (**Strategy 3**). These demonstrated 'powerful and robust treatment effects', but there are doubts as to whether they generalize to other untrained peers.
- *Comprehensive interventions.* These included components from two or more of the foregoing. The research shows that such interventions directed at both learners with autism and their typically developing peers produced pronounced effects on social interactions in the intervention settings, with some evidence of generalization to other settings.[18]

 ## Addressing risks

Two cautions need to be taken into account:

- While some social skills can be taught to some learners in 'social skills classes', these seem to have limited value. As far as possible, social skills should be taught in natural contexts.
- In order to ensure that learners receive clear messages about what constitutes acceptable and unacceptable social behaviour, it is important that all educators in the school (plus parents) understand and agree on the aims of any social skills training programme and consistently reinforce them.

 ## Conclusion

Social skills training is clearly an important area to work on with many learners with special educational needs. There are several promising approaches to this area, but no definitive strategy that produces long-lasting generalizations. However, I am confident that as strategies become more refined and as research improves, there will be significant developments in the future.

Further reading

McConnell, S. (2002). 'Interventions to facilitate social interaction for young children with autism: review of available research and recommendations for educational intervention and future research'. *Journal of Autism and Developmental Disorders*, 32(5), 351–372.

Key references

1 Mathur, S.R. and Rutherford, R.B. (1996). 'Is social skills training effective for students with emotional or behavioral disorders? Research issues and needs'. *Behavioral Disorders*, 22(1), 21–28.
2 Based on a synthesis presented by Black, R.S. and Langone, J. (1997). 'Social awareness and transition to employment for adolescents with mental retardation'. *Remedial and Special Education*, 18(4), 214–222. This draws heavily on the work of Greenspan and his colleagues, e.g., Greenspan, S.R. (1981). 'Defining childhood social competence: A proposed working model'. In B.K. Keogh (ed.) *Advances in special education: Vol 3. Socialization influences on exceptionality* (pp. 1–39). Greenwich, CT: JAI Press.
3 McGrath, H. (2005). 'Directions in teaching social skills to students with specific EBD'. In P. Clough, P. Garner, J.T. Pardeck and F. Yuen (eds) *Handbook of emotional and behavioural difficulties* (pp. 325–352). London: Sage.
4 Wilson, B.A. (1999). 'Inclusion: Empirical guidelines and unanswered questions'. *Education and Training in Mental Retardation and Developmental Disabilities*, 34(2), 119–133.
5 Collett-Klingenberg, L. and Chadsey-Rusch, J. (1991). 'Using a cognitive-process approach to teach social skills'. *Education and Training in Mental Retardation*, 26, 258–270.
6 Margolis, H. and Freund, L. (1996). 'Implementing cooperative learning with mildly handicapped students in regular classrooms'. *International Journal of Disability, Development and Education*, 38(2), 117–133.
7 For a detailed description of such methods, see Merrell, K.W. (2001). 'Assessment of children's social skills: Recent developments, best practices, and new directions'. *Exceptionality*, 9(1–2), 3–18. For a description of a useful checklist, described as 'Assessment of Social Competence', see Fisher, M. and Meyer, L.H. (2002). 'Development and social competence after two years for students enrolled in inclusive and self-contained educational programs'. *Research and Practice for Persons with Severe Disabilities*, 27(3), 165–174.
8 Nuthall, G. (1999). 'Learning to learn: The evolution of students' minds through the social processes and culture of the classroom'. *International Journal of Educational Research*, 31(3), 139–256.
9 Farrell, P. (1997). 'The integration of children with severe learning difficulties: A review of the recent literature'. *Journal of Applied Research in Learning Disabilities*, 10(1), 1–14.
10 http://en.wikipedia.org/wiki/Theory_of_mind (accessed 12 January 2007).
11 Baron-Cohen, S. (2004). 'Autism: Research into causes and intervention'. *Paediatric Rehabilitation*, 7(2), 73–78.
12 See, for example, Howlin, P., Baron-Cohen, S. and Hadwin, J. (1999). *Teaching children with autism to mind-read: A practical guide*. New York: John Wiley and Sons.

13 Mathur, S.R., Kavale, K.A., Quinn, M.M., Forness, S.R. and Rutherford, R.B. (1998). 'Social skills interventions with students with emotional and behavioural problems: A quantitative synthesis of single-subject research'. *Behavioral Disorders*, 23(3), 193–201.

14 Quinn, M.M., Kavale, K.A., Mathur, S.R., Rutherford, R.B. and Forness, S.R. (1999). 'A meta-analysis of social skill interventions for students with emotional or behavioral disorders'. *Journal of Emotional and Behavioral Disorders*, 7(1), 54–64.

15 Gresham, F.M., Sugai, G. and Horner, R.H. (2001). 'Interpreting outcomes of social skills training for students with high-incidence disabilities'. *Exceptional Children*, 67(3), 331–345.

16 Denham, A., Hatfield, S., Smethurst, N., Tan, E. and Tribe, C. (2006). 'The effect of social skills interventions in the primary school'. *Educational Psychology in Practice*, 22(1), 33–51.

17 Erwin, P.G. (1994). 'Effectiveness of social skills training with children: A meta-analytic study'. *Counseling Psychology Quarterly*, 7(3), 305–310.

18 McConnell, S. (2002). 'Interventions to facilitate social interaction for young children with autism: Review of available research and recommendations for educational intervention and future research'. *Journal of Autism and Developmental Disorders*, 32(5), 351–372.

Chapter 13

Strategy 11: Cognitive strategy instruction

'Teach learners ways of thinking'

Rating

★★★⯪

 The strategy

Cognitive strategy instruction (CSI) refers to ways of assisting learners to acquire cognitive skills, or strategies. It does this by helping them to: (a) organize information so that its complexity is reduced, and/or (b) integrate information into their existing knowledge.[1] It involves teaching learners methods for accomplishing various kinds of tasks. As we shall see, CSI includes teaching skills such as visualization, planning, self-regulation, memorizing, analysing, predicting, making associations, using cues and thinking about thinking (i.e., metacognition). In a nutshell, you are as much concerned with teaching your students *how to learn* as teaching them the subject matter of the curriculum.

CSI is particularly useful with students with learning disabilities, although other learners with special educational needs also benefit. Indeed, all students can benefit from selective use of CSI.

Since cognition permeates the teaching-learning process, you will find considerable overlap between this strategy and others I cover in this book, in particular **Strategies 12: Self-Regulated Learning**, **13**: **Mnemonics and other Memory Strategies**, **14: Reciprocal Teaching** and **16: Cognitive Behavioural Therapy** (especially the section on Meichenbaum's six-step process). For an overview of how these cognitive strategies fit into the overall scheme of things, please refer to the learning and teaching model described in Chapter 2, in particular the section on strategies.

You might find the title a little confusing as it refers to a *teaching* strategy that focuses on a *learning* strategy.

 The underlying idea

Cognition, or 'thinking', refers to how we collect, store, interpret, understand, remember and use information. Acquiring these cognitive skills is fundamental to behaviours such as reading, writing, mathematical problem-solving, comprehension, speech production, creative thought and even social skills.

Most individuals develop efficient and effective cognitive skills through their life experiences, with minimal teaching of how to go about the process of learning. Others, however, don't appear to use good techniques or strategies to help them learn. They either don't know what strategies to use, or they use the wrong ones or they don't spontaneously use strategies.[2] These deficiencies might compound other disabilities or they might constitute the disability itself.

Essentially, students' learning strategies result from two things:

- The development of their knowledge about their own cognitive abilities, e.g., limitations of their short-term memory, how much practice they need, how many strategies they have available.
- The development of their ability to consciously regulate cognition by using self-regulatory strategies such as planning, checking, monitoring, testing and changing strategies. These strategies vary from task to task.

There is considerable evidence that students with learning disabilities have inefficient cognitive strategies. These include:

- A tendency to employ an approach to writing that minimizes the role of planning, gives little consideration to constraints imposed by a topic and shows a lack of awareness of the needs of the reader.[3]
- A general lack of awareness of cognitive processes. This awareness is sometimes referred to as *metacognition*, which can be defined as higher-order thinking that results in a learner actively controlling the cognitive processes involved in thinking.[4]
- Serious reading problems, reflected, for example, in poor phonological awareness (**Strategy 15**).
- Poor test-taking skills.

The above inefficiencies inevitably lead to failure, frustration, embarrassment, anxiety, task avoidance and even to aggressive behaviour. You can arrest this vicious cycle by teaching your learners how to become more proficient in recognizing the need to be strategic and in applying cognitive strategies that are appropriate to the various subject domains.

 The practice

CSI had its origins in the late 1970s and early 1980s when it was seen as an alternative to process training. It has many variants, depending mainly on the subject domain and the needs of different categories of learners. Here, I will describe a generic approach that can apply to many situations, as well as several more specific approaches.

✳ Generic CSI

These strategies apply to most learning situations. Here, CSI has three phases:

Phase 1: think ahead, prepare for learning:
- activate and review background knowledge, compare new information to this knowledge;
- form hypotheses concerning the nature of the new information;
- develop goals or purposes for the learning task;
- analyse the problem;
- predict the best way to solve the problem.

Phase 2: think during:
- work to confirm predictions or hypotheses;
- raise questions to form new predictions;
- search for understanding;
- use processes such as questioning, anticipating, comparing, summarizing.

Phase 3: think back:
- understand the information as a whole;
- consolidate on what was learned, integrate new ideas with prior knowledge in the memory;
- understand how the information or skill could be applied in other settings;
- summarize and synthesize.

At the heart of this generic CSI is the challenge of developing positive 'habits of mind'. You can do this by curbing impulsivity, encouraging reflection, organizing and activating prior knowledge, approaching tasks in an effective and efficient manner, making key cognitive steps more concrete for learners and helping them to self-regulate these processes.[5]

Here are some of the key components of effective CSI:

1 *Give priority to strategy instruction.* Devote instructional time to the processes, as well as the products of learning.
2 *Model effective strategies by thinking aloud while you are working on problems.* This has a double benefit: it demonstrates how you solve particular problems and it shows learners the benefit of self-talk.
3 *Give learners practice in using a strategy immediately after you have modelled it.* This will involve you using prompts and supporting, or 'scaffolding', them as they begin to acquire the strategy.
4 *Carry out task analyses.* Analyse tasks in terms of the cognitive strategies to be taught.
5 *Generalize strategy instruction.* Present cognitive strategies as being applicable in more than one domain of learning.

6 *Embed CSI in all your teaching.* Teach strategies over an entire year, not just in a single lesson or unit. Embed them in all areas of the curriculum.

7 *Give guided practice in the use of strategies.* Give learners opportunities to practise the strategies they have been taught. Move them from conscious to automatic application.

8 *Encourage learners to teach cognitive strategies to their peers.* Encourage them to teach others how best to go about reading, problem-solving, learning and other cognitive processes.

9 *Help learners to become aware of learning processes and strategies.* Suggest that they keep a daily 'learning diary' with their reflections on different learning activities – how they were accomplished, where there was confusion, what questions they have. Encourage self-reports to make essentially covert processes overt (e.g., 'Today we are going to talk about how we think when we are trying to solve a problem . . . What do you mean when you talk about "thinking"?') Encourage learners to consciously regulate their cognition by using self-regulatory strategies such as checking, monitoring, planning, and testing and changing strategies; these strategies vary from task to task.

10 *Encourage learners to self-evaluate the quality of their completed work, their understanding of an area of work or their effort in relation to task demands.* Ask them to check the quality of their work or effort (e.g., by re-working, re-reading, visualizing previously learned material and comparing the picture with the completed work). Ask them to use other sources (e.g., people, computers) to check their work, or to test the extent of their knowledge or ability to perform a task.[6]

✳ Domain-specific CSI

Here, I will explain strategies for three learning domains.

1 First, here is a well-known story-writing strategy:[7]

> Who is the main character; who else is in the story?
> When does the story take place?
> Where does the story take place?
> What does the main character want to do?
> What happens when he or she tries to do it?
> How does the story end?
> How does the main character feel?

These seven questions can be represented in the mnemonic (**Strategy 11**):

> W-W-W
> What = 2
> How = 2

2   A second *domain-specific CSI* is concerned with teaching essay-writing skills:

> Use the mnemonics **STOP** and **DARE**:[8]
>
> **S**uspend judgement: consider each side of an argument before taking a position.
> **T**ake a side: read your ideas and decide which side you believe in.
> **O**rganize: choose which ideas you want to develop, and put them in order.
> **P**lan as you write, using all four essay parts, as in **DARE**:
> **D**evelop your topic sentence.
> **A**dd supporting ideas.
> **R**eject possible arguments on the other side.
> **E**nd with a conclusion.

An approach that I have used with learners is to employ the analogy of an aeroplane flight: first you see a town in the distance (introduction), then you fly over it (the body) and then you look back on where you have been (the conclusion).

3   The third *domain-specific CSI* is concerned with problem-solving, following the mnemonic **IDEAL**, with the following five steps:[9]

> **I**dentify: recognize that there is a problem to be solved.
> **D**efine: define the source of the problem and sort out the relevant information.
> **E**xplore: think about the information and strategies needed to solve the problem.
> **A**ct: use available resources to act to solve the problem.
> **L**ook: see if the solution works and change your strategy if necessary.

 ### Other examples

For other examples of CSI, see brief summaries of those used in various research studies summarized in the next section.

 ## The evidence

There is a considerable literature on the effectiveness of various types of CSI on learners with special educational needs. Much of it focuses on those with learning disabilities and on reading and writing skills.[10]

✓   A US review of several studies of CSI concluded that it was effective for improving the mathematical problem-solving performance of middle and secondary school students with **learning disabilities**. The goal of instruction in the studies was to teach the students a comprehensive cognitive and metacognitive strategy for solving mathematical word problems. In the cognitive strategy students were taught to follow these steps: Read, Paraphrase, Visualize, Hypothesize, Estimate, Compute and Check. In the metacognitive strategy they were taught to Self-instruct, Self-question and Self-monitor.[11]

✓ A Canadian study investigated the effects of CSI on algebra problem-solving in adolescents with **learning disabilities**. It used a combination of a multiple baseline design, and a comparison of an experimental group (N = 12) and a control group (N = 8). The intervention was focused on teaching the experimental group in individual sessions how to represent and solve algebraic problems. Examples of how to represent problems included 'Have I read and understood each sentence?' and 'Have I got the whole picture, for this problem?' Examples of how to solve problems included, 'Have I written an equation?' and 'Have I written out the steps of my solution on the worksheet?' The results showed that the experimental group achieved significant gains over the control group and there was evidence that the taught strategy was maintained and transferred to other problems.[12]

✓ A Dutch study investigated the effects on secondary school mathematics education of training in the use of CSI and social strategies in cooperative learning situations (**Strategy 2**). The results showed that **low achieving learners** in both experimental conditions outperformed their counterparts in a control group.[13] This led the researchers to carry out another experiment that combined instruction in social *and* cognitive strategies. This study also focused on secondary school mathematics classes and involved 444 learners aged 12–13 years. Those in the experimental condition received a programme that combined cooperative learning and CSI. They spent some of the time in mixed-ability groups and some in ability groups. Learners in the control condition were not trained in these procedures but were merely told to help each other. The results were somewhat mixed, with low achieving learners showing gains in some measures (e.g., information gathering), but not others (e.g., mathematical reasoning ability). The latter finding was attributed to 'cognitive overload' when those learners have to deal with a new mathematics topic, as well as CSI and cooperative strategies.[14]

✓ In a US study, elementary school students with **learning disabilities** were taught to restate in their own words, and in writing, what happened in each paragraph of a story as they read it. Compared with a control group, the restatement intervention group was found to recall more story information, answer more comprehension questions and show evidence of transferring the skill to other situations.[15]

✓ Notwithstanding the previous finding about transfer, there is some evidence that teaching general metacognitive strategies to students with **learning disabilities** does not generalize to specific learning situations. For example, such learners even need specific guidance on, say, strategies for solving different types of mathematics problems.[16]

✓ A small-scale study of five elementary school students with **mild learning handicaps** investigated a form of CSI involving analysing the structure of texts. The students were taught via a 'story map', which included giving attention to the setting (time, place and characters), the theme or problem portrayed in the story, the actions and the outcome. Four of the five students showed improved comprehension, which was maintained when they were no longer required to use the story map technique.[17]

✓ In a Canadian study of 166 learners, aged seven to 13 years, with **developmental reading disability**, three groups were identified: (a) those with deficits in phonological awareness, (b) those with deficits in visual naming speed (i.e., word recognition speed) and (c) those with both deficits. A metacognitive phonics programme resulted in improvements, especially for learners with only phonological deficits. This programme instructed the learners in the acquisition, use and monitoring of four word identification strategies. These included, for example, a 'compare/ contrast' strategy in which the learners were taught to compare an unfamiliar word with a word they already knew.[18]

✓ A 1996 meta-analysis of study skills interventions found that effect sizes were greatest for learners in the middle of the academic distribution and those classified as **underachieving**, with **low-ability** learners less able to benefit. The latter was attributed to the difficulties such learners might have in comprehending instructions. The study also noted that younger students benefited most from such interventions, probably because their study skills behaviours had not stabilized.[19]

✓ However, the value of CSI for **low-achieving** learners has been shown in some studies. For example, in one study of mathematics problem-solving, learners were assigned to one of two interventions: one emphasizing high task engagement, the other instruction in CSI. The results showed that learners receiving CSI were helped more than those in the task engagement condition.[20]

✓ A recent US study examined the effectiveness of a highly explicit, teacher-directed CSI programme on fourth- and fifth-grade students with **learning disabilities**. In comparison to peers who received process writing instruction, the students who were taught three planning strategies – goal-setting, brainstorming and organizing – spent more time planning stories and produced qualitatively better stories. These gains were maintained one month after the programme. However, the skills did not transfer to an uninstructed genre, persuasive essay writing.[21]

✓ In a similar vein, another US study examined the effects of a CSI programme on informative report writing by adolescents with **learning disabilities** and **low achievement**. The students were taught to search their memory for topics and ideas, visualize events, experience relevant emotions, diagnose writing problems and evaluate the clarity of the central theme of the report. The result was more clearly written reports with better developed themes than shown by the control group.[22]

✓ In another study of writing – this time narrative and expository writing – with elementary and middle school students with **learning disabilities**, a self-regulating strategy was used. This included goal-setting, brain-storming, semantic webbing, generating and organizing writing content and reading to locate information. This form of CSI led to improvements in four aspects of the learners' performances: quality of writing, knowledge of writing, approach to writing and self-efficacy.[23]

✓ Adolescents with **learning disabilities** who were taught test-taking strategies scored higher on tests across content areas.[24]

✓ In recent years, computer-assisted CSI has emerged as a topic in several studies with students with **learning disabilities**. For example, some studies have examined the extent to which metacognitive strategies for monitoring and planning could be linked to health education using computer simulation (**Strategy 22**).[25]

✓ Based on an extensive review of research into teaching strategies for students with **learning disabilities**, a major conclusion was that a model that combines direct instruction (**Strategy 19**) and CSI was an effective procedure with that category of learners. Whereas direct instruction alone and CSI alone both yielded substantial effect sizes (0.68 and 0.72, respectively), the combined strategy effect size was 0.84.[26]

 Addressing risks

Five risks need to be considered:

- Employing CSI in heterogeneous groups may not always be viable. It could well be that when you are intensively teaching a particular strategy you should bring together all those who need this instruction.
- When using CSI with cognitively less able learners, the processes being taught need to be simplified and frequently reviewed.
- CSI seems to work best with younger learners, so should be used selectively with older learners.
- CSI should be seen as an active and dynamic process and not the rote imposition of static routines on passive learners.[27] It should be taught in context and not as an isolated topic.
- Although it might seem that the process of teaching CSI is linear (i.e., one step at a time), in fact it should be seen as a recursive process (i.e., repeating steps when necessary).

Conclusion

There is substantial evidence that CSI can improve the performances of learners with special educational needs, especially those with learning disabilities, in a wide range of subject domains. As expressed by some leaders in the field: 'Good strategy instruction entails making students aware of the purposes of strategies, how and why they work, and when and where they can be used.'[28]

 Further reading

Ashman, A.F. and Conway, R.N.F. (1997). *An introduction to cognitive education: Theory and application*. London: Routledge.

Dockrell, J. and McShane, J. (1993). *Children's learning difficulties: A cognitive approach*. Oxford: Blackwell.

Presley, M. and Woloshyn, V. (1995). *Cognitive strategy instruction that really improves children's academic performance*. Cambridge, MA: Brookline Books.

University of Kansas Center for Research on Learning. URL: www.ku-crl.org (accessed 20 December 2006).

Key references

1 Ashman, A.F. and Conway, R.N.F. (1997). *An introduction to cognitive education: Theory and application*. London: Routledge, p. 43.

2 Sugden, D. (1989). 'Skill generalization and children with learning difficulties'. In D. Sugden (ed.) *Cognitive approaches in special education*. London: Falmer Press.

3 Troia, G.A. and Graham, S. (2002). 'The effectiveness of a highly explicit, teacher-directed strategy instruction routine: Changing the writing performance of students with learning disabilities'. *Journal of Learning Disabilities*, 35(4), 290–305.

4 Scruggs, T.E. and Mastropieri, M.A. (1993). 'Special education for the twenty-first century: Integrating learning strategies and thinking skills'. *Journal of Learning Disabilities*, 26(6), 392–398.

5 Ellis, E.S. (1993). 'Teaching strategy sameness using integrated formats'. *Journal of Learning Disabilities*, 26(6), 448–481.

6 Purdie, N. and Hattie, J. (1996). 'Cultural differences in the use of strategies for self-regulated learning'. *American Educational Research Journal*, 33(4), 845–871.

7 Harris, K.R. and Presley, M. (1991). 'The nature of cognitive strategy instruction: Interactive strategy construction'. *Exceptional Children*, 57(5), 392–404; and Harris, K.R. and Graham, S. (1999). 'Programmatic intervention research: Illustrations from the evolution of self-regulated strategy development'. *Learning Disability Quarterly*, 22(4), 251–262.

8 De La Paz, S. (1997). 'Strategy instruction in planning: Teaching students with learning and writing disabilities to compose persuasive and expository essays'. *Learning Disability Quarterly*, 20(3), 227–248.

9 Bransford, J. and Stein, B. (1984). *The IDEAL problem solver: A guide for improving thinking, learning, and creativity*. New York: W.H. Freeman.

10 For an extensive review of the literature, see Gersten, R., Fuchs, L.S., Williams, J.P. and Baker, S. (2001). 'Teaching reading comprehension strategies to students

with learning disabilities: A review of research'. *Review of Educational Research*, 71(2), 279–320.

11 Montague, M. (1997). 'Cognitive strategy instruction in mathematics for students with learning disabilities'. *Journal of Learning Disabilities*, 30(2), 164–177.

12 Hutchinson, N.L. (1993). 'Effects of cognitive strategy instruction on algebra problem solving of adolescents with learning disabilities'. *Learning Disability Quarterly*, 16(1), 34–63.

13 Hoek, D.J., Terwel, J. and Van Der Eeden, P. (1997). 'Effects of training in the use of social and cognitive strategies: An intervention study in secondary mathematics in cooperative groups'. *Educational Research and Evaluation*, 3(4), 364–389.

14 Hoek, D., Van Den Eeden, P. and Terwel, J. (1999). 'The effects of integrated social and cognitive strategy instruction on the mathematics achievement in secondary education'. *Learning and Instruction*, 9(5), 427–448.

15 Jenkins, J.R., Heliotis, J.D., Stein, M.L. and Haynes, M.C. (1987). 'Improving reading comprehension by using paragraph restatements'. *Exceptional Children*, 54(1), 54–59.

16 Mastropieri, M.A., Scruggs, T.E. and Shiah, S. (1991). 'Mathematics instruction for learning disabled students: A review of research'. *Learning Disabilities Research and Practice*, 6(1), 89–98.

17 Idol, L. and Croll, V.J. (1987). 'Story-mapping training as a means of improving reading comprehension'. *Learning Disability Quarterly*, 10(3), 214–229.

18 Lovett, M.W., Steinbach, K.A. and Frijters, J.C. (2000). 'Remediating the core deficits of developmental reading disability: A double-deficit perspective'. *Journal of Learning Disabilities*, 33(4), 334–358.

19 Hattie, J., Biggs, J. and Purdie, N. (1996). 'Effects of learning skills interventions on student learning'. *Review of Educational Research*, 66(2), 99–137.

20 Swing, S.R., Stoiber, K.C. and Peterson, P.L. (1988). 'Thinking skills versus learning time: Effects of alternative classroom-based interventions on students' mathematics problem solving'. *Cognition and Instruction*, 5(2), 123–131.

21 Troia and Graham, op. cit.

22 Wong, B.Y.L. (1997). 'Research on genre-specific strategies for enhancing writing in adolescents with learning disabilities'. *Learning Disability Quarterly*, 20(2), 140–159.

23 Graham, S., Harris, K.R., MacArthur, C.A. and Schwartz, S.S. (1991). 'Writing and writing instruction with students with learning disabilities: A review of a program of research'. *Learning Disability Quarterly*, 14(2), 89–114.

24 Hughes, C. and Schumaker, J.B. (1991). 'Test-taking strategy instruction for adolescents with learning disabilities'. *Exceptionality*, 2(44), 205–221.

25 Woodward, J. and Rieth, H. (1997). 'A historical review of technology research in special education'. *Review of Educational Research*, 67(4), 503–536.

26 Swanson, H.L. (2000). 'What instruction works for students with learning disabilities? From a meta-analysis of intervention studies'. In R. Gersten, E.P. Schiller and S. Vaughn (eds) *Contemporary special education research: Syntheses of the knowledge base on critical instructional issues* (pp. 1–30). Mahwah, NJ: Lawrence Erlbaum Associates.

27 Harris and Presley, op. cit., p. 394.

28 Harris and Presley, op. cit., p. 401.

Chapter 14

Strategy 12: Self-regulated learning

'Help learners take control of their own learning'

Rating

★★★✫

 The strategy

Self-regulated learning (SRL) aims at helping learners to define goals for themselves, to monitor their own behaviour, and to make decisions and choices of actions that lead to the achievement of their goals.[1] This strategy can be used in a variety of settings, across a range of subjects, and with learners with and without special educational needs.

SRL is a broad concept, which includes within its span a range of strategies, including *self-monitoring, self-reinforcement, self-awareness, self-efficacy, self-directed learning, self-determined learning, self-management* and *self-evaluation.*

This strategy relates most closely to the executive system component of the learning and teaching model outlined in Chapter 2.

 The underlying idea

One of the features of maturity and a good quality of life in most societies is the ability to take personal responsibility for one's own actions. In free, democratic societies, people expect, and are expected, to exercise autonomy by making choices and taking decisions over most aspects of their lives. Of course, this is not absolute freedom as we also expect to have a degree of interdependence as we adjust to the needs and wants of others around us.[2] It follows from this that a major objective of education should be to assist all learners to be increasingly involved in making decisions about their own learning and to act on these decisions, while at the same time taking account of their interdependence.

Although self-determination is a valued attribute, it is frequently the case that many learners with special educational needs seem to have little control over their lives, depending instead on others around them to make decisions on their behalf. Unfortunately, too, many of them have been over-protected and taught to be 'helpless'. This need not remain the case for, as we shall see, there is growing evidence that such learners, including those with major learning disabilities, can be helped to take more control over their own learning. Since many of them might have experienced prolonged failure and have low self-esteem, this is a particularly challenging task for educators.

As I mentioned in Chapter 2, a lack of SRL suggests that a learner's executive system is not being sufficiently activated, which, in turn, is associated with a lack of general cognitive strategies that can develop self-regulation. Also, you will note that SRL involves motivation factors, particularly goal-setting and personal agency beliefs.

Let me give a personal example of SRL. I recently joined a gym, with the goal of losing some weight and regaining some of the fitness that I have lost by sitting too long in front of a computer, writing this book among other things! Thus, it was my decision (influenced a little by my wife, admittedly). When I joined up, I set several targets to do with weights and speeds in various exercises. I monitor these targets every time I go to the gym and revise them as my fitness level increases. As my achievements become apparent, I reinforce myself with self-praise, and sometimes with a coffee, even feeling a little morally superior to those who have not converted to the fitness movement. I believe that my gym-attending behaviour illustrates many of the components usually associated with the SRL, namely:

- *Self-awareness*: awareness that one is a unique person with thoughts and feelings that are distinct from others (I have a body that needs looking after).
- *Motivation*: preparedness to exert effort and to persist in the face of difficulty (I have moved physical fitness up my list of priorities to the point where I attend the gym even when I feel a little tired or out-of-sorts).
- *Emotional control*: ability to limit anxiety about task difficulty (occasionally I have to say to myself, 'Come on David, you can do it. Don't give up!').
- *Goal-setting skills*: defining short- and long-term goals and setting priorities among them (I want to lose weight and gain fitness).
- *Decision-making skills*: deciding what actions to take that would increase the likelihood of achieving the goals (I will attend the gym at least four times a week, and take care with my diet).
- *Problem-solving skills*: dealing with unexpected events and working out solutions (how do I manage this exercise: should I adjust the weight and/or the speed and/or its duration?).
- *Self-monitoring skills*: observing one's own target behaviours and recording them (I record my performance on the exercises and monitor changes that have occurred over the period I have attended the gym).

- *Self-reinforcement skills*: (see my comments about coffee and enjoying the moral high ground!).[3]

I am sure that you can think of many examples of your own SRL.

 ## The practice

 ### SRL development

SRL can be developed in three main ways, through:

1   school experiences, e.g., learners realizing the value of checking their work and educators modelling SRL in their own activities;
2   learners being engaged in activities that require SRL, e.g., in cooperative group learning; and
3   explicit instruction about SRL, as in the following point.[4]

 ### A self-regulated problem-solving strategy

A *Self-Determined Learning Model of Instruction* involves teaching learners a self-regulated problem-solving strategy. This involves learners: (a) setting their own goals based on their preferences and needs, (b) developing and implementing action plans to achieve those goals, (c) self-evaluating their progress toward achieving their goals and (d) revising their goals or action plans accordingly.[5]

 ### Other ideas

For other ideas, see the research evidence below. Also, many of the suggestions contained in **Strategy 11: Cognitive Strategy Instruction** lead to SRL once they become part of learners' repertoires.

SRL in the classroom

As with all the strategies outlined in this book, it is important that, as far as possible, SRL is embedded in all classroom activities, so that they are meaningful and not divorced from real problem-solving.

 ## The evidence

✓   In a descriptive review of research conducted up to the early 1990s, 27 studies pertaining to the use of self-monitoring for behaviour management purposes in special education classrooms were analysed. It was found that self-monitoring can be used **with learners with special educational**

needs of various ages in various settings to increase: (a) attention to tasks, (b) positive classroom behaviours and (c) some social skills.[6]

✓ In a meta-analysis of 99 studies that used interventions to decrease **disruptive classroom behaviour**, self-management strategies yielded an effect size of 1.00. In other words, there was a reduction of disruptive behaviour for about 85 per cent of the students treated by this method.[7]

✓ In a US programme referred to as Self-Regulated Strategy Development, sixth-grade **learning disabled** students were taught to use self-directed prompts to compose argumentative essays. These required them to: (a) consider their audience and reasons for writing, (b) develop a plan for what they intended to say using various frameworks, (c) evaluate possible content by considering its impact on readers and (d) continue the process of planning during the writing itself. The results showed that strategy instruction had a positive effect on students' writing performance and self-efficacy. These effects were maintained over time and transferred to a new setting and teacher. Furthermore, there was evidence for generalization to a second genre, story writing.[8]

✓ In another US study, a Self-Determined Learning Model of Instruction (see above in The Practice section) was used in a field test by 21 teachers with 40 learners with a mean age of 17 years and with a range of disabilities, including **mental retardation**, **learning disabilities** and **emotional or behaviour disorders**. The results showed that the learners receiving instruction in the model attained educationally relevant goals, showed enhanced self-determination and communicated their satisfaction with the process. Teachers also indicated their satisfaction and suggested that they would continue to use the model.[9]

✓ In a follow-up study of 80 learners with **mental retardation** or **learning disabilities**, data on their levels of self-determination on graduation from high school were compared with outcomes one year later. In this US study self-determination was measured on a scale that included items on student autonomy, self-regulation, psychological empowerment and self-realization. It was found that self-determined learners were more likely to have achieved more positive adult outcomes, including being employed at a higher rate and earning more per hour than peers who were not self-determined.[10]

✓ Two separate US studies of the effects of self-monitoring on on-task behaviours have shown positive results. In the first of these, data from a multiple baseline experiment with four **at-risk** learners aged 13 to 15 showed increases in on-task behaviour as each learner began to self-monitor. As well, small improvements in academic performance were noted.[11] In the second study, four elementary school students with **learning disabilities** were put on a self-monitoring programme. This was a simple procedure whereby the learners heard a recorded tone every 60 seconds and noted whether or not they were on-task. The results showed a positive relationship between self-monitoring and on-task behaviour, although the relationship between self-monitoring and written language performance was less convincing.[12]

✓ However, another study has shown a positive impact of self-monitoring on written language. This involved students with **learning disabilities** who ranged in age from 10 to 12 years. The results showed that self-monitoring of both on-task behaviour and the number of words in stories increased on-task behaviour, the number of words in stories and the quality of writing. These results were explained in terms of motivating students to write more and providing them with concrete, immediate feedback.[13]

✓ The effectiveness of self-monitoring across a classroom of learners who were **severely emotionally disturbed** was investigated in another US study. Six boys, aged 11 to 13, placed in a special class were the focus of the study. The programme involved each learner monitoring his on-task behaviour and one additional selected behaviour throughout a 45-minute period. A tape recorder sounded a bell every five minutes when the learners were required to record whether or not they were on-task and to respond to a statement concerning his other target behaviour (e.g., 'I had a positive attitude'). Within a multiple baseline design, all learners improved their on-task behaviour and other targeted behaviours. These results were more effective than a behaviour management system conducted solely by the classroom teacher.[14]

✓ Two recent reviews of the use of self-management strategies with learners with **autism** reported studies showing that it has positive effects on: (a) social skills and social interactions, (b) reducing disruptive behaviour, (c) independent work skills, (d) responsiveness to others' initiations in homes and classrooms, (e) independent work skills, (f) daily living skills, (g) on-task behaviour and (h) reducing stereotypic and self-stimulatory behaviours.[15] An example of a study involving young, low-functioning learners with autism successfully used a pictorial self-management strategy (see also **Strategy 23**). This involved using picture prompts to perform daily living tasks and to self-reinforce upon the completion of tasks.[16]

✓ A US study examined the effects of self-monitoring on selected social and academic behaviours of four high school learners with **mental retardation** who were enrolled in general education classes. The self-monitoring training used a combination of modelling, direct instruction, guided practice, corrective feedback and picture prompts. Self-monitoring was associated with improved behaviours in all the learners, these improvements also being perceived by their teachers and their classmates.[17]

✓ Finally, a study investigated the effects of peer-delivered self-monitoring strategies on the participation of five learners with **severe disabilities** in regular education classrooms. In this case, the peers were given basic training in instructing the disabled learners in self-monitoring and in giving cues and praise. They also kept a record of the learners' classroom behaviour, which was later compared with their self-monitoring record. In a multiple baseline experimental design the results showed increased occurrence of 'academic survival skills' and participation in the classroom.[18]

 ## Addressing risks

Perhaps the biggest risk with SRL is to *under*-estimate the capacity of learners with special educational needs to acquire the skill and the will to use the strategy. Having said that, it is important to implement the strategy under careful supervision, especially with cognitively challenged and younger learners.

 ## Conclusion

Self-regulated learning is a strategy that can be used in a variety of settings, across a range of subject areas and with learners with and without special educational needs. It is a low-cost strategy that is relatively easy to implement. Once taught to learners, it can free educators for other tasks. Although self-regulated learning improves with age, since older learners are better able to match their goals with their actions and are better able to reflect on their behaviour, it also has an important place in the education of young learners.

 ## Further reading

Paris, S.G. and Paris, A.H. (2001). 'Classroom applications of research on self-regulated learning'. *Educational Psychologist*, 36(3), 89–102.
Wehmeyer, M.L., Agran, M. and Hughes, C. (1998). *Teaching self-determination skills to students with disabilities: Basic skills for successful transition*. Baltimore, MD: Paul H. Brookes.

Key references

1 Derived from Zimmerman, B.J. (2000). 'Attaining self-regulation: A social-cognitive perspective'. In M. Boekarts, P. Pintrich and M. Zeidner (eds) *Self-regulation: Theory, research, and applications* (pp. 13–39). Orlando, FL: Academic Press.
2 While most Western cultures place a high value on autonomy, individuality and self-regulation, other cultures, such as Japanese, other Asian, African and Latin American, tend to place more emphasis on 'self-in-relation-to-others', according to Markus, H.R. and Kitayama, S. (1991). 'Culture and self: Implications for cognition, emotion and motivation'. *Psychological Review*, 98(2), 224–253.

3 Based on the following sources: Paris, S.G. and Paris, A.H. (2001). 'Classroom applications of research on self-regulated learning'. *Educational Psychologist*, 36(3), 89–102; and Wehmeyer, M.L. (1999). 'A functional model of self-determination: Describing development and implementing instruction'. *Focus on Autism and Other Developmental Disabilities*, 14(1), 53–61.
4 Paris and Paris, op. cit.
5 Agran, M., Blanchard, C. and Wehmeyer, M. (2000). 'Promoting transition goals and self-determination through student self-directed learning: The self-determined learning model of instruction'. *Education and Training in Mental Retardation and Developmental Disabilities*, 35(4), 351–364.
6 Webber, J., Scheuermann, B., McCall, C. and Coleman, M. (1993). 'Research on self-monitoring as a behavior management technique in special education classrooms: A descriptive review'. *Remedial and Special Education*, 14(2), 38–56.
7 Stage, S.A. and Quiroz, D.R. (1997). 'A meta-analysis of interventions to decrease disruptive classroom behavior in public education settings'. *School Psychology Review*, 26(3), 333–369.
8 Graham, S. and Harris, K.R. (1989). 'Improving learning disabled students' skills at composing essays: Self-instructional strategy training'. *Exceptional Children*, 56(3), 201–214.
9 Wehmeyer, M.L., Palmer, S.B., Agran, M., Mithaug, D.E. and Martin, J.E. (2000). 'Promoting causal agency: the self-determined learning model of instruction'. *Exceptional Children*, 66(4), 439–453.
10 Wehmeyer, M. and Schwartz, M. (1997). 'Self-determination and positive adult outcomes: A follow-up study of youth with mental retardation or learning disabilities'. *Exceptional Children*, 63(2), 245–255.
11 Wood, S.J., Murdock, J.Y., Cronin, M.E., Dawson, N.M. and Kirby, P.C. (1998). 'Effects of self-monitoring on on-task behaviours of at-risk middle school students'. *Journal of Behavioral Education*, 8(2), 263–279.
12 Wolfe, L.H., Heron, T.E. and Goddard, Y.L. (2000). 'Effects of self-monitoring on the on-task behaviour and written language performance of elementary students with learning disabilities'. *Journal of Behavioural Education*, 10(1), 49–73.
13 Harris, K.R., Graham, S., Reid, R., McElroy, K. and Hamby, R. (1994). 'Self-monitoring of attention versus self-monitoring of performance: Replication and cross-task comparison'. *Learning Disability Quarterly*, 17(2), 121–139.
14 Kern, L., Dunlap, G., Childs, K.E. and Clarke, S. (1994). 'Use of a classwide self-management program to improve the behavior of students with emotional and behavioral disorders'. *Education and Treatment of Children*, 17(4), 445–458.
15 Harrower, J.K. and Dunlap, G. (2001). 'Including children with autism in general education classrooms: a review of effective strategies'. *Behavior Modification*, 25(5), 762–784; and Matson, J.L., Benavidez, D.A., Compton, L.S., Paclawskyj, T. and Baglio, C. (1996). 'Behavioral treatment of autistic persons: A review of research from 1980 to the present'. *Research in Developmental Disabilities*, 17(6), 433–465.
16 Pierce, K.L. and Schreibman, L. (1994). 'Teaching daily living skills to children with autism in unsupervised settings through pictorial self-management'. *Journal of Applied Behavior Analysis*, 27(3), 471–481.
17 Hughes, C., Copeland, S.R., Wehmeyer, M.L., Agran, M., Rodi, M.S. and Presley, J.A. (2002). 'Using self-monitoring to improve performance in general education high school classes'. *Education and Training in Mental Retardation and Development Disabilities*, 37(3), 262–272.
18 Gilberts, G.H., Agran, M., Hughes, C. and Wehmeyer, M. (2001). 'The effects of peer delivered self-monitoring strategies on the participation of students with severe disabilities in general education classrooms'. *Journal of the Association for Persons with Severe Handicaps*, 26(1), 25–36.

Chapter 15

Strategy 13: Mnemonics and other memory strategies

'Help learners to remember important information'

This strategy will mainly be devoted to mnemonics, one of the highest rated of all the strategies described in this book. Brief attention will also be paid to several other memory strategies that have a good record in working with learners with special educational needs.

Before reading about these strategies I suggest you refresh your understanding of the learning and teaching model in Chapter 2, particularly the sections on primary memory, short-term memory and long-term memory.

MNEMONICS

Rating
★★★★

 The strategy

Mnemonics simply refers to a method for enhancing the memory of specific content that has been learned in various contexts, especially school lessons.

Given that memory of factual information is essential for school success – and for life in general – it is vital that your learners develop effective memory strategies. While most learners seem to independently develop these strategies, others will require your assistance.

Many learners with special educational needs have difficulties in remembering information. In some cases, these difficulties reflect organically based problems in processing information, but in many cases they reflect a lack of strategies for remembering information.

Mnemonic strategies comprise one of the most effective methods you can employ in assisting the latter group of learners – indeed, any learners – how to remember factual material. You have probably employed mnemonics to assist your own learning.

Since mnemonics rely on learners having some language skills, including reading, this strategy is generally not appropriate for those with severe intellectual disabilities. It is, however, particularly recommended for students with learning difficulties.

The underlying idea

According to the modern proponents of the idea,[1] mnemonic strategies are effective because they form sounds or image links between stimuli and responses. Because many memory deficits are language based, the goal of memory training using mnemonic strategies is to make links between difficult-to-remember words and easy-to-remember sounds or visual images.

The word 'mnemonics' is derived from the Ancient Greek word *mnemikos* ('of memory'). Its origins can be traced back to antiquity, when the highly valued activity of oratory called upon advanced memory skills. The first recorded system of memory aids was developed by Simonides of Ceos (556–468 BC). His system, which became known as 'Visual Imagery Mnemonics', involved encoding information into memory by conjuring up vivid mental images and then mentally placing them in familiar locations, such as in the rooms of a house. Simonides became aware of this process during a tragic event in which he was requested to remember the exact locations of people who were killed by a roof collapsing at a banquet he had attended. He was able to remember where each person was seated, due to his visual memory associations. This was a precursor to the broader system of mnemonics.[2]

In the case of students with **learning difficulties**, mnemonics help them to make a bridge between their areas of relative cognitive strength (e.g., memory for pictures or memory for sounds) and their areas of relative weaknesses (e.g., recall of prior knowledge and independent strategy use).

The practice

Four main strategies fall under mnemonics:

The keyword strategy

In this strategy a new word that you want your learners to remember is recoded into a keyword that is easy to picture and that has a similar sound to the target word. For example, if you want your learners to remember the definition of cirrus clouds (the high, thin feathery formations), ask them to think of a circus top. It sounds similar and it is high and thin.

The pegword strategy

Pegwords are rhyming substitutes for numbers (e.g., one is bun and two is shoe, etc.). They are used to assist students remember numbered or ordered information. For example, if you want them to remember that there are 12 people in a jury, draw a picture of 12 elves sitting near a judge (in this case the pegword for 12 is *elf*). Or, if you want them to remember that there are 11 players in a cricket team, draw a bat-shaped lever (the pegword for 11).

The letter strategy

You are probably more familiar with this mnemonic strategy. As its name suggests, the letter strategy prompts you to remember lists of things. One of the commonly learned lists is for North America's Great Lakes. Most of you probably learned them by using the acronym HOMES. I can recall a slightly different way of remembering them, however. My method was to learn the nonsense word SMHEO ('ess-em-ach-ee-oh'), which had the advantage of placing the lakes in the correct order. Similarly, my way of learning the colours of the rainbow was via the nonsense word ROYGBIV. What was your strategy?

Yet another example is provided by approaches to learning the order of the planets from the sun outwards: MVEMJSUNP. Obviously, this does not even approximate a word in any language, so what is to be done? The writers that figure prominently in promoting mnemonic strategies suggest the creation of what they call an 'acrostic' which, in this case, would be the sentence 'My Very Educated Mother Just Sent Us Nine Pizzas'. Unfortunately, now that poor old Pluto has been demoted from the planetary system, we will have to find another acrostic. Any ideas?

The letter strategy can also be used to help students remember the steps to be taken in performing certain tasks. For example, two such strategies have been used to assist students to recall particular sets of social skills (**Strategy 10**). First, a FAST strategy (*F*reeze and think, *A*lternatives, *S*olution, *T*ry it) was used to assist students to solve interpersonal problems. Second, a SLAM strategy (*S*top whatever you're doing, *L*ook the person in the eye, *A*sk the person a question if you don't understand what he/she means, *M*ake an appropriate response to the person) has been used to enable students to accept and assimilate negative feedback from others.[3]

If you are interested in pursuing other mnemonics, you could check on *Wikipedia*, the free encyclopedia.[4] As a psychologist, one that particularly took my fancy was a mnemonic for child psychologist Urie Bronfenbrenner's ecological systems theory. This defines the contexts of development in terms of microsystems, mesosystems, exosystems, macrosystems and chrono-systems: MICe and Men Eat MACaroni and Cheese!

The picture strategy

Simonides's invention of visual imagery mnemonics draws our attention to the power of associating visual images with verbal constructs. This association can be a powerful method for teaching students who may experience difficulty in remembering certain letters or words. For example, the letter 's' might be recalled as being associated with a snake, which its shape resembles.

 ## The evidence

✓ Several research studies have shown that students (including those with a range of **disabilities**) can be trained to use mnemonic strategies independently across a range of different content areas, including science and social studies.[5]

✓ A social skills intervention programme used FAST and SLAM strategies (described above) to increase peer acceptance of students with **learning disabilities** in general elementary classrooms. Compared with controls, the results showed modest intervention effects, with increased peer ratings of acceptance of the learning disabled students by their peers.[6]

✓ In an analysis of 19 meta-analyses of various interventions, mnemonic training, with an effect size of 1.62, was rated the highest.[7] This effect size can be translated to mean that the average student receiving mnemonic instruction was better off than 95 per cent of the students not receiving such instruction.

✓ A recent review of 34 studies confirmed the above effect size. This analysis showed that neither grade-level nor type of disability had an apparent influence on the effectiveness of mnemonic instruction. However, in the case of students with **mental retardation**, it was necessary to ensure that the instruction was more carefully sequenced, more structured and delivered at a slower pace using less content than when students with **learning disabilities** were taught the same content.[8]

✓ There is evidence that the keyword strategy has value in teaching social studies content. In a comparison of mnemonic and non-mnemonic methods in an inclusive elementary school classroom it was found that non-disabled students scored an average of 83 per cent on non-mnemonic content, compared with 89 per cent on mnemonic content. Significantly, the students with disabilities **(learning disabilities, emotional disturbance, speech and language impairments)** scored 37 per cent and 75 per cent, respectively.[9]

✓ Another study involved teaching first-grade **learners with special needs** letter recognition and letter-sound relationships using picture mnemonics. For example, as noted above, the letter 's' was drawn using a snake while the letter 'a' resembles an apple. Using a multiple baseline across students research design, the authors found that this picture mnemonics method was an effective technique and that learning was maintained after a four-week delay.[10]

✓ In a US study of inclusive life sciences classes in secondary schools, 11 teachers were trained to use a teaching strategy that focused on finding and using mnemonics to enhance learners' recall of information. The results showed that the trained teachers who used the strategy, as well as their students (especially those with **learning disabilities**), were better than controls at selecting and explaining mnemonics.[11]

 Addressing risks

You need to consider three risks:

*   Perhaps the main risk is that more is expected of mnemonic strategies than they are capable of delivering. It is important to note that they are not an overall teaching method. They are simply intended to help learners to recall information that they have already learned through other strategies.
*   A second risk is that you might go overboard in requiring your students to generate their own mnemonics. While there are some advantages in getting students to generate their own mnemonic strategies, it is better that you have a class-wide set of mnemonics developed under your guidance.
*   Also, generating mnemonics can be very time-consuming, as you will appreciate when you try to develop them yourself. I personally find the keyword and pegword strategies can be quite complicated, and would be much happier asking students to assist with developing letter and picture strategies – in moderation.

 Conclusion

Mnemonic strategy instruction is a valuable component of instruction, especially for students with learning disabilities, but also for students with other disabilities. It is particularly valuable when recall of factual material is required, for example in test-taking.

 Further reading

Uberti, H.Z., Scruggs, T.F. and Mastropieri, M.A. (2003). 'Keywords make the difference! Mnemonic instruction in inclusive classrooms'. *TEACHING Exceptional Children*, 35(3), 56–61.

OTHER MEMORY STRATEGIES

While space does not permit a full treatment of other memory strategies in the depth of the discussion of mnemonics, here are several points for you to consider:[12]

Attention is a key feature of memory

Obviously, we cannot remember things that we don't notice, so ensuring that learners attend is critical to remembering. However, what is important is not merely paying attention in some global way, but attending to critical features of a task. This is strongly influenced by your skill in drawing learners' attention to important ideas and ignoring the 'noise' that might surround them. By noise, I mean all the irrelevant events that might be occurring inside and outside the classroom.

Rehearsal is usually necessary for memory

How long and how well something is stored in the learner's long-term memory is often determined by how often it has been attended to. As I point out in **Strategy 20**, building regular rehearsal into your lessons is necessary. This need not be tedious, but should be made fun and its purpose made clear to learners.

Key facts should be available in the learner's primary memory

As I discuss in the learning and teaching model, the presence of key facts in our primary memory frees our cognitive processing resources for more important activities. Therefore, learners should be given ample practice with repetition and drills to build up their store of associations. The aim here is to help the learner have a range of automatic responses available. This is a little different from the previous point where the aim is to extend the learner's long-term memory.

Transform material into mental representations

Long-term memory is helped by the use of *graphic organizers*.[13] These are visual representations of knowledge, concepts or ideas. There are literally dozens of different types of graphic organizers. Let me describe a few of them.

- *Story boards*: these are a series of illustrations displayed in a time sequence to portray a story, as, for example, in a film or a comic strip. They can be a fun way of helping learners to plan writing a story.
- *Concept mapping*: sometimes referred to as *mental mapping*, this is a technique for visualizing the relationships between different concepts or ideas. Concepts are connected with labelled arrows, in a downward-branching hierarchical structure. The relationship between concepts is expressed in linking phrases, e.g., 'gives rise to', 'results in', 'is required

by' or 'contributes to'. They can be an aid to note-taking and brain-storming.

- *Mind mapping*: this is a procedure for using a diagram to represent words or ideas arranged around a key word or idea to show how they are connected. It typically takes the form of branches, like a tree or a network of roads.[14]
- *Flow charts*: are schematic representations of processes. Examples include instructions for assembling a bicycle or for planning an event. Generally the start point, end points, inputs, outputs, possible paths and the decisions that lead to these possible paths are included. In classrooms they could have many uses, including charting the process of writing a story or the process of conducting a chemistry experiment.
- *Visualization*: encourage learners to create representational images when reading texts (e.g., you could ask them to 'draw a picture in your head' to depict the important relations specified in the text, by reading it first and then imagining it).[15]

Chunking helps long-term memory

My telephone number is 8557261. Even though its length fits the 'magic number' of seven digits, I find it much easier to recall when I remember it as 8557 261. I would guess that you do something similar to remember telephone numbers. This method of grouping the numbers together, in my case into two groups, is called 'chunking'. There are many other examples of recoding information into easily remembered chunks.

Finally, I am confident that if you implement the other strategies in this book, particularly those to do with cognitive strategy instruction, you will greatly enhance your students' memories. In making this point, I would like to emphasize that although the strategies are described separately, they are interconnected, with the common theme of helping students to become more effective and efficient learners.

Key references

1 Scruggs, T.E. and Mastropieri, M.A. (2000). 'The effectiveness of mnemonic instruction for students with learning and behavior problems: An update and research synthesis'. *Journal of Behavioral Education*, 10(2/3), 163–173.
2 Yates, F.A. (1966). *The art of memory*. Chicago, IL: The Chicago University Press.
3 McIntosh, R., Vaughn, S. and Bennerson, D. (1995). 'FAST social skills with a SLAM and a RAP: Providing social skills training for students with learning disabilities'. *TEACHING Exceptional Children*, 28(1), 37–41.
4 http://en.wikipedia.org/wiki/Mnemonic (accessed 30 September 2006).

5 Mastropieri, M.A. and Scruggs, T.E. (1989). 'Constructing more meaningful relationships: Mnemonic instruction for special populations'. *Educational Psychology Review*, 1(2), 83–111.
6 Bennerson, D., McIntosh, R. and Vaughn, S. (1991). 'Increasing positive interpersonal interactions: A social intervention for students with learning disabilities in the regular classroom'. Paper presented at the annual conference of the Council for Exceptional Children, Atlanta, Georgia. (ERIC Document Reproduction Service No. ED 333 666).
7 Lloyd, J.W., Forness, S.R. and Kavale, K.A. (1998). 'Some methods are more effective than others'. *Intervention in School and Clinic*, 33(4), 195–200. The authors cite Mastropieri, M.A. and Scruggs, T.E. op. cit. In the latter study, a total of 24 experiments involving mnemonics were analysed. These studies involved students with learning disabilities, mild mental retardation and behavioural disorders.
8 Scruggs and Mastropieri, op. cit.
9 Mastropieri, M.A., Sweda, J. and Scruggs, T.E. (2000). 'Teacher use of mnemonic strategy instruction'. *Learning Disabilities Research and Practice*, 15(2), 69–74.
10 Fulk, B.J.M., Lohman, D. and Belfiore, P.J. (1997). 'Effects of integrated picture mnemonics on the letter recognition and letter-sound acquisition of transitional first grade students with special needs'. *Learning Disability Quarterly*, 20(1), 33–42.
11 Bulgren, J.A., Deshler, D.D. and Schumaker, J.B. (1997). 'Use of a recall enhancement routine and strategies in inclusive secondary classes'. *Learning Disabilities Research and Practice*, 12(4), 198–208.
12 Hirsch, E.D. (2002). Classroom research and cargo cults. *Policy Review*, No. 115.
13 What follows has been adapted from wikipedia, op. cit.
14 See Buzan, T. (1991). *The mind map book*. New York: Penguin.
15 Harris, K.R. and Presley, M. (1991). 'The nature of cognitive strategy instruction: Interactive strategy construction'. *Exceptional Children*, 57(5), 392–404.

Chapter 16

Strategy 14: Reciprocal teaching

'Help learners understand what they read'

Rating
★★★☆

 The strategy

Reciprocal teaching involves teaching learners, by means of guided practice, how to improve their reading comprehension, in all subject areas, by predicting, clarifying, questioning and summarizing what is in a text. It takes place in a dialogue between an educator and learners, in which the educator models and explains in the early stages and gradually passes more and more responsibility to the learners as they become more competent. Reciprocal teaching is an example of the cognitive strategy instruction techniques discussed in **Strategy 11**. It is relevant for many subjects, including social studies, science, the languages, as well as reading.

In the learning and teaching model described in Chapter 2, this strategy relates to the executive system and strategies.

 The underlying idea

Reciprocal teaching is based on the principle that cognitive development is strongly influenced by interacting with more knowledgeable people (experts, educators, parents and more skilled peers). These interactions lead to strategies becoming internalized and made one's own.

Reciprocal teaching typically involves an educator being very active initially, assisting learners to use strategies for comprehending written material, and then gradually reducing support as learners become more skilled.

The strategy, first described in the early 1980s by Palincsar and Brown,[1] had its origins in three related theories of guided learning:

• *'zone of proximal development'*: according to the Russian psychologist, Vygotsky, this is the area between the actual development of a learner and his/her level of potential development, and is the area where instruction should take place;[2]

- *'proleptic teaching'*: this takes place in apprenticeship instruction where the learner participates first as a spectator, then as a novice responsible for very little of the actual work and finally as a competent worker;[3]
- *'expert scaffolding'*: here the expert acts as a guide, shaping the learning of the novice and supporting him/her until no longer needed.[4]

 The practice

 Intention of the reciprocal teaching strategy

The reciprocal teaching strategy is mainly intended to improve the comprehension skills of learners who can decode texts (i.e., read the words) but have difficulty in comprehending them.

The following sequence typically takes place:[5]

- Ask the learners to read a passage of the text silently, or you read it orally, depending on the decoding ability of the learners.
- Begin the discussion by asking *questions* about the content of the passage, and give the learners an opportunity to raise additional questions. These will help to focus attention and help each member of the group gain deeper meaning and understanding from the text. These questions often become interesting predictions, or springboards, for further inquiry. Point out that questions are ways in which we can test ourselves to make sure we understand what we have read and they help us to focus on important information in a passage.
- Move on to work out the gist of the passage and *summarize* it. Initially, you would offer a summary and ask the learners to discuss it in order to achieve consensus about it. Point out that summaries are one or two or three sentences that tell the most important ideas of what we have read.
- *Clarify* words or phrases that are unclear or ambiguous so that everyone understands what the passage is about. Point out that it is very important that we understand what we're reading and that if we don't we should ask for help.
- Finally, suggest and ask for *predictions* regarding what might occur next in the text. The learners might base their predictions on their prior knowledge of the topic, clues that are provided in the passage (e.g., pictures, headings, subtitles) or issues that they hope the author will address in the remainder of the text. Tell the learners that we use clues in what we read to form a picture of what might happen next and that this helps to keep us interested.

Initially, you would model the entire process, explaining each part of the strategy and coaching the learners on how to ask good questions, construct summaries and make appropriate predictions, etc. Gradually, your role would reduce, so that the 'hunt for meaning' becomes a joint process, with you providing 'scaffolds' (see below) where necessary. The emphasis throughout should be on cooperative effort involving you as an educator and all the learners in the class. The aim, of course, is for the learners to take increasing responsibility, until they become self-regulated. As they become more competent, you could increase your expectations.

Once you have initially taught the strategies involved in reciprocal teaching, they can be used in cooperative group teaching (especially in mixed-ability groups) and in peer tutoring (see **Strategies 2** and **3**, respectively).

✳ *Scaffolding*

As mentioned above, scaffolding (sometimes referred to as 'scaffolded instruction' or 'cognitive bootstrapping') is an important element of reciprocal teaching. According to the originators of reciprocal teaching, the metaphor of scaffolding captures the idea of a temporary support that can be removed when no longer necessary. Scaffolding methods include controlling the difficulty level of tasks, pointing out critical features, giving prompts or cues, maintaining learners' interest, providing feedback, providing additional modelling, coaching, giving explanations and using partners. The precise nature of the scaffolds is determined by the learner's needs and they are withdrawn once mastery has been shown.[6]

Here are some other suggestions for scaffolded instruction:

- Identify what learners already know and determine which competencies are within their zones of proximal development and which are beyond their current ability. The former can be scaffolded, the latter cannot.
- Help learners achieve success quickly to give them confidence that they can learn a particular skill.
- Be as unobtrusive as possible in providing scaffolding, so that you don't undermine learners' self-confidence. Learn to 'read' their reactions and adapt your instruction accordingly.
- Know when it is time to stop or to change direction so that the learners don't become bored or frustrated.
- Help learners to be self-regulated when they can carry out the scaffolded activity by gradually withdrawing or reducing the scaffolding.
- Assist learners to generalize their newly acquired skill to other contexts. This might mean discussing other similar activities to which the skill could be applied or it might mean you being alert to those activities when they occur and reminding them how they could apply their new skill.[7]

Other ideas

For other ideas on implementing reciprocal teaching, see the research evidence below, particularly the last two items.

 The evidence

✓ In an early study by the originators of reciprocal teaching, this approach was compared with 'typical practices'. This US study involved 24 seventh-grade learners with **reading difficulties**. The results showed that the majority of the learners in the reciprocal teaching programme made substantial gains in reading comprehension.[8]

✓ A comprehensive review of 16 reciprocal teaching studies, including six with **below-average** learners, found a median effect size of 0.88 when experimenter-developed comprehension tests were used. The effect size was somewhat lower (0.32) when standardized tests were used.[9]

✓ In a US study of six first-grade teachers, the teachers worked with groups of learners identified as being **at risk for academic failure**. Each teacher used reciprocal teaching with one group of children, reading stories to them, asking questions about the content and discussing the stories. The same teachers also worked with a matched control group, who received the identical programme, except they did not engage in discussions on the content. Learners in the reciprocal teaching groups showed improvements in their ability to understand texts and identify the gist of what they read.[10]

✓ In another early US study, 12 intermediate-grade learners with **learning disabilities** received 28 reciprocal teaching sessions. An effect size of 0.36 was obtained for reading performance.[11]

✓ A further US study examined the effectiveness of reciprocal teaching during social studies lessons with 25 students with **learning disabilities** in regular fourth- to sixth-grade classrooms. The results indicated that all learners, including those with learning disabilities, improved their performance on comprehension compared with those in control groups.[12]

✓ A New Zealand study investigated the efficacy of a tape-assisted reciprocal teaching programme, referred to as 'cognitive bootstrapping'. The study's subjects were learners aged from eight to ten years with **poor comprehension skills**, half of whom also had poor decoding skills. The results showed that the poor decoders improved their use of cognitive strategies and their comprehension. These results were maintained after ten weeks and transferred to other material.[13]

✓ In another New Zealand study, 18 fourth- and fifth-grade learners with six months to two years **reading delays** were taught in a reciprocal teaching programme. This involved: (a) discussions based on the title of a story to stimulate the learners to make predictions, (b) summarizing segments of the story after silent reading, (c) thinking of 'teacher-like' questions about the segment, (d) making predictions about what might occur in the next segment and (e) asking for clarification if necessary. During the first part of the intervention, the teachers were involved in extensive modelling of the strategies and the learners actively answered questions and discussed the passages. As a result of the programme the learners showed improvements in comprehension, which were maintained at an eight-week follow-up and were transferred to other genres.[14]

✓ A US study of 26 seventh- and eighth-grade **students with learning disabilities who used English as a second language** investigated the effects of reciprocal teaching of reading comprehension strategies. All students participated in reciprocal teaching for 15 days. This involved them using six strategies while they were reading social studies material: (a) predict what a given passage would be about, (b) brainstorm what they already knew about the topic or passage, (c) clarify words or phrases they did not understand, (d) highlight the main idea of a paragraph, (e) summarize the main ideas and (f) ask and answer questions about a passage. The students were then randomly placed in one of two groups for 12 days, one using the comprehension strategies in cooperative groups and the second tutoring younger peers in the strategies. The results showed that both groups made significant progress in reading comprehension, but there was no significant difference between them, both being equally effective. Unfortunately, no control group was employed.[15]

 Addressing risks

Some cautions to bear in mind:

*   Since reciprocal teaching relies on cooperation between 'experts' and 'novices', it is probably better to use it in mixed-ability groups rather than same-ability groups.
*   It is important to plan for progressive phasing out of scaffolds, so that learners do not become too dependent on educators or more expert peers.
*   Reciprocal teaching is a method for teaching comprehension, not word recognition skills.

 Conclusion

Reciprocal teaching is an effective strategy for teaching a range of learners with special educational needs how to improve their reading comprehension. It does this by teaching them how to predict, clarify, question and summarize what is in a text. A key feature of the process involves passing more and more responsibility to the learners as they become more competent.

Further reading

Larkin, M.J. (2001). 'Providing support for student independence through scaffolded instruction'. *TEACHING Exceptional Children*, 34(1), 30–35.
Palincsar, A.S. and Brown, A. (1984). 'Reciprocal teaching of comprehension-fostering and comprehension-monitoring activities'. *Cognition and Instruction*, 1(2), 117–175.

Key references

1 Palincsar, A.S. and Brown, A.L. (1984). 'Reciprocal teaching of comprehension-fostering and monitoring strategies'. *Cognition and Instruction*, 1(2), 117–175.
2 Vygotsky, L.S. (1978). *Mind in society: The development of higher psychological processes*. Cambridge, MA: Harvard University Press.
3 Wertsch, J.V. and Stone, C.A. (1979). 'A social interaction analysis of learning disabilities remediation'. Paper presented at the International Conference of the Association for Children with Learning Disabilities, San Francisco. Cited by Rosenshine, B. and Meister, C. (1994). 'Reciprocal teaching: A review of the research'. *Review of Educational Research*, 64(4), 479–530.
4 Wood, D.J., Bruner, J.S. and Ross, G. (1976). 'The role of tutoring in problem solving'. *Journal of Child Psychology and Psychiatry*, 17, 89–100.
5 Based on Palincsar and Brown, op. cit., plus Lederer, J. (2000). 'Reciprocal teaching in inclusive elementary schools'. *Journal of Learning Disabilities*. 33(1), 91–106; Kelly, M. and Moore, D. (1993). ' "I've found my memory" Reciprocal teaching in a primary school'. *Set*, 2, item 8, 1–4; and Moore, D. (1988). 'Reciprocal teaching and reading comprehension: A review'. *Journal of Research in Reading*, 11(1), 3–14.
6 See, for example, Swanson, H.L. (1999). 'Instructional components that predict treatment outcomes for students with learning disabilities: Support for a combined strategy and direct instruction model'. *Learning Disabilities Research and Practice*, 14(3), 129–140; Larkin, M.J. (2001). 'Providing support for student independence through scaffolded instruction'. *TEACHING Exceptional Children*, 34(1), 30–35; Coyne, M.D., Kame'enui, E.J. and Simmons, D.C. (2001). 'Prevention and intervention in beginning reading: Two complex systems'. *Learning Disabilities Research and Practice*, 16(2), 62–73; and Winn, J.A. (1994). 'Promises and challenges of scaffolded instruction'. *Learning Disability Quarterly*, 17(1), 89–104.
7 Partly based on Larkin, op. cit. and Presley, M., Hogan, K., Wharton-McDonald, R., Mistretta, J. and Ettenberger, S. (1996). 'The challenges of instructional scaffolding. The challenges of instruction that supports student thinking'. *Learning Disabilities Research and Practice*, 11(3), 138–146.
8 Palincsar and Brown, op. cit.
9 Rosenshine and Meister, op. cit.
10 Palincsar, A.S. and Klenk, L. (1992). 'Fostering literacy learning in supportive contexts'. *Journal of Learning Disabilities*, 25(4), 211–225, 229.
11 This was a re-analysis of a study by Labercane and Battle (1987) carried out by Rosenshine and Meister, op. cit.
12 Lederer, op. cit.
13 Le Fevre, D.M., Moore, D.W. and Wilkinson, A.G. (2003). 'Tape-assisted reciprocal teaching: Cognitive bootstrapping for poor decoders'. *British Journal of Educational Psychology*, 73(1), 37–58.

14 Kelly, M., Moore, D.W. and Tuck, B.F. (1994). 'Reciprocal teaching in a regular primary school classroom'. *Journal of Educational Research*, 88(1), 53–61.
15 Klinger, J.K. and Vaughn, S. (1996). 'Reciprocal teaching of reading comprehension strategies for students with learning disabilities who use English as a second language'. *The Elementary School Journal*, 96(3), 275–293.

Chapter 17

Strategy 15: Phonological awareness and phonological processing

'Use a sound reading strategy'

Rating
★★★⯪

 The strategy

In this chapter I will concentrate on phonological and phonemic awareness (hereafter, for the sake of simplicity, referred to as phonological awareness) and phonological processing.

Briefly, here are the key definitions:

- *Phonological awareness* is an oral language skill that involves the ability to notice, reflect upon and manipulate (move, combine and delete) the individual sounds in words.[1] It involves two aspects: (a) the awareness that speech is made up of sounds and (b) the ability to break down these sounds and manipulate them.
- *Phonemic awareness* is a subset of phonological awareness. It refers to the awareness that words in reading are made up of separate sounds, or phonemes. In other words, phonemic awareness is the recognition that sounds that are paired with letters are one and the same as the sounds of speech.[2]
- *Phonological processing* is the ability to separate, remember, blend and manipulate speech sounds. It involves the use of phonology (the sounds of language) to process verbal information in oral or written form in one's short- and long-term memory.[3] Its components include the awareness and coding of sounds for storage in memory and the subsequent retrieval of sounds from memory codes.[4]

This strategy most closely relates to the section on primary memory in my learning and teaching model, but the executive system also comes into play.

The underlying idea

It is generally accepted that there are five components of reading:[5]

- *phonological and phonemic awareness*;
- word decoding and phonics;
- fluency;
- vocabulary; and
- comprehension.

Learners might have difficulties with one or more of these components. As well, they might have difficulties with:

- processing (auditory processing, language processing and *phonological processing*);
- memory;
- attention;
- English language learning (or French, Spanish, Chinese, etc.).

Although I have elected to focus on phonological/phonetic awareness and phonological processing, I recognize that reading problems might reflect a range of the above factors, singly and in combination.

Importantly, the reading process calls upon learners' ability to segment words into syllables and sounds, to recognize and produce rhyming words, to identify where a specific sound occurs in a word and to blend sounds (phonemes) into words.[6] Weaknesses in phonological awareness and, hence, phonological processing account for a significant proportion of beginning reading problems and related difficulties in reading comprehension, memory and vocabulary.[7] In order to prevent these reading-related problems from occurring, phonological awareness and processing instructional strategies need to be implemented.

I am fully aware that, in choosing to focus on phonological processing, it might appear that I am entering one side of what some refer to as the 'Great Debate' or the 'Reading War' that has been, and is still being, waged in many countries between the proponents of phonics and whole-language approaches to teaching reading. Personally, I don't see this as an 'either-or' issue, but one where both approaches have merit, the mix depending on the age of the learners and their individual characteristics. My approach to this issue is best summarized in the words of a group of my fellow New Zealanders:

> Although a naturalistic, informal, whole language approach to reading instruction (in which word analysis activities arise *incidentally* from the child's responses during text reading) may be suitable for many children,

at-risk children appear to require a more highly structured, systematic approach, with particular attention focussed on the development of phonologically-based skills and strategies.[8]

 The practice

There is a large literature on teaching activities and materials designed to enhance learners' phonological skills (see the Further Reading section later for a selection). A useful framework is to divide activities into the following four groups:

- listening strategies;
- word-level strategies;
- syllable strategies;
- phonemic/rhyming strategies.[9]

 Listening strategies

The goal is to help learners to develop active, attentive and analytical listening skills. Here are some activities you could employ:

- Bring in recordings of various everyday sounds familiar to the learners and ask them to identify them.
- Ask learners to listen to familiar poems and songs and occasionally replace certain words with nonsense words. See if they can identify what did not make sense.
- In order to develop memory for sounds, ask learners to listen to a series of sounds, and after they have heard the sounds twice, omit a particular sound.
- With learners sitting in a circle, ask them to begin whispering certain words to the learner next to them one at a time. The same sentence or words are repeated throughout the circle until it comes to the last person. This student says aloud what was heard. I am sure you have played this game, sometimes referred to as 'Chinese Whispers'.

 Word-level strategies

These activities have the aim of helping learners become aware that words can stand alone. They include:

- Have learners count the number of words in a particular sentence.
- Read a sentence to the learners, then read the sentence a second time but omit a word and ask them to identify the missing word. Or, read

out a list of words, then read it again, but omit one of the words and ask the learners, 'What word is missing?'

- Say a phrase with misplaced words, and ask the learners to put the words in the right order. For example, 'I the beach to went' becomes 'I went to the beach'.

Syllable strategies

In order to help learners become aware that words are made up of segments called syllables, you could:

- Have them count and distinguish syllables in a word. You could do this by clapping each syllable: '*Bean* has one syllable, so we clap once. *Beanstalk* has two syllables, so we clap twice . . .'
- Have them add and delete syllables from a word. For example, ask them what happens when you remove the syllable *bed* from the word *bedroom* or what happens when you add the syllable *un* to *happy*.
- Ask them to replace parts of a word with different syllables. For example, with the word *today*, replace the syllable *day* with the syllable *morrow*.

Phonemic/rhyming strategies

To facilitate learners' awareness of sound structures in words and rhyming, you could:

- Help them become familiar with beginning sounds of words by asking them to find words that begin with particular sounds. For example, *cat*, *candy* and *car* all begin with the /k/ sound, whereas *sun*, *sit* and *sand* begin with /s/. (Use the sound of the letters, not the letter name.)
- Have them say what is left when a given sound or syllable is dropped from a word. For example, omitting the /s/ sound from the word *school* results in the word *cool*. (They will probably see the joke!)
- Have them select words that sound alike from a variety of pictures/words. For example, a picture of a *frog* rhymes with the written word *log*. Also, giving learners plenty of opportunities to hear poems, riddles and songs that rhyme can enable them to become familiar with rhyming words.
- Have them blend sounds in single-syllable words that can be classified as 'onset-rime' (i.e., words that begin with a single consonant (i.e., 'onset') followed by a vowel and any following consonants (i.e., 'rime'), such as *h* + *ot*). For example, you could say, 'I am going to say a word very slowly. You put the sounds together to make a word, like *h* + *ot* is *hot*, and *c* + *oat* is *coat* and *m* + *an* is – ?' (Note that in these exercises not every letter is sounded out.)

The evidence

There is a substantial body of research showing that instruction in phonological awareness and phonetic awareness has positive effects on both phonological skill and word-reading skills for learners with **specific learning disabilities**[10] and **complex communication needs**.[11]

✓ In a meta-analysis carried out by the US National Reading Panel, an effect size of 0.22 was obtained for phonemic processing instruction.[12]
✓ An Australian study evaluated the effects of phonological processing skills training for learners aged 9–14 years with **persistent reading difficulties**. The results showed that improvement in the learners' phonological processing skills led to considerable improvement in their reading accuracy and reading comprehension. Extending the length of the training time significantly improved the transfer of skills to the reading process, especially for those with severe phonological processing skill difficulties.[13]
✓ In an earlier study by the same researchers, ten learners aged 10–12 years with **severe difficulties in written and spoken language** participated in an intervention programme. One group received phonological training followed by semantic-syntactic training and a second group received the training programmes in reverse order. It was found that training in phonological processing skills had a greater impact on reading accuracy than training in semantic-syntactic skills, but both programmes contributed to improved reading comprehension.[14]
✓ In a US study, five- and six-year-old learners were given phonological awareness training in 40 ten-minute sessions spread over two years. The training included such exercises as: (a) learners being shown a picture of a bus and asked to pick another picture of a word starting with the same sound, (b) learners being shown four pictures and asked to choose the one that began with a different sound from the others and (c) learners being asked to tell whether two words rhymed. A comparison group received the same number of lessons involving the same words, but the tasks involved activities such as sorting the pictures into categories. The group receiving the phonological awareness training showed improvement in that area, as well as on reading tests.[15]
✓ In another US study, 99 first-grade learners were identified as **being at risk for reading difficulties**. Half of them received a phonological processing intervention, which included syllable discrimination training, phonemic blending and phonemic segmentation. The results supported the early identification of reading difficulties and the effectiveness of the intervention.[16]
✓ A third US study investigated the relative effectiveness of three instructional approaches for the prevention of **reading disabilities** in

young learners with weak phonological skills. Two of the programmes varied the intensity of phonemic decoding and the third continued the regular classroom reading programme. The intervention comprised 88 hours of one-to-one instruction in first and second grades. The results showed that learners receiving the most intensive phonemic programme made the strongest growth in word-level reading skills, but there were no differences between the groups in reading comprehension.[17]

✓ A New Zealand study investigated the effects of a phonological processing instructional programme on **severely disabled readers**, compared with a matched group who received instruction in the use of context cues to identify unfamiliar words. The phonological instruction took the form of training in 'rime spelling units' (for the definition of 'rime', see The Practice section above). The results showed significantly greater gains in phonological skills and reading achievement for the experimental group, and these performances were maintained at a one-year follow-up.[18]

✓ The same group of New Zealand researchers also studied learners in their first year of schooling (usually commencing at the age of five years in New Zealand). An experimental group received supplementary instruction designed to help them develop awareness of sound sequences in spoken words and to make greater use of letter-sound patterns in reading unfamiliar words. The matched comparison group received 'standard' whole-language instruction. By the end of the first year, the learners receiving phonological instruction significantly outperformed the comparison group on a range of reading measures. After one further year these differences were maintained, the experimental group achieving a reading age 14 months ahead of the comparison group. It was concluded that the presence of phonological processing skills instruction greatly improves whole-language literacy programmes, as well as reducing the number of learners **at risk for failure**.[19]

✓ A recent review by the US Department of Education's What Works Clearinghouse identified a computer-assisted programme of instruction in phonological awareness as being very effective. This programme, *DaisyQuest*, targets learners aged three to seven years and includes instructional activities, framed in a fairy tale involving a search for a friendly dragon named Daisy, to teach learners how to recognize words that rhyme; words that have the same beginning, middle and ending sounds; and words that can be formed from a series of phonemes presented separately, as well as how to count the number of sounds in words. The four studies that met the evidence standards set by the Clearinghouse included 223 learners, some of whom were **below average readers**. On average, they yielded an effect size of 0.60 for a range of phonological and phonics measures.[20]

Addressing risks

There are three main risks:

- First, a risk can occur if the phonological processing activities are not carefully chosen to meet the needs and interests of all the learners in your class. It is important to present alternative activities, or to modify a given activity by making it more challenging for higher-level learners or easier for children with special educational needs.
- Second, if the activities are not well thought out and monitored, they may become no more than exercises.
- Third, you might over-emphasize the use of phonological processing. Rather, you should recognize that instruction in phonological processing only plays a part in an effective overall reading curriculum, and should not become the main focus. Vocabulary development, fluency and comprehension are also critical for developing reading skills.

 Conclusion

Phonological processing strategies constitute a valuable component in a balanced reading curriculum. These strategies are most effective when the instruction is provided at an early age and in a direct, explicit and systematic manner. Learners at risk for reading failure are the most likely to benefit from the strategy.

 Further reading

Adams, M., Foorman, B., Lundberg, I. and Beeler, T. (1998). *Phonemic awareness in young children*. Baltimore, MD: Paul H. Brookes.

Goldsworthy, C.L. (1998). *Sourcebook of phonological awareness activities: Children's Classic Literature*. San Diego, CA: Singular Publishing Group.

McCormick, C., Throneburg, R. and Smitley, J. (2002). *A sound start: Phonemic awareness lessons for reading success*. New York: The Guilford Press.

Torgesen, J. and Mathes, P. (1998). *What every teacher should know about phonological awareness*. Florida Department of Education: Bureau of Instructional Support, Division of Public Schools and Community Education. URL: www.firn. edu/doe/commhome/pdf/phon9872.pdf (accessed 8 January 2007).

Key references

1 Torgesen, J. and Mathes, P. (1998). *What every teacher should know about phonological awareness*. Florida Department of Education: Division of Public Schools and Community Education. URL: www.firn.edu/doe/commhome/pdf/ phon9872.pdf (accessed 8 January 2007).

2 Adams, M.J., Foorman, B.R., Lundberg, I. and Beeler, T.D. (1998). 'The elusive phoneme: Why phonemic awareness is so important and how to help children develop it'. *American Educator*, 22(1 and 2), 18–29.
3 Smith, S.B., Simmons, D.C. and Kame'enui, E.J. *Synthesis of research on phonological awareness: Principles and implications for reading acquisition.* Eugene, OR: University of Oregon. URL: http://idea.uoregon.edu/~ncite/documents/techrep/tech21.html (accessed 8 January 2007).
4 Ibid.
5 The material in this section represents a synthesis of several sources, including: The Learning Disabilities Association of America: URL: www.ldaamerica. org/aboutld/teachers/teaching_reading/phonology.asp (accessed 20 December 2006); The Learning Disabilities Association of Ontario: URL: www.ldao.ca/ resources/education/pei/defsupp/e4.php (accessed 20 December 2006); Reading Rockets: URL: www.readingrockets.org/helping/target/otherissues (accessed 20 December 2006); and Reading Success Lab: URL: www.readingsuccesslab. com/PhonologicalAwareness.html (accessed 21 December 2006).
6 Alba, L. (2002). 'Glossary of speech- and language-related terms'. Children's Speech Care Center. Torrance, CA. URL: www.childspeech.net/glossary.html (accessed 6 January 2007).
7 Goldsworthy, C.L. (1998). *Sourcebook of phonological awareness activities: Children's Classic Literature.* San Diego, CA: Singular Publishing Group.
8 Tunmer, W.E., Chapman, J.W., Greaney, K.T. and Prochnow, J.E. (2002). 'The contribution of educational psychology to intervention research and practice'. *International Journal of Disability, Development and Education*, 49(1), 11–29.
9 Based on Goldsworthy, op. cit.; and the Learning Disabilities Association of America. URL: www.ldamerica.org/aboutld/teachers/teaching_reading/phonology. asp (accessed 23 December 2006).
10 Coyne, M.D., Kame'enui, E.J. and Simmons, D.C. (2001). 'Prevention and intervention in beginning reading: Two complex systems'. *Learning Disabilities Research and Practice*, 16(2), 62–73.
11 Clendon, S., Gillon, G. and Yoder, D. (2005). 'Initial insights into phoneme awareness intervention for children with complex communication needs'. *International Journal of Disability, Development and Education*, 52(1), 7–31.
12 National Reading Panel (2000). *Report of the National Reading Panel: Teaching children to read.* Washington, DC: National Institute of Child Health and Human Development. It is worth noting the overall conclusion of this panel, reached after reviewing 125,000 research studies on reading and analysing those that were experimental or quasi-experimental in design:

> The panel determined that effective reading instruction includes teaching children to break apart and manipulate the sounds in words (phonemic awareness), teaching them that these sounds are represented by letters of the alphabet which can then be blended together to form words (phonics), having them practice what they've learned by reading aloud with guidance and feedback (guided oral reading), and applying reading comprehension strategies to guide and improve reading comprehension.
> (www.nichd.nih.gov/new/releases/nrp.htm, accessed 8 January 2007)

13 Gillon, G. and Dodd, B. (1997). 'Enhancing the phonological processing skills of children with specific reading disability'. *European Journal of Disorders in Communication*, 32(2), 67–90.

14 Gillon, G. and Dodd, B. (1995). 'The effects of training phonological, semantic, and syntactic processing skills in spoken language on reading ability'. *Language, Speech and Hearing Services in Schools*, 26(1), 58–68.

15 Research carried out by Bradley and Bryant, as summarized by Meyer, R.E. (2001). 'What good is educational psychology? The case of cognition and instruction'. *Educational Psychologist*, 36(2), 83–88.

16 Hurford, D.P., Johnston, M., Nepote, P., Hampton, S., Moore, S., Neal, J., Mueller, A., McGeorge, K., Huff, L., Awad, A., Tatro, C., Juliano, C. and Huffman, D. (1994). 'Early identification and remediation of phonological processing deficits in first-grade children at risk for reading disabilities'. *Journal of Learning Disabilities*, 27(10), 647–659.

17 Torgeson, J.K., Wagner, R.K., Rashotte, C.A., Rose, E., Lindamood, P., Conway, T. and Garvan, C. (1999). 'Preventing reading failure in young children with phonological processing disabilities: Group and individual responses to instruction'. *Journal of Educational Psychology*, 91(4), 579–593.

18 Greaney, K., Tunmer, W. and Chapman, J. (1997). 'The effects of rime-based orthographic analogy training on the word recognition skills of children with reading disability'. *Journal of Educational Psychology*, 89(4), 645–651.

19 Summarized in Tunmer *et al.*, op. cit. (2002). 'The contribution of educational psychology to intervention research and practice'. *International Journal of Disability, Development and Education*, 49(1), 11–29.

20 What Works Clearinghouse. URL: www.whatworks.ed.gov (accessed 11 February 2007); for one of the four studies, see Barker, T. and Torgesen, J.K. (1995). 'An evaluation of computer-assisted instruction in phonological awareness with below average readers'. *Journal of Educational Computing Research*, 13(1), 89–103.

Chapter 18

Strategy 16: Cognitive behavioural therapy

'Help learners change their negative thinking'

Rating

★★★★

  The strategy

Cognitive behavioural therapy (CBT) is an active process of changing a person's negative thinking patterns, which in turn leads to changes in behaviour and, ultimately, to a reduction or elimination of feelings of anxiety or depression. It is a brief, systematic form of psychotherapy that teaches people to change the way they think about themselves and act. It does not involve them examining possible root causes of problems that might lie in the past.

CBT is sometimes extended to include other related therapies, such as *cognitive behavioural intervention, family-focused CBT, trauma-focused CBT, cognitive behavioural group therapy, cognitive-behaviour modification, rational emotive behaviour therapy, rational behaviour therapy* and *cognitive therapy*.

Originally developed for adults with depression or anxiety conditions, CBT has successfully been extended to children and adolescents in recent years. As with adults, it has also been used to treat depression and anxiety disorders, as well as aggressiveness, school refusal and post-traumatic stress disorders resulting from such events as sexual and physical abuse, divorce in the family, violence and natural disasters. Because of the difficulties learners with attention deficit hyperactivity disorder (ADHD) experience in controlling their behaviours, some studies have found that CBT has been successfully used to treat this disorder, although the evidence is not unanimous for this group of learners.

In all cases, when CBT reduces or eliminates behavioural deficits or excesses, it benefits the learners' own sense of well-being and improves their relationships with adults and peers.

This strategy is probably of greater relevance to psychologists and counsellors, but I believe that classroom educators should also understand its fundamental principles: (a) because they can be applied to some of their teaching and (b) because they would need to work closely with any professionals who are treating learners in their classes with CBT.

This strategy relates most closely to the motivation, executive system and strategies sections of the learning and teaching model.

 ## The underlying idea

CBT is based on the assumption that it is our thinking (hence *cognitive*) that causes us to feel and act (hence *behavioural*) the way we do. Therefore, if we are experiencing unwanted or destructive feelings and behaviours, we must learn how to replace the thinking that leads to them with more realistic or helpful thoughts that lead to more desirable behaviours.[1]

For example, if learners fail a mathematics test, they might think, 'I am useless at maths' or, even worse, 'I am a useless person'. This could lead them into a vicious cycle of failure to the point where they avoid maths lessons, or even school in general, eventually generating feelings of depression or even aggressive behaviours. To break this cycle, educators must ensure that learners can achieve successes. In some cases, they might have to be referred for more intense CBT where 'I am a failure' thoughts can be replaced with more positive 'I can do' thoughts. In this strategy, in order to control their behaviour, learners are taught to use inner speech (often referred to as 'self-talk') to modify faulty cognitions. Thus, the central idea is self-regulation (**Strategy 12**).[2]

Support for this approach can be found in social information processing models that describe how children process information in a social situation before they enact a competent or incompetent behaviour. The steps that typically occur are as follows: (a) notice the social cues, (b) interpret these cues, (c) select a goal, (d) consider the response options, (e) decide on a response and (e) carry out the response. Of course, this process takes place at varying durations – some very short, some much more deliberate. It can go wrong for some children, with distorted judgements being possible at any step. Research shows, for example, that aggressive children attend to fewer social cues and often selectively direct their attention to hostile social cues; also, they are more confident than non-aggressive children that aggression will produce a satisfying outcome. CBT is aimed at addressing these dysfunctional cognitions.[3]

This approach to therapy had its recent origins in the work of Albert Ellis who, as a reaction against psychoanalytic and humanistic approaches, developed a technique known as Rational Emotive Behavioural Therapy in the 1950s. Aaron Beck extended this in the 1960s with his work on Cognitive Therapy. In its earliest form, rational emotive and cognitive therapies were often contrasted with behavioural approaches to therapy, but in recent years the two have been combined into CBT.

The practice

Although CBT is essentially a therapy approach undertaken by trained specialists such as counsellors and psychologists, I believe that many of its features could guide your practices as an educator. Every day you are working with learners who might not feel good about themselves as a result of difficulties they experience with the curriculum or in relating to their peers. Your challenge is to: (a) anticipate such difficulties and take steps to avoid them, (b) equip learners with skills to deal with them when they occur by helping them to 'think' their way through problems. In more serious cases, you should be alert to the problem and take steps to discuss it with the learner's parents and refer the case for specialized counselling or therapy, in this case CBT.

 The ABC Technique of Irrational Beliefs

Over 30 years ago, Albert Ellis described what he referred to as 'The ABC Technique of Irrational Beliefs'. It begins with an analysis of the problem:

A: Activating event: the situation that leads to negative thinking (e.g., failing a mathematics test);

B: Belief: the negative thoughts that occur (e.g., 'If I cannot do maths, I am useless');

C: Consequence: the negative feelings and dysfunctional behaviours (e.g., 'I really am useless – in fact, I am worthless', and the person is therefore at risk for depression, anger and anxiety).

Following such an analysis, the therapist works with the person to 'reframe' the problem. This involves challenging the negative thoughts to reinterpret them in a more realistic light, leading, one expects, to more rational beliefs and more appropriate behaviours.[4]

 The six-step process

Meichenbaum was one of the earliest proponents of what became a forerunner of CBT and also cognitive strategy instruction (**Strategy 11**). He argued that the traditional versions of classical and operant conditioning (**Strategy 17**) needed to be supplemented to include underlying cognitions. He and his colleagues argued that 'thinking aloud' and the internalization of self-statements formed the basis of self-control. In this process, adults play a critical role in modelling the cognitive skills, particularly how to think aloud and then to make these thoughts covert (i.e., internal). They described a six-step process as follows.[5] I will illustrate this with reference to teaching italic handwriting, which I have used with my students:

This is what italic script looks like: *abc*

- Step 1: *Cognitive modelling*: you model the behaviour and describe it at the same time:

    'This is how you hold the pen. The nib is always at 45 degrees when making the letters. Start with the top of the letter *a*. Draw a line across, curl around and come straight down . . . .'

- Step 2: *External guidance*: the learner performs the task while the educator describes the actions:

    'Now you write the letter *a* while I tell you the steps. Hold the pen so that it is always at 45 degrees. Start with the top . . .'

- Step 3: *Overt self-guidance*: the learner performs the task and describes it at the same time:

    'This time I want you to draw the letter and describe each step as you go' (prompt if necessary).

- Step 4: *Faded overt self-guidance*: the learner performs the task, while whispering the action at the same time:

    'Now do it again, but this time I want you to whisper the steps as you go.'

- Step 5: *Simultaneous covert self-instruction and task performance*: the learner performs the task while 'thinking' the actions at the same time:

    'Last time! Could you now do it again, but just think about the steps.'

- Step 6: *Self-reinforcement*: acknowledge the performance:

    'Finished? The last thing to do is give yourself a pat on the back for a job well done!'

While this example is a long way from dealing with conduct disorders or anxiety, I hope it illustrates the essential features of CBT. Such an activity could also serve as a neutral way to introduce learners to the steps involved in dealing with such disorders.

Another example

In another example of CBT, learners were taught to use the following steps when approaching a problem situation, in this case those that provoke aggressive responses:

1   Stop and think before acting: restrain aggressive responses through the use of covert speech.
2   Identify the problem: distinguish the specific aspects of a problematic situation that might bring out an aggressive response.
3   Develop alternative solutions: generate at least two alternative solutions to a problematic situation; e.g.:
    •   think about something else until able to relax; and/or
    •   move to another location in the room to avoid further provocation.
4   Evaluate the consequences of possible solutions: assess the benefits of each possible solution.
5   Select and implement a solution: carry out the selected alternative.[6]

 The evidence

CBT is one of the most widely researched therapies for children and young people.[7]

✓   Of particular importance for educators, a meta-analysis of school-based studies was reported in 1999. This study surveyed 23 investigations of the effect of CBT on learners with **hyperactivity-impulsivity** and **aggression**. The mean effect size across all the studies was 0.74, with 89 per cent of the studies reporting that those in treatment groups experienced greater gains than those in control groups. In all bar one of the studies, the children were treated in self-contained special classes in regular schools or in regular classes. All of the studies incorporated strategies designed to assist children increase self-control, mostly by using covert self-statements to regulate their behaviours (see previous section for a description of this method).[8]
✓   A recent English review reported similarly positive results for CBT.[9] This review reported on the research evidence on the outcomes of four approaches to counselling children and young people: CBT, person-centred, psychodynamic and creative therapies. More high-quality evidence was found for the effectiveness of CBT than the other approaches. In a breakdown of the studies reviewed, CBT was found to be an effective therapy for the following problem areas: behavioural and conduct disorders, anxiety, school-related issues, self-harming practices and sexual abuse. Examples of the studies cited included the following:
    •   Anxiety: a study showed evidence of the effectiveness of CBT in the 6–13 years age group with generalized anxiety, separation anxiety and avoidant disorders.[10]
    •   Depression: better results were achieved with CBT with 13–18 year olds than 6–11 year olds, probably reflecting adolescents' higher levels of cognitive functioning.[11]

- • Self-harm: a study found that brief CBT was effective in reducing drug use.[12]
- ✓ In an earlier comprehensive summary of 14 meta-analyses of CBT carried out between 1983 and 1991, the effect size ranged from 0.15 to 0.99, with a mean of 0.66.[13]
- ✓ A more recent meta-analysis, carried out by Dutch researchers, reviewed the outcomes of CBT for **anti-social behaviour** in children, as reported in 30 studies. The mean effect size was 0.48 at the end of treatment and 0.66 at follow-up (12 studies only reporting on this). There was a positive relationship between children's age and effect size, suggesting that CBT is more effective with older children. Given the cognitive requirements of CBT, this is not altogether surprising. The researchers also commented that since the outcomes for CBT for children with anti-social behaviour appeared to be smaller than those achieved with parent management training (see **Strategy 5**), CBT might be more useful as a component of a multi-modal approach. They also mentioned that it could be combined with medication, which falls outside the coverage of this book.[14]
- ✓ A Cochrane review, considered to be one of the most prestigious ratings of therapies, noted that anxiety disorders are relatively common, occurring in between 5–18 per cent of all children and adolescents. They are associated with significant impairment in social and academic functioning and, when persistent, there is a risk of depression, suicide attempts and substance abuse in adulthood. In its review, 13 studies with 498 subjects and 311 controls were included in the analyses. The authors found that CBT appears to be an effective treatment for childhood and adolescent **anxiety disorders** in comparison to waiting list controls. Their results showed that 56 per cent of those in the CBT group improved, compared with only 28 per cent in the control group. There was no evidence for a difference between CBT delivered in individual, group or parental/family formats. The review concluded by recommending CBT for the treatment of childhood anxiety disorders, although with only just over half the participants improving, a need for further therapeutic developments was noted.[15]
- ✓ These findings were confirmed, with a slight difference, in an Australian study of the effects of CBT alone and CBT plus family management on children aged seven to 14 years diagnosed with **separation anxiety**, **overanxious disorder** or **social phobia**. At the six-month follow-up, the researchers found that 70 per cent of the children in both treatment conditions were no longer classified as anxious, compared with only 26 per cent in a control group. Unlike the Cochrane review, this study found that the family management component had an additive effect. After 12 months, while the CBT alone group maintained the 70 per cent improvement rate, 95.6 per cent of the CBT plus family management group had improved.[16]

✓ A US study compared family-focused CBT with traditional child-focused CBT for children with **anxiety disorders**. It reported a similar outcome to the previous study. Forty children aged 6–13 years were randomly assigned to the two conditions. The main difference between the two was the inclusion of parent communication training in family-focused CBT. Both groups showed improvement on all outcome measures, such as anxiety symptoms, but family-focused CBT provided additional benefits.[17]

✓ Child- and family-focused cognitive behavioural therapy was employed to help children (mean age 11.33 years) with **bipolar disorders**. This approach integrated principles of family-focused therapy with those of CBT. Parents and children were actively engaged in the therapy over 12 hour-long sessions. Symptom severity and functioning were evaluated before and after treatment. On completion of the therapy, the children showed significant reductions in severity scores compared to pre-treatment results. Unfortunately, no control groups were employed.[18]

✓ Group and individual CBT were compared in another study. The researchers randomly assigned 37 children aged 8–14 years with **anxiety disorders** to group CBT, individual CBT and a control group. After the nine-week treatment period, significantly more of those receiving treatment (73 per cent of the individual condition and 50 per cent of the group condition) had improved, compared with only eight per cent in the control group. These results were maintained at a three-month follow-up.[19]

✓ A Spanish study examined the efficacy of CBT with and without anger management training in the treatment of 32 children with **ADHD, with and without accompanying aggressiveness**. Thus, there were four matched groups. All groups received CBD, which included behavioural self-control training (i.e., self-instructional training via modelling and behavioural contingencies). The results showed significant improvements on several measures for all four groups. The improvements in the ADHD children with aggressiveness were slightly better when CBT was accompanied by anger management training.[20]

✓ A Canadian study investigated effects of a variant of CBT, referred to as Cognitive Orientation to daily Occupational Performance (CO-OP), on the motor performances of children with a mean age of 9.05 years with **developmental coordination disorders**. The CO-OP programme emphasized strategies where the child was taught to use self-talk and problem-solving strategies to solve motor problems. This approach was compared with a Contemporary Treatment Approach (CTA), which focused on the motor aspects of skill acquisition. Both treatments led to improved performances, with gains in the CO-OP group being greater than those in the CTA group. This advantage was maintained on follow-up measures.[21]

✓   A review of Trauma-Focused CBT reported that over 80 per cent of **traumatized children** showed significant improvement with 12–16 weeks of CBT. The essential components of this treatment included assisting the child to acquire emotional regulation skills, stress management skills, ways of sharing stories about trauma, adaptive cognitive and emotional processing of trauma experiences and ways of coping with future reminders of trauma.[22]

 Addressing risks

Four factors might limit the use of CBT:

- First, since it requires cognitive maturity to be able to understand concepts such as self-talk and self-instruction, its effectiveness will be limited with young children and should therefore be used with caution with that age group.
- Second, the learner must be prepared to practise the skills being taught in CBT, which, in turn, requires a high level of cooperation from parents. This might not always be readily forthcoming.
- Third, as noted earlier, there is some doubt as to the effectiveness of CBT in treating ADHD, with the suggestion that it might be more advantageous to combine it with other treatments such as pharmacological interventions and behaviour therapy.[23]
- Fourth, as will be apparent in the above description, if CBT intervention is to be systematically implemented in classrooms, educators need training and supervision.

 Conclusion

CBT is well established as a treatment of choice for many conditions, particularly for adolescents with depression and anxiety disorders, as well as aggressiveness, school refusal and post-traumatic stress disorders. It can be used with some caution with younger children. It is advisable to consider combining CBT with parent training.

 Further reading

British Association for Counselling and Psychotherapy. URL: www.bacp.co.ukemotional (accessed 17 January 2007).

Kendall, P.C. (ed.) (2005). *Child and adolescent therapy: Cognitive-behavioral procedures*. 3rd edn. New York: Guilford Publications.

National Association of Cognitive-Behavioral Therapists: www.nacbt.org/whatiscbt.htm (accessed 17 January 2007).

Reinecke, M.A., Dattilio, F.M. and Freeman, A. (eds) (2003). *Cognitive therapy with children and adolescents: A casebook for clinical practice*. 2nd edn. New York: Guilford Publications.

Key references

1 National Association of Cognitive-Behavioral Therapists: www.nacbt.org/whatiscbt. htm and Wikipedia: http://en.wikipedia.org/wiki/Cognitive_therapy (accessed 17 January 2007).
2 Meichenbaum, D.H. (1977). *Cognitive-behavior modification: An integrative approach*. New York: Plenum Press; and Meichenbaum, D.H. and Goodman, J. (1971). 'Training impulsive children to talk to themselves: A means of developing self-control'. *Journal of Abnormal Psychology*, 77, 115–126.
3 Van de Wiel, N., Mattys, W., Cohen-Kettenis, P.C. and Van Engeland, W. (2002). 'Effective treatments of school-aged conduct disordered children: Recommendations for changing clinical and research practices'. *European Child and Adolescent Psychiatry*, 11, 79–84.
4 Ellis, A. (1975). *A new guide to rational living*. New York: Prentice Hall.
5 Meichenbaum, op. cit.; and Meichenbaum and Goodman, op. cit.
6 Etscheidt, S. (1991). 'Reducing aggressive behavior and increasing self-control. A cognitive-behavioral training program for behaviorally disordered adolescents'. *Behavioral Disorders*, 16(2), 107–115.
7 Pattison, S. and Harris, B. (2006). 'Added value to education through improved mental health: A review of the research evidence on the effectiveness of counselling for children and young people'. *The Australian Educational Researcher*, 33(2), 97–121.
8 Robinson, T.R., Smith, S.W., Miller, M.D. and Brownell, M.T. (1999). 'Cognitive behavior modification of hyperactivity-impulsivity and aggression: A meta-analysis of school-based studies'. *Journal of Educational Psychology*, 91(2), 195–203.
9 Pattison and Harris, op. cit.
10 Compton, S.N.B., Burns, B.J., Egger, H.L. and Robertson, E. (2002). 'Review of the evidence base for treatment of childhood psychopathology: Internalising disorders'. *Journal of Consulting and Clinical Psychology*, 70(6), 1240–1266.
11 Compton *et al.*, op. cit.
12 Breslin, C., Li, S., Sdao-Jarvie, K., Tupker, E. and Ittig-Deland, V. (2002). 'Brief treatment for young substance abusers: A pilot study in an addiction treatment setting'. *Psychology of Addictive Behaviours*, 16(1), 10–16.
13 Lipsey, M.W. and Wilson, D.B. (1993). 'The efficacy of psychological, educational, and behavioral treatment: Confirmation from meta-analysis'. *American Psychologist*, 48(12), 1181–1209.
14 Van de Wiel *et al.*, op. cit.
15 James, A., Soler, A. and Weatherall, R. (2005). 'Cognitive behavioural therapy for anxiety disorders in children and adolescents' (Cochrane Review). *The Cochrane Database of Systematic Reviews*, Issue 4. Art. No.: CD004690. DOI:10.1002/14651858.CD004690.
16 Barrett, P.M., Dadds, M.R. and Rapee, R.M. (1996). 'Family treatment c childhood anxiety: A controlled trial'. *Journal of Consulting and Clinica Psychology*, 64, 333–342.
17 Wood, J., Piacentini, J.C., Southam-Gerow, M., Chu, B.C. and Sigman, M. (2006] 'Family cognitive behavioural therapy for child anxiety disorders'. *Journal of the American Academy of Child and Adolescent Psychiatry*, 45(3), 314–321.
18 Pavuluri, M.N., Graczyk, P.A., Henry, D.B., Carbray, J.A., Heidenreich, J.L. and Miklowitz, D.J. (2006). 'Child- and family-focused cognitive-behavioral therapy for pediatric bipolar disorder'. *Journal of the American Academy of Child and Adolescent Psychiatry*, 43(5), 528–537.
19 Flannery-Schroeder, E.C. and Kendall, P.C. (2000). 'Group and individual cognitive behavioural treatment for youth with anxiety disorders: A randomised clinical trial'. *Cognitive Therapy and Research*, 24(3), 251–278.

20 Miranda, A. and Presentacion, M.J. (2000). 'Efficacy of cognitive-behavioral therapy in the treatment of children with ADHD, with and without aggressiveness'. *Psychology in the Schools*, 37(2), 169–182.
21 Miller, L.T., Polatajko, H.J., Missiuna, C.A., Mandich, A.D. and MacNab, J.J. (2001). 'A pilot trial of a cognitive treatment for children with developmental coordination disorder'. *Human Movement Science*, 20, 183–210.
22 National Child Traumatic Stress Network (USA). URL: www.NCTSNet.org (accessed 20 January 2007).
23 Pelham, W.E. and Gnagy, E.M. (1999). 'Psychosocial and combined treatments for ADHD'. *Mental Retardation and Developmental Disorders*, 5(3), 225–236.

Chapter 19

Strategy 17: Behavioural approaches

'Control antecedents and consequences to change behaviours'

Rating

★★★★

 The strategy

Behavioural approaches focus on how events that occur either before or after learners engage in a verbal or physical act affects their subsequent behaviour. These events are referred to as antecedents and consequences, respectively.

Although not exact synonyms, behavioural approaches as discussed in this strategy draw upon a similar theoretical position to *classical conditioning*, *operant conditioning*, *applied behaviour analysis*, *functional analysis*, *experimental analysis of behaviour*, *behaviour modification* and *behaviour therapy*.

Within this book two other strategies draw directly upon behavioural principles: Direct Instruction (**Strategy 19**) and Functional Behavioural Assessment (**Strategy 18**). Another one, Cognitive Behavioural Therapy (**Strategy 16**), blends behavioural approaches with cognition. School-wide Positive Behaviour Support (**Strategy 7**) also calls upon behavioural principles.

 The underlying idea

The behavioural approach had its origins in the experimentation of American Edward Thorndike around the beginning of the twentieth century and the subsequent work of another American, J.B. Watson, and the Russian physiologist, Ivan Pavlov. It gained impetus in the 1930s with American psychologist B.F. Skinner and later, in the 1960s, with such researchers as Lovas, Bijou and Baer.

The essence of the behavioural approach is summarized in the acrostic S-R-S (Stimulus-Response-Stimulus), sometimes expressed in the near-equivalent A-B-C (Antecedent-Behaviour-Consequence). For the purposes of this book, I will use the latter.

In the US, behavioural approaches (specifically applied behaviour analysis) have received official recognition, the Surgeon General stating in 1999 that it is the treatment of choice for autism: 'Thirty years of research demonstrated the efficacy of applied behavioural methods in reducing inappropriate behavior and in increasing communication, learning, and appropriate social behavior.'[1]

This strategy relates to two elements of my learning and teaching model. External task demands, when formulated by an educator, equate with antecedents in behavioural approaches, and external responses to learners' external performances equate with consequences.

The practice

Central to the behavioural approach are three procedures:

- controlling antecedents;
- controlling reinforcement; and
- a three-step implementation.

Controlling antecedents

In setting up tasks for learners, you have several options of antecedents to choose from.[2] For example, you can:

- control the level of task difficulty;
- provide advance organizers;
- use prompts to supplement your general instructions;
- ensure a positive learning context (**Strategies 8** and **9**);
- provide suitable, stimulating materials; and
- use picture schedules to remind the learner about the steps (**Strategy 23**).

Controlling reinforcements

When a learner does something, either on his or her own initiative or in response to another person's behaviour, you have several choices as to your responses:

1 You can respond by adding something pleasant; i.e., give *positive reinforcement*. This can be defined as any pleasant event that occurs after a behaviour, which reinforces it and increases the probability of it recurring in the future. For example, if you give a positive reinforcer (say, praise for good ideas) to a learner after writing a good story, you might assume that he or she is likely to write good stories in the future. This is by far the most successful behavioural strategy and you should use it when possible.

2   I would like to emphasize two points about positive reinforcement. First, it is very important that you select appropriate reinforcers, which can be defined as something that is important, significant or meaningful to the learner at the time. Whether or not your praise, in the above example, acts as a positive reinforcer depends on its significance for a particular learner at a particular time and in a particular place. Some learners might like it to be given publicly, while others would find it embarrassing.

Second, there is the question of how often you should give positive reinforcement. Do you have to give it after every behaviour you want to see continued? No, for if you do, the currency of your positive reinforcement will become devalued and it will lose its potency. As a rule of thumb, you should give *continuous positive reinforcement* (i.e., on as many occasions as practicable) while a child is learning a particular behaviour. Once that behaviour is established and you are seeking to maintain it, then *intermittent positive reinforcement* (i.e., reinforcing occasional correct responses) is all that is required.

Given the substantial amount of research pointing to the effectiveness of positive reinforcement, it is surprising that praise for appropriate social behaviour is rarely observed.[3] Perhaps it reflects the belief some educators have that the use of rewards might undermine intrinsic motivation, i.e., the desire to do something for the sake of the activity. There is contrary evidence to show this does not occur.[4]

3   You can respond by adding something unpleasant; i.e., *punishment type I*. This can be defined as any aversive event that occurs after a behaviour, which decreases the probability of it recurring in the future. For example, if you punish a learner (say, by giving a reprimand) after off-task behaviours, you might assume that such behaviours might stop or diminish in the future. (Please note that this is *not* negative reinforcement – see below.) You should also be aware of the legal aspects of punishment. In most countries corporal punishment is forbidden – and rightly so, not only on moral and ethical grounds, but also on efficacy grounds.

The risk here is that what you consider to be a punishment turns out, in fact, to be positively reinforcing in the eyes of some learners. For example, if you are trying to eliminate calling out in class by reprimanding any miscreant, learners who bask in additional attention may perversely see this as positive reinforcement. Similarly, by sending him or her from the classroom, you may be inadvertently applying positive reinforcement in the eyes of peers who rejoice in you losing your cool! This strategy is of limited effectiveness but provided it is not too punitive, it does have a place on occasions.

4   You can respond by removing something pleasant; i.e., *punishment type II*. This can be defined as any pleasant event removed after a behaviour, which decreases the probability of it recurring in the future. In technical

terms, this is sometimes referred to as *response cost*. For example, a mother might take away a privilege such as watching television after her children begin quarrelling. This, of course, assumes that the children really want to watch television. Like punishment type I, this form of punishment can be useful in some situations, particularly if the learner is given a chance to redeem him/herself and have the pleasant stimulus (tv) reinstated – the theme of the next technique.

5   You can respond by removing something unpleasant; i.e., *negative reinforcement*. This can be defined as any unpleasant event that, once removed after a behaviour, increases the probability of a behaviour occurring in the future. To take up the example of the television again, let's assume that having the television turned off during a favourite programme is pretty undesirable to the kids sitting in front of it. Their salvation is to be quiet for five minutes and then their mother will switch it back on. This is negative reinforcement. Another example is where you might be training a football team and they are getting very tired. You insist that they perfect a particular move before stopping the session. In this case, the removal of the demand to keep running, once they perform the move, acts as a negative reinforcer.

As I mentioned above, negative reinforcement is sometimes confused with punishment. The key difference is that punishment is designed to reduce or extinguish certain behaviours, whereas negative reinforcement, like positive reinforcement, is designed to increase the occurrence of certain behaviours. To complicate matters even further, some reinforcement can be both positive and negative. For example, a drug addict might take a drug because of the euphoric effect (positive reinforcement), but also to get rid of withdrawal symptoms (negative reinforcement).[5]

6   You can respond by withholding any positive reinforcement for any behaviour. This is referred to by the somewhat draconian term, *extinction*. An example of extinction is when a learner climbs under a desk to get attention, but is ignored until he returns to his or her seat. Of course, both you and the rest of the class have to do the ignoring to ensure that the behaviour is not positively reinforced by attention. On occasions, ignoring behaviours can lead to a temporary upsurge, even a raising of the ante, so you have to be patient and trust in the strategy eventually succeeding. Again, this strategy has to be used very carefully, lest the learner see it as punishment or positive reinforcement.

A variant of extinction is *time-out from positive reinforcement*. This occurs when a learner is already in a positive situation, for example, playing a game. If he or she engages in some antisocial act, such as ignoring a particular rule, time-out would involve being withdrawn from the game for a few minutes.

There are other varieties of reinforcement that can be very useful in school settings. Here are the main ones:[6]

7 *Differential reinforcement of incompatible behaviour* (DRI). Here a reward is presented when the learner performs a behaviour that is incompatible with the undesired behaviour. For example, a learner who frequently engages in self-injurious behaviour such as hitting his head may be reinforced for playing with toys with his hands for a predetermined period of time. In this case, playing with toys is incompatible with head hitting.

8 *Differential reinforcement of alternative behaviour* (DRA). This means reinforcing a behaviour that has the same function as one you want to extinguish, for example, inappropriately calling out answers to your questions in class. In this case, you would pay more attention to learners who put up their hand to answer questions. This, of course, assumes that gaining your attention is positively reinforcing.

9 *Differential reinforcement of low response rate* (DRL). Here a behaviour is reinforced only if it occurs infrequently. 'If you only call out in class no more than twice in every lesson [compared with, say, ten times], I will let you play a game on the computer. If you call out more often, no game!'

10 *Shaping* involves reinforcing *successive approximations* of a desired response, which become increasingly accurate. As training progresses, the responses reinforced become progressively more like the desired behaviour. Here, I think of the example of my five-year-old grandson learning to swim. This involved him going through various stages: getting wet up to his chest, putting his head under the water, floating at the side of the pool, floating with a flotation device, propelling himself by kicking, 'dog paddle' and now he is ready for the crawl stroke – perhaps next summer! In behaviour shaping, follow the dictum: positively reinforce success and ignore failure.

11 *Chaining* involves linking behaviours together in a series, so that the result of each behaviour acts both as the reinforcement for the previous behaviour and the antecedent for the next behaviour. For example, in learning the alphabet, each letter after A reinforces the preceding letter and acts as a cue for the following letter, and so on to Z.

There are two main ways to teach chaining. First, you can use *forward chaining*, where you start from the first behaviour in the chain. Take the example of learning the alphabet, where you start with 'A', then proceed to 'A, B', then to 'A, B, C', and so on. Second, in *backwards chaining* you start from the last behaviour and work backwards until all the chain is completed. A good example is a jigsaw puzzle of, say, five pieces where you present the learner with four pieces completed and ask him or her to put in the last one, then proceed to the puzzle with three pieces completed and two to be fitted, and so on. This method of backwards chaining helps the learner to understand the final target to be achieved.

12   *Fading* involves reducing the number of times reinforcement is given within a task and also changing the type of reinforcement so that eventually the only reinforcement used is intrinsic in the task itself. For example, a learner may initially require continuous reinforcement for taking part in a game. Once you consider that his or her participation was satisfactory, you could then reduce the reinforcement to be intermittent (see earlier), and then you could eliminate your reinforcement altogether and rely on the enjoyment of participation to be its own reward. The 'trick' to effectively fading reinforcement is to provide only the amount that is necessary to ensure that the behaviour continues.

 ## A three-step implementation

The behavioural approach requires that you focus on particular behaviours that you expect children to learn or unlearn and that you carefully plan and record what occurs as you seek to achieve these goals. The acid test is always that the learners' behaviours tell you how successful your intervention is and whether you need to try another way. Indeed, this is a common theme in all of the strategies I have presented in this book, but it is an integral part of the behavioural approach.

In using this approach there are three main phases:

1   *Pre-modification phase.* This involves these steps:
    - Identify the target behaviour and its antecedents and consequences.
    - Take baseline measurements of how often the target behaviour occurs over a range of settings.
    - Decide on the ethics of modifying that behaviour.
    - Specify the sub-skills of the target behaviour and sequence them from simple to complex. This is called *task analysis*.
    - Find out which sub-skills the learner can already perform.
    - Decide on suitable reinforcers.
    - Decide which method or combination of methods from the above 12 reinforcement regimes you will use.
    - Plan for the subsequent two phases.
2   *Modification phase.* Here you should implement the behavioural method you have chosen, keeping careful records of the learner's behaviour. These should be identical to the categories you employed in the baseline measurements.
3   *Post-modification phase.* Four steps are involved in this phase:
    - Remove the modification procedure and observe the learner's behaviour. Compare these behaviours with those you recorded during the earlier two phases. If they show appreciable improvements with

the target behaviours, reward yourself with a cup of coffee! If not, this means you might have to go back to the drawing boards. For example, you might have to change the reinforcer, revise your task analysis, or ensure that the tasks do not have too steep a gradient between the sub-skills.

- Carry out long-term follow-up, say after two weeks, a month and six months. This is to check on *maintenance*. After all, you want to be sure that any changes are permanent.

- Check to see if there has been *generalization* of the behaviour to other settings (e.g., from classroom to playground and home) and from one domain to another (e.g., from mathematics to science). You would not want it to be limited to the context in which it was learned.

- If either maintenance or generalization data cause you concern, you should design other interventions to rectify this.

 ## The evidence

Research studies have shown convincingly that behavioural approaches work successfully with a wide range of learners with special educational needs. There is an enormous literature on this strategy, the following just being a sample.

✓ In a comprehensive review of meta-analyses involving 20 different intervention strategies, behaviour modification came out with the third highest effect size (after mnemonic strategies (**Strategy 13**), reading comprehension (**Strategy 14**) and just ahead of direct instruction (**Strategy 19**)). The effect size of 0.93 for behaviour modification represented the average of effect sizes for social outcomes (0.69) and academic outcomes (1.57).[7]

✓ A review of research on behavioural interventions for learners with **autism** aged eight years and younger published between 1996 and 2000 concluded there were grounds for significant optimism. The authors noted that the five existing summaries of research in this area showed that the early use of behavioural interventions can result in the reduction of problem behaviours in this group of learners by 80–90 per cent in 50 per cent of the studies. Their own analysis of nine studies showed that nearly 60 per cent of the comparisons reported 90 per cent reduction in problem behaviour.[8]

The research reviewed points to the following elements being important in designing behavioural supports for young children with autism:

- prevent problem behaviours by organizing the environment to minimize the presence of aversive events, maximize access to rewarding outcomes and minimize the likelihood that problem behaviours will be rewarded;

- given that learners with autism are less likely to find social praise or attention rewarding, it is vital to identify and use reinforcers that function well for individuals.

✓ In an earlier review of the effectiveness of behavioural approaches with learners with **autism**, it was concluded that such intervention was effective not only in reducing problematic behaviours such as aggression, stereotypy, echolalia and self-injurious behaviour, but also in building repertoires of functional skills in such areas as language, daily living skills and social behaviour.[9]

✓ In a review of research on effective classroom management for dealing with **serious or chronic misconduct**, the following points were made with regard to corporal punishment:
  - its effects are unpredictable;
  - even when it succeeds in inhibiting inappropriate behaviour, it does not foster appropriate behaviour;
  - it is sometimes unintentionally reinforcing, since it brings attention to its recipient;
  - it creates resentment and hostility;
  - it is associated with undesirable outcomes such as increased vandalism, truancy and dropping out.[10]

✓ Typical of many studies conducted since the 1970s is one that summarized research on using behavioural approaches to improve the classroom conduct of **misbehaving learners**. This review identified reinforcement – whether it be verbal, symbolic or tangible – as being effective.[11]

 ## Addressing risks

You will probably agree that using behavioural approaches can be quite labour intensive and time consuming if they are to be employed correctly. Against that, however, they hold out considerable promise for helping learners with special educational needs learn new behaviours and unlearn inappropriate ones.

 ## Conclusion

Behavioural approaches have been successfully employed with a wide range of learners with special educational needs and across diverse areas of behaviour. It is a strategy that can be readily employed by classroom educators by controlling the antecedents and consequences of learners' behaviours.

 ## Further reading

Gardner, R., Sainato, D.M., Cooper, J.O., Heron, T.E., Heward, W.L., Eshleman, J. and Grossi, T.A. (eds) (1994). *Behavior analysis in education: Focus on measurably superior instruction*. Monterey, CA: Brooks/Cole.

Troutman, A. and Alberto, P.A. (2005). *Applied behavior analysis for teachers*. 7th edn. Upper Saddle River, NJ: Pearson/Prentice Hall.

Journals
Behavior Modification
Journal of Applied Behavior Analysis
Journal of Behavioral Education

Key references

1 US Department of Health and Human Services (1999). *Mental health: A report of the surgeon general*. Rockville, MD: US Department of Health and Human Services.
2 See, for example, Conroy, M.A. and Stichter, J.P. (2003). 'The application of antecedents in the functional assessment process: Existing research, issues, and recommendations'. *The Journal of Special Education*, 37(1), 15–25.
3 Beaman, R. and Wheldall, K. (2000). 'Teachers' use of approval and disapproval'. *Educational Psychology*, 20(4), 431–446.
4 Cameron, J. and Pierce, W.D. (1994). 'Reinforcement, reward, and intrinsic motivation'. *Review of Educational Research*, 64(3), 363–423.
5 Wikipedia. URL: www.answers.com/negative%20reinforcement (accessed 28 January 2007).
6 Sources: Oliver, C., Moss, J., Petty, J., Sloneem, J., Arron, K. and Hall, S. (2003). *A guide for parents and carers: Self-injurious behaviour in Cornelia de Lange Syndrome*. Birmingham: University of Birmingham and Community Fund; Carr, J. *Behaviour management*. London: St George's, University of London. URL: www.intellectualdisability.info/mental_phys_health/behaviour_jc.html (accessed 28 January 2007); BBB Autism Support Network. URL: www.bbbautism.com/aba_shaping_and_chaining.htm (accessed 28 January 2007); and Society for the Treatment of Autism (1998). URL: www.autism.ca/educsugg.htm (accessed 28 January 2007).
7 Forness, S. (2001). 'Special education and related services: What have we learned from meta-analysis?' *Exceptionality*, 9(4), 185–197. The original meta-analysis was carried out by White, W.A.T. (1988). 'A meta-analysis of effects of direct instruction in special education'. *Education and Treatment of Children*, 11(4), 364–374.
8 Horner, R.H., Carr, E.G., Strain, P.S., Todd, A.W. and Reed, H.K. (2002). 'Problem behavior interventions for young children with autism: a research synthesis'. *Journal of Autism and Developmental Disorders*, 32(5), 423–446.
9 Matson, J.L., Benavidez, D.A., Compton, L.S., Paclawskyj, T. and Baglio, C. (1996). 'Behavioral treatment of autistic persons: A review of research from 1980 to the present'. *Research in Developmental Disabilities*, 17(6), 433–465.
10 Doyle, W. (1989). 'Classroom management techniques'. In O.C. Moles (ed.) *Strategies to reduce student misbehavior* (pp. 11–31). Washington, DC: Office of Educational Research and Improvement.
11 Brophy, J.E. (1983). 'Classroom organization and management'. *The Elementary School Journal*, 83(4), 265–285.

Chapter 20

Strategy 18: Functional behavioural assessment

'Change problem behaviours by changing their antecedents and consequences'

Rating

★★★☆

 The strategy

Functional behavioural assessment (FBA) refers to the procedures used to determine the function or purpose of a learner's repeated undesirable behaviour. More specifically, it examines why a learner acts in a specific way, and what he or she obtains or avoids when acting this way. This information is then used as a basis for substituting more desirable behaviour in a behaviour support plan.[1]

FBA is one of the components of applied behaviour analysis (**Strategy 17**) and is an integral part of positive behavioural support (**Strategy 7**).

Although not identical, FBA is closely related to *functional assessment, functional analysis, descriptive analysis* and *behavioural assessment.*

In terms of the learning and teaching model it relates to external task demands and external responses.

 The underlying idea

FBA has its roots in applied behaviour analysis during the 1960s, which gave rise to the well-known paradigm A – B – C, when A = Antecedent, B = Behaviour and C = Consequence.

In 1997 FBA received considerable impetus in the US when the re-authorization of the Individuals with Disabilities Education Act (IDEA) specifically mentioned it. This Act requires that if a child's behaviour is affecting his or her learning or that of peers, an IEP meeting should be requested so that an intervention plan or an FBA plan can be carried out.[2]

The key idea of FBA is the assumption that problem behaviours occur as a result of *triggering antecedents* and/or *maintaining consequences.* Once these causes are determined, it becomes possible to reduce the problem behaviour by either: (a) changing the antecedents or consequences for that behaviour, and/or (b) substituting more desirable behaviour.[3]

There is some debate as to how far you should go in diagnosing causes. Most proponents of FBA argue that you should focus on the immediate (i.e., *proximal*) causes, while others say you should also give consideration to less immediate (i.e., *distal*) causes such as family conflict, as well as to physiological factors such as depression and intrapsychic factors such as thoughts and feelings.[4] I favour the latter position, which suggests that multi-disciplinary teams should carry out assessment of learners' problem behaviours, particularly if those behaviours are very challenging. However, for the purposes of this book, I will focus mainly on the proximal approach, which is appropriate for all learners with challenging behaviours.

 ## The practice

FBA requires a careful analysis of three factors and how they are linked:

- problem behaviours;
- antecedents;
- consequences.

 ### Problem behaviour(s)

Your first challenge is to define as precisely as possible the behaviours that are of concern to you as an educator and your colleagues. These then become the *negative target behaviours* for intervention, with a view to eliminating or reducing them. Next you should define with equal precision the behaviours you wish to replace the negative behaviours with; these are your *positive target behaviours*.

 ### Antecedents

The next challenge is to determine the antecedent events (i.e., those that precede the negative target behaviours), which might seem to 'cause' the occurrence of these behaviours.

 ### Consequences

The third task is to describe the consequent events (i.e., those that follow the negative target behaviours), which seem to maintain them.

In summary, here are the six steps to be taken in FBA:[5]

- *Step 1.* A team should determine what behaviours are most disruptive or problematic and describe them accurately. Depending on the learner and the target behaviour(s), this team would include some or all of the following: educator(s), the school principal, the learner's parents, a counsellor, a behavioural consultant, a psychologist, paraprofessionals/ teacher aides and the learner himself/herself. One person should be designated as the FBA coordinator, but all members of the team should have responsibilities.

> For example, Maria, aged 11 years, might be causing you concern because of her frequent off-task behaviour during reading, associated with her wandering around the classroom and even leaving it at times.

• *Step 2.*   These behaviours are then the subject of further investigation. Information on them can be obtained in a variety of ways, indirectly via existing school reports, learners' work samples and interviews. Best of all, information should be obtained directly via observations carried out in a range of settings. In the latter, the frequency (how often), intensity (the force or power), duration (how long), the locus (where) and consequences of the target behaviours should be noted.[6]

> In the case of Maria, her school reports going back since the time she entered school might reveal she had consistently scored poorly on reading tests and had not responded to remedial work. When she was interviewed she said she hated reading. Observations of her during a whole school day showed that her off-task behaviour was most marked during reading and when she was required to follow a textbook in other subjects. In activity-based lessons such as science and physical education, she concentrated as well as most in her class. Her off-task behaviour was usually treated with reprimands in the early parts of lessons and then ignored. Some of her peers engaged her in conversation when she was out of her seat.

• *Step 3.*   The team then determines the functions of the behaviours and develops hypotheses about what factors in the environment seem to cause them. This involves considering: (a) the common antecedents that seem to trigger the behaviours and (b) the consequences that seem to maintain them. For example, antecedents might include certain tasks or peer behaviours, while consequences might include such things as attention, the exercise of power over others and the opportunity to avoid a task by being 'referred to the school office'. As well as considering the antecedents and consequences of the *negative target behaviours*, attention should also be paid to the antecedents and consequences of *positive target behaviours*, or the non-occurrence of negative target behaviours, as these are the ones you want to increase.

> Maria's off-task behaviours seemed to be triggered by reading materials that were too difficult for her and maintained by teacher

and peer attention. On the other hand, her positive target behaviours seemed to be triggered by lessons involving active performances with materials and maintained by success.

- *Step 4.*   An intervention plan is then developed, which would include: (a) an operational definition of the problem behaviour(s), (b) behaviour teaching strategies (see, for example, **Strategies 7: School-wide Positive Behavioural Support, 10: Social Skills Training** and **16: Cognitive Behavioural Therapy**) and (c) strategies for manipulating antecedents and consequences (see **Strategy 17: Behavioural Approaches**). Here the aim is two-fold: to decrease or eliminate negative target behaviours *and* to increase positive target behaviours. Such plans should specify how, when, where and by whom the intervention is to be implemented.

  Maria's plan would probably include such features as: (a) a progressive target for reducing the occurrence of off-task behaviour, which is carefully defined, (b) ensuring that reading materials are more closely adapted to suit her skill level and age interests, (c) the inclusion of more practical activities (e.g., directions for making objects) in lessons involving reading, (d) seeking the cooperation of other members of the classroom to ignore any students who inappropriately engage them in conversation during lessons, etc.

- *Step 5.*   The intervention plan is then carefully implemented, and systematic records kept.
- *Step 6.*   Finally, the plan is critically evaluated and modified where necessary. Essentially, this is formative evaluation (**Strategy 21**).

 The evidence

Research studies have shown that FBA is generally effective in reducing negative target behaviours and, correspondingly, increasing positive target behaviours in a range of learners.

✓   In a comprehensive analysis of school-based functional assessment it was shown that this approach was useful for: (a) ascertaining the factors that control high-frequency problem behaviours in learners with **low-incidence disabilities** and (b) designing effective interventions for those behaviours. A total of 100 studies were reviewed, with most (69 per cent) of them manipulating both antecedents and consequences. In descending order, the most common functions of target behaviours were to: (a) escape from task demands, (b) gain adult attention, (c) gain an object/activity, (d) gain sensory stimulation and (e) gain peer attention. In nearly a quarter of all participants in the studies, multiple functions were indicated. In all but two of the 148 intervention cases reported, outcome data showed that the intervention was successful.[7]

✓ In a review of **high-incidence behaviour problems** in school settings, 14 studies were identified. Twelve of these showed that 'the effects of FBA were clear', with only slight improvements in the remaining two. These results were often attributed to modifications to academic tasks, such as giving learners a choice of activity, moderating task difficulty and adding prompts.[8]

✓ In another review, 22 studies of FBA-based interventions for learners with or at risk for **emotional and behavioural disorders** were reported. These studies comprised a mix of antecedent-based interventions (N = 6), consequence-based interventions (N = 6), a combination of antecedent-based and consequence-based procedures (N = 4) and other related approaches (N = 6). Regardless of the type of intervention, 18 of the 22 studies showed positive results, with clear reductions of problem behaviours and/or increases in appropriate behaviours.[9]

✓ In an early application of FBA, the functions of self-injurious behaviour for learners with **severe developmental disabilities** were shown to include attention, self-stimulation and demands. These assessments led to successful interventions, resulting in the reduction of self-injurious behaviour.[10]

 ## Addressing risks

I would like to draw your attention to two related risks in FBA:

• First, as I mentioned earlier, by focusing on proximal causes of behaviour, there is a risk that more complex causes are overlooked or downplayed. In the case of learners with severe behavioural problems, it is critical that a more comprehensive multi-disciplinary analysis and treatment plan be implemented, alongside the approach described in this chapter.

• Second, I recognize that FBA is quite labour intensive and can be expensive to implement. Against this point, however, is the cost of not intervening to reduce or eliminate problem behaviours, both for the individual learner and the wider society. This point needs to be driven home to educational administrators and politicians responsible for school budgets.

 ## Conclusion

FBA is an effective and positive strategy to use when addressing challenging behaviours. It is concerned with both eliminating or reducing negative behaviours and increasing positive behaviours in all learners.

 ## Further reading

Chandler, L.K. and Dahlquist, C.M. (2002). *Functional assessment: Strategies to prevent and remediate challenging behavior in school settings*. Upper Saddle River, NJ: Merrill/Prentice Hall.

Cooperative Educational Service Agency 12 and FBA Task Force. (1999). *Functional behavioral assessment: A study guide.* URL: www.dpi.state.wi.us/een/doc/fba-study.doc (accessed 25 January 2007).
Crone, D.A. and Horner, R.H. (2003). *Building positive behavior support systems in schools: Functional behavioral assessment.* New York: The Guilford Press.
Journal of Applied Behavior Analysis (1994). Special issue on functional analysis approaches to behavioural assessment and treatment, 27(4).
Shapiro, E.S. and Kratochwill, T.R. (2000). *Conducting school-based assessments of child and adolescent behavior.* New York: The Guilford Press.
Steege, M.W. and Watson, T.S. (2003). *Conducting school-based functional behavioral assessments: A practitioner's guide.* New York: Guilford Press.

Key references

1 Zirpoli, T.J. and Melloy, K.J. (1997). *Behaviour management: Applications for teachers and parents.* 2nd edn. Upper Saddle River, NJ: Merrill/Prentice Hall; and OSEP Center on Positive Behavioral Intervention: Sugai, G., Horner, R.H., Dunlap, G., Hieneman, M., Lewis, T.J., Nelson, C.M., Scott, T., Liaupsin, C., Sailor, W., Turnbull, A.P., Turnbull, H.R., Wickham, D., Wilcox, B. and Ruef, M. (2000). 'Applying positive behavior support and functional behavioral assessment in schools'. *Journal of Positive Behavior Interventions*, 2(3), 131–143.
2 Public Law 105–17, Section 615 (k)(1)(B)(i).
3 OSEP Center on Positive Behavioral Intervention, op. cit.
4 Carr, E.G. (1994). 'Emerging themes in the functional analysis of problem behavior'. *Journal of Applied Behavior Analysis*, 27(2), 393–399; and Miller, J.A., Tansy, M. and Hughes, T.L. (1998). 'Functional behavioural assessment: The link between problem behavior and effective intervention in schools'. *Current Issues in Education*, 1(5). URL: http://cie.ed.asu.edu/volume1/number5 (accessed 25 January 2007).
5 See Miller *et al.*, op. cit.; OSEP, op. cit.; and Cooperative Educational Service Agency 12 and FBA Task Force (1999). *Functional behavioral assessment: A study guide.* URL: www.dpi.state.wi.us/een/doc/fba-study.doc (accessed 25 January 2007).
6 Cooperative Educational Service Agency 12 and FBA Task Force, op. cit.
7 Ervin, R.A., Radford, P.M., Bertsh, K., Piper, K., Andrew, L., Erhardt, K.E. and Poling, A. (2001). 'A descriptive analysis and critique of the empirical literature on school-based functional assessment'. *School Psychology Review*, 30(2), 193–210.
8 Reid, R. and Nelson, R. (2002). 'The utility, acceptability, and practicality of functional behavioral assessment for students with high-incidence problem behavior'. *Remedial and Special Education*, 23(1), 15–23.
9 Heckaman, K., Conroy, M., Fox, J. and Chait, A. (2000). 'Functional assessment-based intervention research on students with or at risk for emotional and behavioural disorders in school settings'. *Behavioral Disorders*, 25(3), 196–210.
10 Iwata, B.A., Dorsey, M.F., Slifer, K.J., Bauman, K.E. and Richman, G.S. (1982). 'Toward a functional analysis of self-injury'. *Analysis and Intervention in Developmental Disabilities*, 2(1), 3–20.

Chapter 21

Strategy 19: Direct instruction
'Make lessons highly structured, briskly paced and successful'

Rating

★★★★

 The strategy

Direct Instruction (DI) is a multi-component instructional strategy centring on teacher-directed, explicit, systematic teaching based on scripted lesson plans and frequent assessment. Its best-known applications are the commercially available programmes for teaching reading, spelling, language arts and mathematics.[1]

Although not exact synonyms for DI, the following strategies have much in common with it: *precision instruction/teaching*, *explicit teaching/instruction*, *structured teaching/instruction* and *systematic teaching/instruction*.

DI relates to external task demands and external responses in the learning and teaching model.

 The underlying idea

DI originated in the 1960s in the USA with the work of Bereiter and Engelmann at the University of Illinois. It gained momentum as part of the US Office for Education's Project Follow Through, a follow-up to Head Start. Since then it has expanded in its use, but not without controversy.

Project Follow Through was a major educational study carried out in the USA from 1968 to 1976. It was designed to compare different educational strategies for low-income, at-risk children. The goal was to raise the level of performance of the poorest schools from the 20th to the 50th percentile. This target was largely achieved for learners receiving DI and Behaviour Analysis (**Strategy 17**), but not for those receiving other models of instruction, broadly labelled as 'child-centred'.[2]

DI had its origins in three analyses: the analysis of behaviour, the analysis of communication and the analysis of knowledge systems:[3]

- The analysis of behaviour seeks to understand how the environment influences behaviour. This concerns such factors as how to motivate learners, how to prompt and reinforce responses and how to correct errors.
- The analysis of communications seeks to understand how to logically define effective teaching sequences so that they prevent mis-rules, restricted generalization or over-generalization.
- The analysis of knowledge systems seeks to logically organize or classify knowledge and how to communicate skills to a learner.

 ## The practice

DI has ten main features.[4]

 ### Explicit, systematic instruction

DI lessons are planned in the most logical, developmental order. They are highly structured and targeted skills are taught in a pre-planned manner. Lesson sequences are based on a careful analysis of the content of various knowledge systems making up the school curriculum (e.g., mathematics, literacy) and breaking down new material into small steps.

 ### Scripted lesson plans

In DI, educators work through a carefully graduated sequence of tasks with carefully timed comments. The educator knows exactly what to say and what to ask to enable learners to reveal their understanding and/or the help they need. Scripts (which teachers in time generally memorize) ensure that educators present exercises using the exact wording that most clearly communicates the task at hand. Teacher talk is kept to a minimum. Specific correction procedures are prescribed.

 ### Emphasis on pace

In order to maximize students' engagement and learning potential, DI lessons include many opportunities to respond. They move at a brisk pace, with 15 learning opportunities per minute being common.

 ### High level of success

Although a brisk pace is maintained, the over-arching aim of every DI lesson is mastery: for all learners to perform each skill independently and without mistakes. Lessons should be completed with 90 per cent or better engagement and success rates. Educators are alert to errors and teach learners how to immediately identify and correct them. The assumption is that uncorrected errors will be learned, which makes it harder and harder for students to learn new material and requires much time to remedy later.

Frequent opportunities to practise targeted skills

As well as the rapid pace within lessons, DI provides many opportunities for learners to practise and review material, i.e., to over-learn content and skills. A part of this process is 'choral responding', when all learners give an answer at exactly the same time. It is argued that this method makes sure all learners are active participants and have maximum opportunities to practise all content, as well as minimizing off-task behaviour and giving educators opportunities to detect misunderstandings. Individual responses are also included in DI.

Frequent curriculum-based assessment

Short mastery tests are used periodically (about every ten lessons) to ensure that all learners have mastered the material and to determine which concepts, rules or cognitive strategies require additional instruction.

Ability grouping

Generally, in DI, learners are taught in small groups of about eight to 12 so that the educator can more easily monitor progress and provide individual help. They are grouped and re-grouped on the basis of their rate of progress. Proponents of DI are at pains to emphasize that these temporary skill groups are not permanent tracks or streams.

Mediated scaffolding

Gradually, the DI educator moves from an educator-guided to a more learner-guided approach. This is accomplished by first ensuring learners master the tasks at hand, then teaching them problem-solving strategies and fading the level of assistance.[5]

Embedded in other instructional strategies

A school that uses DI does not use it all day. Rather, it would most likely be used at the beginning of some class periods, to review previous concepts and to give instruction that builds on previous learning. The rest of a class period would be individual or small-group work to practise, generalize or adapt what was learned.

Strategic integration

In DI, concepts, rules and cognitive strategies are not taught in isolation from each other. Instead, instruction involves strategic integration within and across subjects.[6]

 The evidence

Research studies have consistently shown that DI has a positive effect across a range of learners and across various subject areas.

✓ In Project Follow Through (referred to earlier) DI was compared with 12 other models of pre-school education, which included a behaviour analysis model, a parent education model and the High Scope cognitive model. The results showed that DI was superior not only to the other models, but also to comparison schools in fostering basic reading and mathematics skills, higher order cognitive skills and self-esteem.[7] Furthermore, there is evidence that these gains are maintained over time. One study, for example, found that learners who had been taught reading and mathematics using DI in elementary school were still one year ahead of controls in reading and seven months ahead in mathematics in the ninth grade.[8]

✓ In a meta-analysis of 25 studies on the effects of DI on learners with **mild, moderate and severe disabilities**, an effect size of 0.84 was yielded. In other words, learners taught via DI would be expected to gain about 30 percentile ranks. However, there was a difference according to subject area with an effect size of 0.85 for reading but only 0.50 for mathematics.[9]

✓ In another meta-analysis, 37 studies were reported on. When the 21 studies involving **special education learners** were analysed separately, the effect size was 0.90, a large magnitude of change from pre-assessment to post-assessment.[10]

✓ Another meta-analysis produced a similar effect size to that obtained for reading in the previous study: 0.82.[11]

✓ In a meta-analysis of research into **learning disabilities**, four intervention models were compared: DI alone, strategy instruction (SI) alone (**Strategy 11**), DI combined with SI, and neither DI nor SI. The results showed that the combined model had significantly higher effect sizes (0.84) than DI alone (0.72), SI alone (0.72) or non-DI and non-SI (0.62). DI yielded higher effect sizes than SI for word recognition, but not comprehension. The combined method was more effective with reading-related material (especially reading comprehension) than with other material, such as mathematics and social skills.

The important instructional components making up the combined approach included:

- attention to sequencing (e.g., breaking down of tasks and sequencing of short activities);
- drill-repetition-practice (e.g., daily testing of skills, review and practice distributed over several sessions and daily feedback);
- controlling of task difficulty through prompts or cues (sequencing tasks from easy to difficult with only necessary hints being provided to learners);
- the educator systematically modelling problem-solving steps (providing demonstrations of processes or steps to solve problems); and
- making use of small groups.[12]

✓ An early study of the relationship between early childhood education approaches and subsequent **juvenile delinquency** found that graduates of a DI programme reported more antisocial behaviour than graduates of other programmes.[13] The present study attempted to replicate the earlier one, but with an improved methodology. A total of 171 learners were randomly assigned to two pre-school models – one using DI and the other a cognitively oriented, child-directed model. At age 15, the groups were found *not* to differ in their level of reported delinquency. The authors of this study criticized the earlier study on several grounds: (a) sample size (18 per group, compared with 77 in the present study), (b) programme characteristics (the earlier study did not employ a valid DI system), (c) sample differences (the DI group in the earlier study had more boys than the other approach, whereas the present study had a balanced gender representation in both comparison groups).[14]

✓ An early review of six studies evaluating the effectiveness of DI with **special education** learners showed that it tended to produce higher academic gains than traditional approaches.[15] In one of these studies, the effects of a DI programme, Distar Language, compared with the Peabody Language Kit, on 28 **moderately to severely retarded** children aged six to 14 years in a state institution was investigated. After two years, the DI group gained 22.5 months in mental age compared with only 7.5 months for the comparison group. In a second study, 23 middle school students with **learning disabilities** were randomly assigned to a DI group or to a traditional special education programme for a period of eight months. The results showed significant differences in favour of the DI group on reading and intelligence tests.

✓ A review of research found eight studies of DI with learners with **low incidence disabilities** (average IQ = 52), covering the ages from six to 16 years. Overall, all eight studies showed that DI had positive effects for this population of learners.[16]

Addressing risks

The main risk with DI is that it is not implemented appropriately. Its originators are at pains to emphasize that educators who wish to include DI in their classrooms receive careful training and monitoring to ensure fidelity of implementation. While I agree that this is the ideal, I recognize that not every school can afford to purchase the commercially available packages and would thus not be able to implement the scripted lesson plans. At the risk of offending DI purists, I would suggest, in that case, the other elements of DI could be put in place. Indeed, I review many of them elsewhere in this book: e.g., emphasis on pace, with a corresponding maximization of opportunities for learners to respond (**Strategy 24**), scaffolding (**Strategies 11** and **14**), frequent assessment (**Strategy 21**) and opportunities to practise targeted skills (**Strategy 20**).

 Conclusion

DI is one of most highly rated of strategies for teaching learners with special educational needs (as well as other learners). It is a multi-component strategy that requires intensive training, carefully developed teaching materials and adherence to a detailed teaching method.

 Further reading

Carnine, D., Silbert, J., Kame'enui, E. and Tarver, S. (2004). *Direct instruction reading*, 4th edn. Upper Saddle River, NJ: Pearson.
Journal of Direct Instruction
Marchand-Martella, N.E., Slocum, T.A. and Martella, R.C. (eds) (2004). *Introduction to direct instruction*. Boston, MA: Allyn and Bacon.
Web sites, accessed 22 January 2007:
 National Institute for Direct Instruction: www.nifdi.org/#top
 Association for Direct Instruction: www.adihome.org/phpshop/members.php
 What the data really show: Direct instruction really works!: www.jefflindsay.com/EducData.shtml
 Direct Instruction Resources: http://people.uncw.edu/kozloffm/DI.html
 SRA/McGraw-Hill: www.sraonline.com/download/DI/Research/General/special_ed.pdf
 Marchand-Martella, N., Kinder, D. and Kubina, R. (N.D.). Special education and direct instruction: An effective combination. SRA. URL: https://www.sraonline.com/download/DI/Research/General/special_ed.pdf
 Zig Engelmann: www.zigsite.com

Key references

1 SRA/McGraw-Hill: www.sraonline.com/download/DI/Research/General/special_ed.pdf (accessed 22 January 2007).

2 Bereiter, C. and Kurland, M. (1981). 'A constructive look at Follow Through results'. *Interchange*, 12(1), 1–22. For a commentary, see also Grossen, B. (1999). *What does it mean to be a research-based profession?* URL: http://darkwing. uoregon.edu/~bgrossen/pubs/resprf.htm (accessed 22 January 2007).

3 Engelmann, S. and Carnine, D.W. (1982). *Theory of instruction: Principles and applications.* New York: Irvington. Cited by Binder, C. and Watkins, C.L. (1990). 'Precision Teaching and Direct Instruction: Measurably superior instructional technology in schools'. *Performance Improvement Quarterly*, 3(4), 74–96.

4 Sources: Wikipedia. URL: http://en.wikipedia.org/wiki/Direct_instruction (accessed 22 January 2007); Association for Direct Instruction: www.adihome. org/phpshop/members.php; http://people.uncw.edu/kozloffm/dihighschool.html (accessed 22 January 2007); Kozloff, M.A., LaNunziata, L., Cowardin, J. and Bessellieu, F.B. (2000). *Direct instruction: Its contributions to high school achievement.* URL: http://people.uncw.edu/kozloffm/dihighschool.html (accessed 22 January 2007); SRA/McGraw-Hill, op. cit.; and Marchand-Martella, N., Kinder, D. and Kubina, R. (N.D.). Special education and direct instruction: An effective combination. SRA. URL: www.sraonline.com/download/DI/Research/General/special_ed.pdf (accessed 23 January 2007).

5 Kame'enui, E.J. and Carnine, D.W. (1998). *Effective teaching strategies that accommodate diverse learners.* Upper Saddle River, NJ: Merrill.

6 Kame'enui and Carnine, op. cit.

7 Becker, W. and Carnine, D.W. (1981). 'Direct instruction: A behavior theory model for comprehensive educational intervention with the disadvantaged'. In S.W. Bijou and R. Ruiz (eds) *Behavior modification: Contributions to education* (pp. 145–210). Hillsdale, NJ: Lawrence Erlbaum Associates.

8 Meyer, L. (1984). 'Long-term academic effects of the Direct Instruction Project Follow Through'. *Elementary School Journal*, 84(4), 380–394.

9 White, W.A.T. (1988). 'A meta-analysis of effects of direct instruction in special education'. *Education and Treatment of Children*, 11(4), 364–374.

10 Adams, G.L. and Engelmann, S. (1996). *Research on Direct Instruction: 25 years beyond DISTAR.* Seattle, WA: Educational Achievement Systems.

11 Hattie, J. (1999). *Influences on student learning.* Inaugural lecture, University of Auckland, Auckland, New Zealand.

12 Swanson, H.L. (2000). 'What instruction works for students with learning disabilities? From a meta-analysis of intervention studies'. In R. Gersten, E.P. Schiller and S. Vaughn, (eds) *Contemporary special education research: Syntheses of the knowledge base on critical instructional issues* (pp. 1–30). Mahwah, NJ: Lawrence Erlbaum Associates.

13 Schweinhart, L., Weikart, D. and Larner, M. (1986). 'Consequences of three preschool curriculum models through age 15'. *Early Childhood Research Quarterly*, 1(1), 15–45.

14 Mills, P.E., Cole, K.N., Jenkins, J.R. and Dale, P.S. (2002). 'Early exposure to direct instruction and subsequent juvenile delinquency: A prospective examination'. *Exceptional Children*, 69(1), 85–96.

15 Gersten, R. (1985). 'Direct instruction with special education students: A review of evaluation research'. *The Journal of Special Education*, 19(1), 41–58.

16 Marchand-Martella, Kinder and Kubina, op. cit.

Chapter 22

Strategy 20: Review and practice

'Practice makes perfect'

Rating
★★★★

  The strategy

Review and practice require planning and supervising opportunities for learners to encounter the same skills or concepts on several occasions. This is to ensure that they become readily available in their primary memory and/or their long-term memory (see the learning and teaching model in Chapter 2).

This strategy is sometimes referred to as *rehearsal, guided practice, explicit practice, mass practice, distributed practice* and *overlearning*. It is closely related to the generalization and transfer section of **Strategy 17**.

 The underlying idea

Review and practice are aimed at helping learners to 'internalize' concepts and skills once they have been initially taught. The ultimate aim is two-fold. First, it is important to make some skills and concepts automatically available to learners' primary, or 'working', memory. Having material available in the primary memory (say, reading vocabulary or number facts) frees a learner's processing resources for more important tasks (say, comprehending a passage or solving a mathematical problem). Second, it is important to ensure that selected skills and concepts are efficiently stored in a learner's long-term memory. This enables them to be readily retrieved or combined when called upon to solve future problems. In both cases, review and practice are necessary strategies to employ. This is particularly the case with basic skills that are taught hierarchically, so that success at any level requires the application of knowledge and skills mastered earlier.[1] It is also particularly important for learners with special educational needs, many of whom need to rehearse strategies and information more frequently than other learners.

A basic assumption of this strategy is that 'one-shot' learning is a rare occurrence. Rather, for much of our learning we require repeated experiences for the skill or the concept to be grasped. This came home to me recently when my gym instructor put me onto a new programme of ten exercises. He showed me once and then left me alone. I remembered about half of them! After a review I remembered all bar two, and after a second review, I recalled all of them. If you have ever tried learning another language, I am sure you will identify with this point.

A distinction can be made between *mass practice* and *distributed practice*. The former involves several repetitions at one time, the latter several repetitions spread over a period of time. Research supports both being used.[2]

The practice

Learners are given adequate opportunities to engage with the same idea on different occasions

Educators recognize that if learners are to remember an idea or a concept, then there have to be at least four different occasions when they engage with that idea or concept in some way. This can be reduced to three for older and more able learners but should be increased to five or more for less able learners, especially when the lesson content involves complex concepts, rather than explicit information. Whatever the number of rehearsals or reviews, each of them should be separated by no more than two days.[3] This goal is achieved, at least in part, through:

- supervised practice of skills that have been taught, immediately after instruction, with frequent checking and feedback;
- reviews of previously learned concepts, providing feedback, and reteaching if necessary, at the beginning of new lessons in the same area;
- regular within-class reviews;
- frequent questions: some calling for specific answers, others for explanations of how the answers were found;
- out-of-class practice, including homework;
- computer-assisted practice; and
- the ultimate goal, independent practice, alone or in groups.[4]

Learners are given adequate opportunities to practise new skills in different contexts

Educators should give learners ample opportunities to practise new skills and to generalize or transfer new skills to several different situations.[5] They should ensure that learners become aware that skills can be applied to solve a range of different problems – at school, at home and in the community.

Learners are given appropriate homework

Homework should be:

- designed to suit the learners' ability and previous knowledge;
- able to be supervised in the learners' homes;
- checked regularly and retaught where necessary; and
- no more than about ten minutes per grade per night.

 The evidence

✓ In a comprehensive meta-analysis of 93 intervention studies targeting adolescents with **learning disabilities**, the single most important strategy was found to be explicit practice, defined as 'treatment activities related to distributed review and practice, repeated practice, sequenced reviews, daily feedback, and/or weekly reviews'.[6]

✓ A recent synthesis examined 24 studies of effective interventions for building reading fluency with elementary students with **learning disabilities**. One of the main factors that emerged was multiple opportunities to repeatedly read familiar text independently and with corrective feedback. This led to improvements in the automatic processing of text and, hence, to improved speed and accuracy (i.e., fluency).[7]

✓ A US study of arithmetic calculation abilities of learners with **specific language impairments** found that, compared with their age mates, they experienced difficulties in rote memory. In particular, they had low scores on automatic number recall tasks, making numerous errors when trying to recall such maths facts as $7 \times 6 = \underline{\quad}$. It was recommended that such learners be given extensive practice in number facts, possibly using computer-assisted programmes.[8]

✓ A recent review found that practice and application opportunities are effective in supporting learning across the curriculum, although the ways this can be done tend to be specific to particular curriculum areas.[9] Various studies in this review reported that practice was critical in areas such as the following:
  - physical education: practice should be at the right level of difficulty and carried out by each learner with mental concentration;
  - gymnastics: learner gains were higher when teachers provided more active learning time and less instruction;
  - literacy skills in learners' first languages;
  - learning second languages: especially practice through meaningful interaction.

✓ In the same review, research on the role of *homework* was summarized. The following were the key points:
  - A meta-analysis found homework to have the fourth largest effect size (0.77) of nine strategies.

- Another review found that 14 of 20 studies reported positive effects for homework, the other six reporting a positive effect for *no* homework. This study found that an average secondary school learner who received homework outperformed 69 per cent of those who did not receive homework. This effect was less significant for junior high school learners and disappeared for elementary school learners.[10]
- In a study of intermediate school students' learning in an integrated science and social studies module, homework tasks played a critical role in enabling working memory to consolidate in-class learning.
- Variability in the results of homework reflects such factors as: (a) differing ability among teachers to design, resource and scaffold appropriate homework tasks for diverse learners, and (b) the provision of support and resources in homes.

   From this review, it would be fair to conclude that *effective* homework has a strong impact on learners' achievement, particularly at the secondary level.

✓ In a very recent review of homework, a wide range of studies was synthesized.[11] Not surprisingly, similar findings to the above were reported. Here are a few of them:

- Of 12 US studies that linked the amount of homework to how well learners performed on national academic tests, 11 found a positive link between time spent on homework and long-term achievement.
- Age makes a big difference, the benefits being twice as large for high school learners than for junior high school learners, and twice as large again for junior high school learners than for elementary school learners.
- A good rule of thumb is to assign up to ten minutes homework per night per grade; i.e., a fourth grader (i.e., ten-year-old) should be doing about 40 minutes per night.

Note: unfortunately, I have been unable to trace any studies of homework involving learners with special educational needs.

 ## Addressing risks

Four risks should be attended to:

- First, and perhaps the main risk, is that this strategy is seen as a licence to teach material by rote. While I am recommending the value of drill and practice exercises, understanding of the content or processes involved must precede all such exercises.[12]
- Second, with reviews and practice comes the risk of boredom, or 'drill and kill'. To avoid this, you should ensure that it is not overdone, to the point where learners are required to rehearse skills or concepts that have already been thoroughly mastered. Here, the 'Goldilocks principle'

should apply: not too little, not too much, but just the right amount of practice. You should also ensure that reviews are fun and not tedious exercises. Many computer programs are emerging that can assist this.[13]

- A third, and related, risk is that you might attempt to put too much into learners' primary memory for automatic recall. Use your judgement as to how much material should reach that level of automatic recall.
- A fourth risk has to do with homework. For all learners, but particularly for those with special educational needs, it is important that homework be carefully planned to be within their abilities, and capable of being carried out in their home environments.

 Conclusion

Review and practice is one of the critical elements of learning. It is well supported in the research literature as a means of helping learners to internalize skills and concepts.

Key references

1 Rosenshine, B. (1983). 'Teaching functions in instructional programs'. *The Elementary School Journal*, 83(4), 335–351.
2 Woodward, J. and Rieth, H. (1997). 'A historical review of technology research in special education'. *Review of Educational Research*, 67(4), 503–536.
3 Nuthall, G. and Alton-Lee, A. (1994). 'How pupils learn'. *Set*, 2. Wellington: New Zealand Council for Educational Research.
4 See Rosenshine, op. cit.; Swanson, H.L. and Deshler, D. (2003). 'Instructing adolescents with learning disabilities: Converting a meta-analysis to practice'. *Journal of Learning Disabilities*, 36(2), 124–136; and Pacchiano, D.M. (2000). 'A review of instructional variables related to student problem behavior'. *Preventing School Failure*, 44(4), 174–178.
5 Ysseldyke, J. and Christensen, S. (1993–1998). *The Instructional Environment System – II: A system to identify a student's instructional needs*. Fifth printing. Longmont, CO: Sopris West; Greeno, J., Moore, J.L. and Smith, D.R. (1993). 'Transfer of situated learning'. In D.K. Detterman and R.J. Sternberg (eds) *Transfer on trial: Intelligence, cognition and instruction* (pp. 99–167). Norwood, NJ: Ablex; and Council for Exceptional Children (1997). *CEC Code of Ethics and Standards of Practice*. Reston, VA: CEC.
6 Swanson, H.L. and Hoskyn, M. (2001). 'Instructing adolescents with learning disabilities: A component and composite analysis'. *Learning Disabilities Research and Practice*, 16(2), 109–119.
7 Chard, D., Vaughn, S. and Tyler, B.J. (2002). 'A synthesis of research on effective interventions for building reading fluency with elementary students with learning disabilities'. *Journal of Learning Disabilities*, 35(5), 386–406.
8 Fazio, B. (1999). 'Arithmetic calculation, short term memory and language performance in children with specific language impairment: A five year follow-up'. *Journal of Speech, Language and Hearing*, 42(2), 420–431.
9 Alton-Lee, A. (2003). *Quality teaching for diverse students in schooling: Best evidence synthesis*. Wellington: Ministry of Education.

10 Cooper, H. (2001). 'Homework for all – in moderation'. *Educational Leadership*, 58(7), 34–38.
11 Cooper, H., Robinson, J.C. and Patall, E.A. (2006). 'Does homework improve academic achievement? A synthesis of research'. *Review of Educational Research*, 76(1), 1–62.
12 For an expansion of this point, see Heward, W.L. (2003). 'Ten faulty notions about teaching and learning that hinder the effectiveness of special education'. *The Journal of Special Education*, 36(4), 186–205.
13 See, for example, Kelly, L. (2003). 'Considerations for designing practice for deaf readers'. *Journal of Deaf Studies and Deaf Education*, 8(2), 172–186.

Chapter 23

Strategy 21: Formative assessment and feedback

'Regularly check and inform learners of their progress'

Rating

★★★★

 The strategy

Formative assessment and feedback is a combined strategy in which you: (a) probe for knowledge within lessons (sometimes referred to as *interactive formative evaluation* or *performance monitoring*), (b) give frequent feedback to learners (sometimes referred to as *corrective feedback*) and (c) adjust your teaching strategies, where necessary, to improve learners' performances.

This strategy relates to external task demands and external responses in the learning and teaching model.

 The underlying ideas

Assessment serves educational purposes

Assessment is increasingly being seen as serving educational purposes by promoting learning and by guiding teaching. It should provide the best possible account of what a learner knows, can do or has experienced. Ideally, assessment is aligned with your intended learning outcomes, which are usually aligned with the curriculum. In the case of learners with special educational needs, individual education plans (IEPs) are used to define the learning outcomes you are seeking to achieve.

How does formative assessment differ from summative assessment?

Briefly, *summative assessment* is concerned with evaluating learners' performances at the end of a module or a course. The results count towards making a final judgement on what the learners have achieved.

Formative assessment evaluates learners' progress during a course or module so that they have opportunities to improve. It is as much assessment *for* learning as assessment *of* learning.

In its pure form, formative assessment does not contribute to the overall grade. However, sometimes assessment serves both summative and formative purposes. How you classify the two types depends on the extent to which assessment leads to feedback that enables learners to improve their performances. The more it does this, the more justified is its classification as formative assessment.

The importance of probing for knowledge

We know that mere exposure to information or concepts does not guarantee that students will learn them. Rather, it is helpful if you frequently probe for knowledge in a variety of ways and at different times to ensure that learners are understanding, retaining and generalizing new concepts.

By systematically using formative assessment, you will gain a better idea of your learners' needs and be able to 'fine-tune' your teaching.

The value of feedback

The whole point of formative assessment is to provide feedback (a) to learners and (b) to you, the educator. Thus, it is important that you frequently monitor and give regular explicit feedback to your students on their levels of understanding, or you ensure that such feedback is given by their fellow learners in group work. Without frequent probes of students' understanding, you will have no idea of the effectiveness of your teaching. Also, giving prompt feedback prevents learners from wasting their time practicing errors.

 ## The practice

 ### Formative assessment

Formative assessment allows educators to diagnose failure and to adapt the curriculum and re-design their teaching to rectify such problems.

Formative assessment should provide descriptions of what has or has not been achieved. This is sometimes referred to as *criterion-referenced assessment*. Several countries have gone down this track. For example, in Scotland the National Certificate provides information on whether or not learners have mastered each specified learning outcome on each module of work. In New Zealand the National Certificate of Educational Achievement serves the same purpose.[1]

There are many ways in which formative assessment can be carried out, some formal and others informal. These include checklists, quizzes, classroom tests, portfolios, observations, learning journals, assignments and conferences/ interviews with individuals or small groups. As a rule of thumb, educators should try to make at least one assessment per subject per learner per week.

Feedback

In formative assessment, you probe for knowledge within lessons and give frequent feedback.[2]

It is important that you convey a sense that feedback is intended to be helpful, not embarrassing, and that it is part of the joint search for success. For this reason, errors can be tolerated as they provide good information on learners' current levels of understanding and misunderstanding. Bridging the gap between the two is your task as a teacher – and a challenge to learners.

Providing plenty of feedback does not necessarily mean that you should use lots of tests and be overly prescriptive in giving directions to learners. Rather, it means providing information on how and why learners understand or misunderstand, and how they can improve.[3] This can be made an enjoyable, fun process.

In a class of mixed ability, it is all too easy to avoid asking questions of students with learning difficulties – partly to avoid embarrassing them, but also to ensure that the lesson flow is not too disrupted. The net effect of this is that such students can go for whole stretches of time without being required to show their level of understanding. Take active steps to avoid this situation.

Feedback can come from a variety of sources: educators (the main focus of this description), peers, books and other written resources, computers, parents and learners themselves.

The purposes of feedback are to motivate learners, to inform them how well they have done, and, above all, to show them how they could improve.[4] To achieve these purposes, feedback should be:

- *Timely*: provide feedback as soon as possible after the assessment has been conducted, so that the material is still fresh in the learners' minds.
- *Explicit*: in your feedback, describe where the learner was accurate or inaccurate ('Good, you used the right formula here.' 'I can see where you went wrong here: you confused New Mexico, the US state, with the country of Mexico. Please check this in your atlas.').
- *Focused on strategy use, rather than on the learner's ability or effort* (i.e., 'You got it right because you applied the steps in the right order', rather than 'You really tried hard on this problem.'):[5] this might mean briefly reviewing the strategy, rather than telling learners the correct answer.
- *Adjusted to the complexity of the task:* research has shown that for low-level skills such as memorizing spelling words, immediate 'correct/

incorrect' feedback (for example, delivered via a computer) is more effective than delayed feedback. On the other hand, more complex tasks, such as drawing conclusions from two statements, lend themselves to more complex feedback, which includes reminding learners about the relevant strategies.[6]

* *Able to be used by learners*: you might need to teach learners how to use feedback and to periodically check that they use previous feedback in their subsequent work.

 The evidence

✓ In an early meta-analysis of 21 studies of the effects of formative evaluation, an effect size of 0.70 was obtained. However, when formative evaluation was combined with positive reinforcement for improvement (i.e., feedback), the effect size was even higher at 1.12.[7]

✓ A US study used a formative evaluation system with **low-achieving** learners in a large urban school system. It resulted in significant gains in maths achievement.[8]

✓ After synthesizing a large number of studies on the effects of a wide range of influences on learner achievement, a New Zealand researcher found 139 that focused on feedback. With an effect size of 1.13, this was the most powerful of all the influences on achievement.[9] He concluded that 'The simplest prescription for improving education must be "dollops of feedback" – providing information how and why the child understands and misunderstands, and what directions the student must take to improve.'[10] Although the meta-analysis was not confined to students with special educational needs, it is highly likely to apply to such learners.

✓ An early study in the USA examined the effects of instructional cues, student participation and corrective feedback on student achievement. A total of 20 studies yielded a very high effect size of 0.94. This result was consistent across elementary and secondary schools and across socio-economic levels and ethnicities. As with the previous study, no data were separately reported for learners with special educational needs, but it is very likely that such learners would fit within the results.[11]

✓ According to a report of a recent UK study, efforts to encourage 'interactive practice' in the National Literacy and Numeracy Strategies have led to an emphasis on teacher questions. This article reports on evidence gathered from a large-scale research project examining classroom interactions during literacy and numeracy lessons. The authors argue that in order to 'open' classroom interaction, emphasis should be less on the questions teachers ask, and more on the manner with which teachers react to pupils' responses to questions. They present evidence of educators' behaviours in reaction to learners' responses that succeed in facilitating a more interactive learning environment.[12]

✓ There is evidence to show that teachers trained in formative assessment are more open to changing their instructional strategies to promote learners' mastery of material.[13] Furthermore, it has been shown that without formative assessment, teachers' perceptions of learners' performances are often erroneous.[14]

 Addressing risks

In formative assessment there are four main risks:

- the assessment is not aligned with intended learning outcomes;
- there is too little assessment, which means that some aims are not being evaluated;
- there is too much assessment, at the expense of actually teaching; and
- the assessment is deficit-driven, with too much attention given to looking for problems in the learners, rather than with the teaching strategies.[15]

Feedback, if not handled carefully, can be:

- de-motivating;
- not understood by learners;
- too little, too late;
- too dominated by tests; and
- placing too much responsibility on the learners for any lack of achievement, rather than sharing responsibility with educators.

 Conclusion

Taken together, formative assessment and its close relative, feedback, comprise one of the most powerful teaching strategies. At its most basic, it simply means regularly checking and informing learners of their progress. This then leads to learners and/or educators changing their strategies to increase the likelihood of improved performances.

 Further reading

Campbell, D.M., Cignetti, P.B., Melenyzer, B.J., Nettles, D.H. and Wyman, R.M. (2006). *How to develop a professional portfolio: A manual for teachers.* Boston, MA: Pearson Education.

Key references

1 www.parliament.nz/en-NZ/PubRes/Research/ (accessed 7 February 2007).
2 Englert, C.S., Tarrant, K.L. and Mariage, T.V. (1992). 'Defining and redefining instructional practices in special education: Perspectives on good teaching'.

Teacher Education and Special Education, 5(2), 62–86; Florian, L. and Rouse, M. (2000). 'Investigating effective classroom practice in inclusive secondary schools in England'. Paper presented at the Special Education World Congress, Vancouver, Canada, April 2000; and Stanovich, P.J. and Jordan, A. (1998). 'Canadian teachers' and principals' beliefs about inclusive education as predictors of effective teaching in heterogeneous classrooms'. *The Elementary School Journal*, 98(3), 221–238.

3 Hattie, J. (1999). *Influences on student learning.* Inaugural lecture, University of Auckland, New Zealand.

4 Brown, G. (2001). *Assessment: A guide for lecturers.* Nottingham: LTSN Generic Centre.

5 Schunk, D.H. and Cox, P.D. (1986). 'Strategy training and attributional feedback with learning disabled students'. *Journal of Educational Psychology*, 78(3), 201–209.

6 Woodward, J. and Rieth, H. (1997). 'A historical review of technology research in special education'. *Review of Educational Research*, 67(4), 503–536.

7 Fuchs, L.A. and Fuchs, D. (1986). 'Effects of systematic formative evaluation: A meta-analysis'. *Exceptional Children*, 53(3), 199–208.

8 Ysseldyke, J.E. (2001). 'Reflections on a research career: Generalizations from 25 years of research on assessment and instructional decision making'. *Exceptional Children*, 67(3), 295–308.

9 Hattie, J. (2003). *Teachers make a difference: What is the research evidence?* Presentation to Australian Council for Educational Research Annual Conference on Building Teacher Quality.

10 Hattie (1999), op. cit.

11 Lysakowski, R.S. and Walberg, H.J. (1982). 'Instructional effects of cues, participation and corrective feedback: A quantitative synthesis'. *American Educational Research Journal*, 19(4), 559–578.

12 Smith, H. and Higgins, S. (2006). 'Opening classroom interaction: The importance of feedback'. *Cambridge Journal of Education*, 36(4), 485–502.

13 Bloom, L.A., Hursh, D., Weinke, W.D. and Wold, R.K. (1992). 'The effects of computer-assisted data collections on students' behaviours'. *Behavioral Assessment*, 14(2), 173–190.

14 Fuchs, L.S., Deno, S.L. and Mirkin, P.K. (1984). 'The effects of frequent curriculum-based measurement and evaluation on pedagogy, student achievement, and student awareness of learning'. *American Educational Research Journal*, 21, 449–460.

15 Ysseldyke, op. cit.

Chapter 24

Strategy 22: Assistive technology

'Compensate for learners' skill deficits'

Rating
★★★☆

 The strategy

An assistive technology (AT) device is defined in US legislation as 'any item, piece of equipment, or product system, whether acquired commercially off the shelf, modified, or customized, that is used to increase, maintain, or improve functional capabilities of children with disabilities'.[1] In the US and most other developed countries such devices must be provided at no cost, a situation which, unfortunately, does not pertain in most developing countries where access to them is severely restricted.[2]

In this chapter, I will outline a range of such devices and how they can be used to assist learners with special educational needs to achieve better performances and independence at school and at home. Since the next chapter on *augmentative and alternative communication* will be devoted to assistive devices aimed at improving learners' communication ability, these will not be considered in any depth in the present chapter. Also, I will not be dealing with *sound-field amplification* as an aid for improving classroom acoustics, which I discuss in Chapter 10.

The field covered by assistive technology encompasses strategies variously referred to as *special access technology*, *adaptive technology*, *accessible digital media*, *augmentative technology*, *special education technology* and *computer-assisted instruction*.

This strategy relates to the biological structures and functions component of the learning and teaching model, in that it attempts to compensate for sensory, physical or intellectual barriers to learning.

 The underlying idea

The use of high-tech AT has been with us only since the 1980s, when the first major developments of computer-assisted instruction began to be used.

Its advantages for such learners was expressed nearly 20 years ago when the US Congress stated that it enables individuals to:

* have greater control over their own lives;
* participate in and contribute more fully to activities in their home, school and work environments, and in their own communities; and
* interact to a greater extent with non-disabled individuals.[3]

Given the rapid advances in technology in general and AT in particular, what we are seeing is an ever-expanding field, with enormous future possibilities.

 The practice

There are literally hundreds of AT devices, so I can only mention a few of them in this book. They range from low-tech (those that are not electronically based or battery-operated and are usually low-cost, such as whiteboards, photo albums) to high-tech (those that are electronically based and are usually high-cost, such as computers, video cameras and voice output devices). In this strategy I will mainly focus on high-tech devices.

 Who needs what assistive technology?

There are several groups of learners with special educational needs who would benefit from having access to AT:[4]

* Those who have some hand function or who can use a mouth-stick or head pointer, but have one or more of the following difficulties: poor accuracy in locating the desired key, prone to accidentally pressing keys adjacent to the required one, inability to drag on the mouse and a tendency to tire easily. These learners could be helped by such adaptations as: (a) an expanded keyboard; (b) a joystick rather than a mouse, which can be moved directly with mouth, fingers, feet, elbows, etc. to control the cursor; (c) 'sticky keys', which allow characters or commands to be typed without having to hold down a modifier key such as Shift and Control, while pressing a second key; (d) a touch screen, where the user can touch objects directly on the screen and move them around; and (e) key-guards, consisting of a metal or plastic plate with punched holes, fitted over the keyboard to reduce accidental key-presses.
* Those who have limited control of their limbs or head and are not able to use the standard keyboard and mouse. They could benefit from using a switch or voice recognition programmes as input devices.
* Those who are partially sighted or blind and who have difficulty in seeing the cursor and information displayed on a screen. Learners with

some vision might benefit from a larger monitor, while blind learners could use screen readers to speak the text via a speech synthesizer.

- Those with specific learning disabilities or who have spatial or perceptual problems might benefit from a simplified keyboard.
- Those who have difficulty processing and remembering spoken language. Such learners could be helped with their listening by: (a) personal FM listening systems (which transmit a speaker's voice directly to the user's ear), or (b) variable-speed tape recorders/players (which allow users to listen to pre-recorded text or to capture spoken information (e.g., a classroom lesson) and play it back).
- Those who struggle with computing, organizing, aligning and copying mathematics problems down on paper. Such learners can benefit from: (a) electronic maths worksheets, (software programs that can help users organize, align and work through maths problems on a computer screen), (b) talking calculators (calculators with built-in speech synthesizers that read aloud each number, symbol or operation key a user presses) and (c) a range of drill-and-practice software.
- Those with reading difficulties. They may be assisted by: (a) audio books (recorded books that allow users to listen to text and are available in a variety of formats, such as audiocassettes, CDs and MP3 downloads), (b) optical character recognition (OCR) (which allows a user to scan printed material into a computer or handheld unit, the scanned text then being read aloud via a speech decoder) and (c) speech synthesizers/screen readers (which display and read aloud text on a computer screen, including text that has been typed by the user, or scanned in from printed material).
- Those who have difficulty with writing. Here AT devices might help learners to circumvent the actual physical task of writing, while others facilitate proper spelling, punctuation, grammar, word usage and organization. These include: (a) abbreviation expanders (which allow users to create, store and re-use abbreviations for frequently used words or phrases), (b) graphic organizers and outlining programs (which help users to organize and outline information as they begin a writing project), (c) speech recognition programs (which work in conjunction with a word processor and allow users to dictate into a microphone, and have their spoken words converted into text) and (d) speech synthesizers (see above outline of AT use with learners experiencing reading difficulties).

✳ Accessing the computer

Depending on the needs of the learner, there are many adaptations that can be made to computers to make them accessible to all. In addition to those I refer to above, here are some others:

- place computers on height-adjustable tables or trolleys;
- provide a footrest;

- provide a wrist-rest; and
- make sure that the computer can work with the curriculum software used by the rest of the class.

See also **Strategy 8** for guidelines on lighting.

 Choosing the right AT device

It is, of course, critical that great care be taken in choosing the most appropriate AT device. Here are some important guidelines:[5]

- involve the learner and his or her parents in selecting the device;
- customize it to suit the requirements of the individual learner and his or her usual environments;
- keep it as simple as possible, and as similar as possible to those already in use;
- ensure that it is durable under the anticipated conditions of use;
- ensure that it is aesthetically pleasing, age-appropriate, fashionable and culturally acceptable;
- give it an evaluation trial.

 Integrating AT into daily lives

Since AT devices have the potential to help learners to be more independent, they and their parents/caregivers and educators face a transition from a situation where they might have been very dependent on others to meet their needs.[6] Changing the habits of all concerned can be quite a challenge, especially when the AT device might be relatively complex to operate at the beginning and its value may not be immediately apparent. Motivation is likely to follow, however, if the preceding guidelines are followed and if the learner is successful in using the device in daily activities and quick solutions are found to any problems that might arise, thus minimizing frustrations.

 Accessing Web sites

In recent years, parents have increasingly turned to the Web for information on their children's special needs – their medical features and education programmes in particular. In addition to providing information, the Web, in the form of on-line discussion groups, also provides avenues for emotional support and advocacy opportunities. The Web has certainly done much to equalize the balance of knowledge-based power between parents and professionals. While this access is usually very helpful in providing free, as-needed support to parents, there are risks associated with the lack of quality monitoring and information overload. Professionals can play a valuable role in helping parents interpret what they obtain from the Web.[7] One way you could do this is to refer parents to Web sites that refer to sites with a high level of trustworthiness (e.g., Healthfinder, a US government site: www. healthfinder.gov).

Learners with special educational needs can also gain a great deal from accessing information on the Web and linking with other people with similar challenges, thus reducing the loneliness that many might experience. Here, too, professionals can play an important role in ensuring that Web access is positive and as risk-free as possible.

Developing Web sites

You might be involved in developing your own Web site or in advising others about them. In that case, you could turn to a series of guidelines about what makes a Web site accessible for learners with special educational needs. These are described in the document 'Web Content Accessibility Guidelines 1.0': www.w3.org/TR/WAI-WEBCONTENT/. The key theme of the guidelines is how to make content understandable and navigable.

Here are the main points to take into consideration:[8]

- ensure accuracy of content;
- ensure ease of use by making the language clear and simple and by providing understandable mechanisms for navigating within and between pages;
- regularly update the site;
- provide links and ensure their current availability;
- include frequently asked questions; and
- provide chat rooms for real-time communication and/or bulletin boards for asynchronous communication.

The preceding points apply to all Web sites, so here are some points that are specific to users with disabilities:

- provide a text equivalent for every non-text element, such as images, animations, objects, sounds and video;
- ensure that all information available in colour is also available without colour;
- use the clearest and simplest language appropriate for a site's content; and
- ensure that foreground and background colour combinations provide sufficient contrast when viewed by someone with colour deficits or when viewed on a black-and-white screen.

Teamwork is essential

As you can see from the above, selecting an AT device requires extensive planning by a multi-disciplinary team of professionals working with the learner and his/her family. This team may well include most, if not all of the following, depending on the learner's needs: a physician and/or medical specialists, a psychologist, a special educator, occupational and/or physio-therapists, speech and language therapists, visual and hearing impairment specialists, relevant AT technicians and a relevant paraprofessional/learning support assistant. Such a team would assess a range of factors, including the learner's: (a) seating and positioning needs, (b) vision and visual perception, (c) motor control and (d) cognitive and linguistic skills.[9] As well, the school and home contexts will need to be assessed to determine attitudes, knowledge and skills relevant to AT. As you can see, implementing AT calls upon teamwork of the highest order (**Strategy 4**).

 The evidence

✓ An early (1985) meta-analysis of 16 studies involving comparisons of computer-assisted instruction (CAI) with traditional forms of instruction with **exceptional children** reported an effect size of 0.52 – a moderately positive effect. It was also found that **language disordered** and **mentally retarded** learners benefited the most from CAI, a finding that should be treated cautiously according to the researchers.[10]

✓ Two more recent reviews of the literature on the use of CAI with learners with **mild and moderate disabilities** found that, although mixed, research supported the potential for CAI to raise academic achievement, particularly when it is used as a tool for extended practice of previously learned concepts.[11]

✓ A Swedish study investigated the effects of an interactive multimedia computer program on reading and communication skills of six-year-old learners, 11 with **autism** and nine with **mixed handicaps**. The former group increased both their word reading and phonological awareness, but these were not sustained during follow-up. A similar, but weaker pattern was found for the second group. It was concluded that such interventions should be individually based.[12]

✓ A recent English study examined the impact of computers with and without animations on learners with **ADHD** working on science tasks. The results showed that the non-animated computerized presentations significantly improved the accuracy of responses and on-task behaviours.[13]

✓ In a recent US study of fifth- to seventh-grade **low-achieving mathematics** learners, an experimental group received an after-school maths programme that made extensive use of commercially available computer programs.

This group performed substantially better than those not receiving the computer program.[14]

✓ In another US study, speech recognition technology was used to assist 39 elementary and secondary school students aged nine to 18 with **learning disabilities** to improve their reading and spelling. As noted earlier, speech recognition programs work in conjunction with a word processor and allow users to dictate into a microphone, and have their spoken words converted into text. Results showed that the speech recognition group showed significantly more improvement than a control group in word recognition, spelling and reading comprehension.[15]

 Addressing risks

There are two main risks attending the use of AT:

• It may not be fully utilized or is not utilized at all. One study, for example, found that one-third of all assistive devices are abandoned.[16]
• Perhaps an explanation of the preceding point lies in AT not being integrated into users' daily lives. In turn, this might reflect a breakdown somewhere along the chain comprising: assessment of the learner's needs, evaluation of devices, customization of the device, and training of the learner and his or her family.[17]

 Conclusion

AT represents one of the most rapidly expanding and promising strategies presented in this book. It has already proven its worth across a diverse range of learners with special educational needs and, with the rapid developments that are taking place in technology, it will continue to expand in its applications.

 Further reading

Edyburn, D., Higgins, K. and Boone, R. (eds) (2005). *Handbook of special education technology research and practice*. Whitefish Bay, WI: Knowledge by Design.

Journals

Assistive Technology Outcomes and Benefits
Journal of Educational Computing
Journal of Special Education Technology
Special Education Technology Practice

Web sites (accessed 14 January 2007)

Australia: http://education.qld.gov.au/curriculum/learning/students/disabilities/process/
  dssu.html
Canada: www.uvatt.org/
Europe: www.aaate.net/index.asp?auto-redirect=true&accept-initial-profile=standard
Scotland: http://callcentre.education.ed.ac.uk/
UK: www.inclusive.co.uk/infosite/index.shtml, www.abilitynet.co.uk/
US: www.seat.ilstu.org/
General: www.eschoolnews.com/toolsforschools/tools4schools011707.htm

Key references

1   Individuals with Disabilities Education Act of 1990, 20 USC. 1401 Definitions, (a) (25).
2   The good news, however, is that a project called 'One Laptop Per Child' aims to have cheap laptops available for developing countries from 2007 onwards. They will be sold to governments and issued to children by schools. They will be rugged, open source and so energy efficient that a child can power them manually. Mesh networking will give many machines Internet access from one connection. The pricing goal will start near US$100 and then steadily decrease. By mid-2007, several million are expected to reach Brazil, Argentina, Uruguay, Nigeria, Libya, Pakistan, Thailand and the Palestinian territory. See the One Laptop Per Child Web site: www.laptop.org/ (accessed 30 January 2007).
3   Technology-Related Assistance for Individuals with Disabilities Act of 1988, PL 100–407 Title 29, USC 2201 *et seq*: *US Statutes at Large*, 102, 1044–1065.
4   See the following: Nisbet, P. and Poon, P. (1998). *Special access technology.* Edinburgh: CALL Centre. URL: http://callcentre.education.ed.ac.uk/ (accessed 14 January 2007). Schwab Learning. URL: wwwschwablearning.org (accessed 15 January 2007). Wikipedia: http://en.wikipedia.org/wiki/Assistive_technology (accessed 14 January 2007).
5   These ideas are derived from a range of sources, including: Kintsch, A. and DePaula, R. Center for Lifelong Learning and Design, University of Colorado at Boulder. URL: www.cs.colorado.edu/~l3d/clever (accessed 14 January 2007).
6   Scherer, M.J. (1996). *Living in a state of stuck: How technology impacts the lives of people with disabilities.* 2nd edn. Cambridge: Brookline Books.
7   Zaidman-Zait, A. and Jamieson, J.R. (2007). 'Providing Web-based support for families of infants and young children with established disabilities'. *Infants and Young Children*, 29(1), 11–25.
8   Zaidman-Zait and Jamieson, op. cit.
9   Nisbet and Poon, op. cit.
10 Schmidt, M., Weinstein, T., Niemic, R. and Walberg, H.J. (1985/1986). 'Computer-assisted instruction with exceptional children'. *The Journal of Special Education*, 19(4), 493–501.
11 Fitzgerald, G. and Koury, K. (1996). 'Empirical advances in technology-assisted instruction for students with mild and moderate disabilities'. *Journal of Research on Computing in Education*, 28(4), 526–553; and Howell, R. (1996). 'Technological aids for inclusive classrooms'. *Theory into Practice*, 35(1), 58–65.
12 Heimann, M., Nelson, K.E., Tjus, T. and Gillberg, C. (1995). 'Increasing reading and communication skills in children with autism through an interactive multimedia computer program'. *Journal of Autism and Developmental Disorders*, 25(5),

459–480.
13 Shaw, R. and Lewis, V. (2005). 'The impact of computer-mediated and traditional academic task presentation on the performance and behaviour of children with ADHD'. *Journal of Research in Special Educational Needs*, 5(2), 47–54.
14 McDonald, N., Trautman, T. and Blick, L. (2005). 'Computer-assisted middle school mathematics remediation intervention: An outcome study'. The American Education Corporation. URL: www.amered.com/docs/buhl_research.pdf (accessed 15 January 2007).
15 Raskind, M.H. and Higgins, E.L. (1999). 'Speaking to read: The effects of speech recognition on the reading and spelling performance of children with learning disabilities'. *Annals of Dyslexia*, 49, 251–281.
16 Scherer, op. cit.
17 Kintsch and DePaula, op. cit.

Chapter 25

Strategy 23: Augmentative and alternative communication

'Utilize all means to develop communication skills'

Rating

★★★★☆

 The strategy

Some learners with special educational needs have significant difficulties in communicating with others using speech. They include learners with cerebral palsy, autism, developmental apraxia, multiple sclerosis, stroke and traumatic brain injury, some of whom have virtually no speech ability while others have some use of their voice.[1] Thus, there are two strategies for assisting these learners: augmentative communication and alternative communication, respectively.

On the one hand, *augmentative communication* is used to supplement whatever existing methods of communication a learner has. For example, a learner with autism or delayed speech might use a touch screen computer or voice output communication aid to communicate with other people.

On the other hand, *alternative communication* represents an attempt to replace the lost means of communication. For example, a learner who is born profoundly deaf can be taught sign language. This will function as their primary alternative method of communication.

These two categories are collectively known as *augmentative and alternative communication* (AAC). As with **Strategy 22**, this strategy relates closely to the biological structures and functions component of the learning and teaching model, in that it attempts to compensate for language barriers to learning.

In most cases, speech and language therapists are most closely involved with AAC, but as an educator you need to be knowledgeable about it if any learners in your classroom are using it.

 The underlying idea

Since the 1980s, AAC has grown in its capacity and popularity as a way of helping learners who cannot speak or have limited speech competence to interact with others. Its central goal is to provide learners with the opportunity and capability to: (a) interact in conversations, (b) participate more fully in activities at home, school and recreation, (c) learn their native language and (d) establish and maintain their social roles (e.g., as a family member, friend and student). In turn, AAC has the potential to maximize such learners' feelings of self-sufficiency, self-respect and worth. Its importance is recognized in the recent UN Convention on the Rights of Disabled Persons, which expects countries to facilitate 'the learning of Braille, alternative script, augmentative and alternative modes, means and formats of communication and orientation and . . . the learning of sign language and the promotion of the linguistic identity of the deaf community'.[2]

It should be noted that learners who use AAC usually employ many modalities (e.g., any existing speech or vocalizations, and gestures), in addition to various devices such as communication boards and speech output communication aids to communicate.[3]

 The practice

There are two main techniques used in AAC to improve learners' ability to communicate effectively: unaided and aided:

Unaided techniques do not require external aids in order to communicate. These include non-verbal means of natural communication, as well as manual signs, such as:

- facial expressions;
- gestures; and
- manual signs.

Aided techniques require some additional external support, such as a physical object or a device, in order for the learner to communicate. Examples include:

- graphic sign systems;
- pictures;
- symbol charts; and
- computerized speech-generating devices, including voice synthesizers and voice output communication aids (VOCAs).

Access to these aided forms of AAC can be via direct selection or scanning. *Direct selection* techniques include pointing with a finger, hand, head (e.g., through an attached head stick), eyes or feet. *Scanning* involves message elements being presented to the learner in a sequence, whether by another person or by the device itself. The learner then makes a choice by specifying yes or no after each element is presented.[4]

Note: there is a limited amount of research into teaching writing skills to learners who use AAC;[5] this aspect will not be dealt with in this chapter.

 Gestures

These range from gestures that are generally understood by everyone in a given culture (e.g., nodding the head, shrugging the shoulders) to those that are understood only by particular groups (e.g., those used by baseball catchers to indicate what kind of ball to throw).

 Sign language or manual signs

These are made of hand shapes developed by people with severe hearing loss or deafness. Many different sign languages exist in different parts of the world. People who do not know sign language will have problems understanding what is being signed.

 Voice synthesizers

Both blind learners and those with minimal or no speech use voice synthesizers. Blind learners use voice synthesizer programmes such as *Kurzweil 3000*, which will read back any printed material that has been scanned into the computer.[6] For people who are mute, voice synthesizers become their voices. All they have to do is type what they want to say and the machine will read out the words for them.

 Voice Output Communication Aids (VOCAs)

These are portable electronic devices that produce synthetic or digitized speech output. A variety of graphic symbols (see next point) can be used in conjunction with VOCAs to represent messages that are activated when an individual uses a finger, hand or some other means to select a symbol from the VOCA's display. It functions as a speech output tool for the AAC user, thereby facilitating interactions.

 Graphic sign systems

There are many different graphic sign systems. Some of these include Blissymbols, Pictogram Ideogram Communication (PIC), Rebus Signs and Picture Exchange Communication System (PECS). Each of these systems has its own unique way of representing words with symbols. Therefore, choosing a graphic sign system is a highly individualized process. These systems can be used by way of a simple communication board (a chart with more frequently used symbol-vocabulary on it) or in more advanced computer programs.[7]

PECS is perhaps the best known and most widely used of all AAC systems. In a nutshell, in PECS learners are taught to pick up cards with line drawings or symbols on them and hand them to another person (educator, parent, peer, etc.), in exchange for the actual item. Once the learner can accomplish this simple request routine, the system is gradually expanded to teach such communication skills as labelling and information-seeking. Behaviourally based teaching strategies (e.g., shaping, prompting and fading) are used to implement the program (**Strategy 17**). In particular, one of the first tasks of an educator using PECS is to identify powerful reinforcers for which the learner will be motivated to communicate.[8]

 ## Pictures

Pictures can also be used on communication boards. They can be actual photographs, magazine clippings, labels, advertisements, etc. that are readily recognized by the learner.

 ## A multi-modal approach is advised

Although each of the above approaches has merit when used alone, the trend is more towards a multi-modal approach to using AAC. This reflects three factors. First, in real life, most communication is, in fact, multi-modal (e.g., combining speech and gestures). Second, inclusion of learners with special educational needs requires methods of communication that can be readily understood by a range of partners. Third, by using a combination of aided and unaided AAC, say, you can capitalize on the strengths of each mode while minimizing their limitations.[9]

 ## Teamwork is essential

Selecting and implementing an AAC strategy requires extensive planning by a multi-disciplinary team of professionals working with the learner and his/her family. This team may well include most, if not all of the following: a speech-language pathologist/therapist, a physical therapist, a physician and/or medical specialists, a special educator, a social worker, a psychologist, a relevant technician and a relevant paraprofessional/learning support assistant. It therefore calls upon teamwork of the highest order (**Strategy 4**).

 ## The evidence

✓ In an analysis of 50 single-subject experimental studies carried out across a wide age range, the effectiveness of AAC was examined. The results showed that interventions were effective in terms of behaviour change and generalization, although to a lesser extent with maintenance over time. Unaided systems were found to be more effective than aided systems.[10]

✓ A brief review of studies comparing the effects of teaching expressive vocabulary using speech, signing or total communication with **autistic** learners found that signing or total communication resulted in quicker and more complex learning of vocabulary than speech training. Those who benefited most seem to be those with more limited communication repertoires.[11]

✓ A US study investigated the effects of a classroom-based augmentative communication intervention with **non-verbal and behaviourally and cognitively challenged** adolescents. Picture communication boards, as well as natural language, were used and resulted in increases in communication and positive behaviours and participation in a more complex curriculum.[12]

✓ Another US study attempted to increase the quantity of social interactions by learners with **cerebral palsy** aged five to nine years, using AAC. The multi-faceted 15-week intervention was found to increase social interactions with peers.[13]

✓ A UK study investigated the views of 23 children and young people, most of whom had **cerebral palsy**, who were using AAC. Most of them reported that their AAC system was useful to them, any negative attitudes being limited to operational issues such as the technical skills required to operate an AAC system.[14]

✓ A US study evaluated the long-term outcomes of using AAC for a group of seven young men with **cerebral palsy**, aged 19–23 years, who had received AAC for at least 15 years. The outcomes were diverse, with individual variations across various measures.[15]

✓ A US study used picture book schedules describing daily classroom routines for three learners with disabilities, including one with **autism**. The results of the study showed that the learners followed their activity schedules 90–100 per cent of the time and required fewer prompts from teaching assistants.[16]

✓ In an extensive review of the literature on the effects of AAC on **autistic learners**, a Canadian researcher summarized studies that included the following points:

  • An early (1983) study reported on the use of pictorial symbols with two learners over a period of 100 days. It found that the learners learned to follow pictorial directions and generalized this learning to new pictures.

  • Several studies successfully used pictorial schedules to assist with the completion of specific activities in school and home settings, for example, using a photographic sequence for dressing.

- Other studies have successfully used pictorial schedules for assisting learners with autism to move from one task to another, eventually resulting in self-management of these tasks.
- Visual symbols have been used as a means of augmenting verbal questions in choice-making, for example in choosing foods.
- In what is referred to as 'aided language stimulation', success has been achieved when an educator points to a symbol for verbs and nouns, as well as communicating verbally with the learner.[17]

✓ There have been several studies (all US) of the Picture Exchange Communication System (PECS) (see The Practice section for a detailed description):

- The originators of the strategy reported that of 69 learners who used PECS for more than a year, 39 developed independent speech, 20 used speech plus PECS and the remaining seven used only PECS. The researchers noted that speech tended to develop once the learners were able to use 30 to 100 symbols to communicate.[18]
- In a study involving 18 children in an inclusive pre-school setting, 11 had **autism**. Of the 18 children, eight developed robust verbal skills (six were autistic), the remainder acquired very little speech but continued to use PECS.[19]
- A recent study investigated the effects of PECS on communication and speech development in three learners with **autistic spectrum disorders**, one at the pre-school level and two at the elementary school level. The results showed that PECS was mastered rapidly by the learners and there were increases in the number of words in their utterances, as well as in the complexity of their grammar.[20]

✓ The above represents but a small selection of research into the effectiveness of different approaches to AAC. A recent overview provides a much more detailed, technical analysis of how to select from the wide range of AAC symbols, devices and strategies for persons with **developmental disabilities**.[21]

 Addressing risks

If learners under your jurisdiction are using AAC or it is being considered, the following points should be taken into account:

- Selecting the AAC system that is best for an individual learner is not an easy task, and requires evaluation by many specialists.
- Professionals need to help the learner and his or her communication partners learn the skills of operating an AAC system effectively and efficiently.[22]
- In order for communication to be truly functional, both familiar and unfamiliar communication partners must understand it.[23]

- Learners with poor fine motor skills are likely to have difficulty learning and using even simple unaided AAC for functional communication and, therefore, might be better suited to an aided system.[24]
- Electronic aids, while highly useful, might break down. The AAC user will then need a back-up form of communication.
- An AAC system selected for use at one age might need to be modified or replaced as the learner develops. A related point is that AAC systems are undergoing rapid development, particularly with the use of computers and potential users need to keep the field under constant review.[25]

Conclusion

AAC methods are useful techniques to help learners with limited or no oral language competence to learn functional communication skills.

Further reading

Augmentative and Alternative Communication
Beukelman, D.R. and Mirenda, P. (1999). *Augmentative and alternative communication: Management of severe communication disorders in children and adults.* 2nd edn. Baltimore, MD: Paul H. Brookes.
Schlosser, R.W. (2003). *The efficacy of augmentative and alternative communication: Toward evidence-based practice.* San Diego, CA: Academic Press.

Key references

1 It is estimated that between 2.5 per cent and 6 per cent of learners with special educational needs could benefit from using augmentative or alternative communication systems (Lue, M.S. (2001). *A survey of communication disorders for the classroom teacher.* Toronto: Allyn and Bacon, p. 213).
2 UN Convention on the Rights of Disabled Persons, Article 24 (3)(a)(b).
3 Lund, S.K. and Light, J. (2006). 'Long-term outcomes for individuals who use augmentative and alternative communication: Part I – What is a "good" outcome?' *Augmentative and Alternative Communication*, 22(4), 284–299.
4 Beukelman, D.R. and Mirenda, P. (1999). *Augmentative and alternative communication: Management of severe communication disorders in children and adults.* 2nd edn. Baltimore, MD: Paul H. Brookes.
5 Millar, D., Light, J.C. and McNaughton, D.B. (2004). 'The effect of direct instruction and writer's workshop on the early writing skills of children who use augmentative and alternative communication'. *Augmentative and Alternative Communication*, 20(3), 164–178.
6 Dyslexia Association of Ireland (2004). *Computers and assistive technology.* URL: www.dyslexia.ie/comp.htm (accessed 11 January 2007).
7 For a more detailed explanation and examples of individual graphic sign systems, see von Tetzchner, S. and Martinsen, H. (1992). *Introduction to symbolic and augmentative communication.* San Diego, CA: Singular Publishing Group.
8 Bondy, A. and Frost, L. (1994). 'The Picture Exchange Communication System'. *Focus on Autistic Behavior*, 9, 1–19. See also URL: www.pecs.com (accessed 11 January 2007).

9 Sigafoos, J. and Drasgow, E. (2001). 'Conditional use of aided and unaided AAC: A review and clinical case demonstration'. *Focus on Autism and Other Developmental Disabilities*, 16(3), 152–161.

10 Schlosser, R.W. and Lee, D.L. (2000). 'Promoting generalization and maintenance in augmentative and alternative communication: A meta-analysis of 20 years of effectiveness research'. *Augmentative and Alternative Communication*, 16(4), 208–226.

11 Goldstein, H. (2002). 'Communication intervention for children with autism: A review of treatment efficacy'. *Journal of Autism and Developmental Disorders*, 32(5), 373–396.

12 Cafiero, J.M. (2001). 'The effects of an augmentative communication intervention on the communication, behavior, and academic program of an adolescent with autism'. *Focus on Autism and other Developmental Disorders*, 16(3), 179–189.

13 Carter, M. and Maxwell, K. (1998). 'Promoting interaction with children using augmentative communication through a peer-directed intervention'. *International Journal of Disability, Development and Education*, 45(1), 75–96.

14 Clarke, M., McConachie, H., Price, K. and Wood, P. (2001). 'Views of young people using augmentative and alternative communication systems'. *International Journal of Language and Communication Disorders*, 36(1), 107–115.

15 Lund and Light, op. cit.

16 Hall, L.J., McClannahan, L.E. and Krantz, P.J. (1995). 'Promoting independence in integrated classrooms by teaching aides to use activity schedules and decreased prompts'. *Education and Training in Mental Retardation*, 30(3), 208–217.

17 Mirenda, P. (2001). 'Autism, augmentative technology and assistive technology. What do we really know?' *Focus on Autism and Other Developmental Disabilities*, 16(3), 141–152.

18 Bondy, A. and Frost, L. (1998). 'The Picture Exchange Communication System'. *Topics in Language Disorders*, 19, 373–390.

19 Schwartz, I., Garfinkle, A. and Bauer, J. (1998). 'The Picture Exchange Communication System: Communicative outcomes for young children with disabilities'. *Topics in Early Childhood Special Education*, 18(3), 144–159.

20 Ganz, J.B. and Simpson, R.L. (2004). 'Effects on communicative requesting and speech development of the Picture Exchange Communication System in children with characteristics of autism'. *Journal of Autism and Developmental Disorders*, 34(4), 395–409.

21 Schlosser, R.W. and Sigafoos, J. (2006). 'Augmentative and alternative communication interventions for persons with developmental disabilities: Narrative review of comparative single-subject experimental studies'. *Research in Developmental Disabilities*, 27(1), 1–29.

22 American Speech-Language-Hearing Association (1997–2004). Augmentative and Alternative Communication Decisions. URL: www.asha.org/public/speech/disorders/Communication+Decisions.htm (accessed 9 January 2007).

23 Mirenda, P. (2003). 'Toward functional augmentative and alternative communication for students with autism: Manual signs, graphic symbols, and voice output communication aids'. *Language, Speech, and Hearing Services in Schools*, 34, 203–216.

24 Beukelman and Mirenda, op. cit.

25 Beukelman and Mirenda, op. cit.

Chapter 26

Strategy 24: Opportunities to learn

'Provide sufficient quantity and quality of time for learning'

Rating

★★★★

 The strategy

This brings me to the last strategy I present in this book: opportunities to learn (OTL). It is fitting that it brings together most, if not all, of the other strategies I have described, as well as a new one centring on adequate active learning time. Hence, the strategy relates to the total learning and teaching model described in Chapter 2.

 The underlying idea

It is essential that you ensure that learners with special educational needs do not have their problems compounded by reduced opportunities to learn within lessons and across the school year. In other words, you do what you can to remove or reduce any barriers to learning that might be present and you provide a stimulating, quality education experience, based on evidence-based teaching strategies. Within this context, one of your major challenges is to make sure that adequate time is devoted to instruction for all learners in your class.[1]

 The practice

There are four aspects of OTL for learners with special educational needs:

1 they have access to education;
2 the core curriculum for the particular year level is accessible;
3 the quality of instruction is high; and
4 adequate active learning time is provided.

Ensure access to education

At the most basic, all children should have access to free education, at least at the primary/elementary level. According to a recent South African report,[2] this involves the state ensuring that education is:

- *Physically accessible.* This 'physical' refers to the distances that learners must travel to school and also their safety when travelling. This has both a poverty aspect as well as a gender aspect, with girls being more vulnerable to violence and sexual abuse.
- *Economically accessible.* Free schooling does not refer only to the absence or minimization of fees, but also to minimizing the many indirect costs borne by parents and caregivers in ensuring that their children attend school. These indirect costs include school uniforms, transport, learner materials and the opportunity cost of the child's labour to the family.
- *Accessible to minorities.* Schools should be accessible to all children, including those from minorities and vulnerable sectors such as refugees, child migrants, working children and those with disabilities.
- *Linguistically accessible.* Clearly, for education to take place, both learners and educators must be able to speak the same language or dialect. Unfortunately, this is not always the case. For example, in a recent South African report, 42 per cent of children in poor, rural and township schools said that they had difficulty understanding their teachers.[3]
- *Provided by well-trained teachers.* Learners need to be taught by teachers who are well trained in pedagogy and the content of various subjects in the curriculum. This, unfortunately, is not always the case, even in developed countries such as the US where 1996 data showed that 27 per cent of newly hired teachers were not fully licensed and nearly 25 per cent of secondary teachers did not have a college major or minor in their main teaching subject.[4]

 Provide access to the core curriculum

As I emphasized in **Strategy 1**, I believe that all learners with special educational needs should have access to their country's core curriculum, albeit in a modified form to suit their cognitive and other skills. This suggests, in turn, that the curriculum is designed so that it is accessible to all learners, i.e., that it is an inclusive curriculum. It also suggests that curriculum and achievement standards are reasonable and appropriate for all learners.

 Provide high-quality instruction

Here are the main points I have made in this book that are relevant to this criterion:

- Most learners with special educational needs will benefit from a well-designed inclusive education programme, which is characterized by adaptations to the curriculum, assessment and teaching methods and is well supported by special education advisers (**Strategy 1**).
- Cooperative group teaching and peer tutoring will benefit all learners, particularly when reviewing material (**Strategies 2** and **3**).
- Planning and delivering instruction requires the active collaboration of a range of professionals and parents, with a clear delineation of responsibilities (**Strategies 4** and **5**).
- A favourable learning environment requires a school culture that accepts and celebrates diversity, is sensitive to cultural issues and sets high but realistic standards (**Strategy 6**). It provides a positive and motivating classroom climate with high, but reasonable, expectations and comprehensible language (**Strategy 9**). It provides classrooms that are physically accessible, well-lit, reasonably quiet and properly ventilated with healthy air (**Strategy 8**).
- Behavioural problems can be reduced by preventative school-wide positive behavioural support (**Strategy 7**).
- Many learners with special educational needs require social skills training to help them to establish and maintain positive interactions with others (**Strategy 10**).
- Many learners with special educational needs require assistance in acquiring cognitive strategies (**Strategy 11**), self-regulated learning (**Strategy 12**) and memory skills (**Strategy 13**).
- Some learners need help with reading comprehension, and benefit from reciprocal teaching (**Strategy 14**), while some, in the early stages of learning to read, need training in phonological awareness and phonological processing (**Strategy 15**).
- Some older learners who are experiencing anxiety or depression and other emotional or behavioural disorders benefit from cognitive behavioural therapy to help them change the ways they think about themselves (**Strategy 16**).
- Most learners with challenging behaviours benefit from interventions based on systematic analyses of the antecedents and consequences of their behaviour (**Strategies 17** and **18**).
- All learners benefit from multi-faceted direct instruction, with explicit, systematic instruction (**Strategy 19**), opportunities to systematically review and practise what they initially learn (**Strategy 20**) and from formative assessment and feedback during the learning process (**Strategy 21**).
- Some learners with physical or sensory impairments benefit from assistive technology (**Strategy 22**), while other learners with difficulties in communicating with speech need access to augmentative and alternative communication (**Strategy 23**).

Provide learners with adequate active learning time

In this strategy, the emphasis is on your effective management of students' learning time within lessons, across the school day and across the school year.[5] Here are some ways of maximizing your students' learning time:

- Set clear learning objectives for your students (usually through an IEP for those with high needs), and regularly assess how well these are being achieved.
- Prepare your teaching materials well in advance of lessons and train your learners in accessing them and replacing them after the lessons.
- Emphasize active responses rather than passive responses.[6]
- Maintain a brisk pace within your lessons. Here the 'Goldilocks principle' should apply: not too slow and not too fast, but just right, according to individual students' needs. Research with autistic learners, for example, that compared the length of time between instructional trials (sometimes referred to as 'inter-trial intervals') has shown that shorter intervals (around two seconds) result in better learning and attention to tasks than longer intervals.[7]
- Provide sufficient time for learners to respond to questions and comments within your lessons. Research has found that when educators ask learners questions, they typically wait less than one second for a response. Further, after a learner stops speaking, educators react or respond with another question in less than one second. When these periods of silence (referred to as 'wait-time' or 'think-time') last three to five seconds, many benefits seem to accrue. For learners, the length and correctness of their responses increases, the number of 'I don't know' and no responses decreases, and their scores on academic achievement tests increase. For educators, there are also benefits: for example, their questioning strategies became more varied and flexible and they asked additional questions requiring higher-level thinking on the part of their learners. In following this '3–5 second rule' in your own interactions, you should also ensure that the learners in your class also observe it.[8]
- In the UK, the notion of wait-time has been incorporated into the Primary National Strategy.[9] It also underpins a well-researched teaching pro-gramme developed in New Zealand: *Pause, Prompt, Praise*, used when a learner is reading aloud with educators, parents or peers.[10] Briefly, it takes this form. *Pause*: when the learner makes an error, wait for at least five seconds for him or her to self-correct; *Prompt*: if the learner still does not know the word, give two or three hints before saying the word; *Praise*: give praise for attempts at saying the word.
- Make the transitions between activities or classes as efficient as possible. As I emphasized in **Strategy 9**, 'messy' transitions provide many

opportunities for disruptive students to disrupt and for task-avoiding students to delay the beginning of the next task.

- One of your important tasks, therefore, is to set up routines so minimal time is lost on administrative matters or behavioural corrections.[11] You should keep transition times within and between lessons or activities as short as possible. For example, you could establish clear routines and behavioural expectations for transitions and inform the class when an activity or lesson is about to end. You should see the transition time as an important target of your teaching, not just a time outside of 'real' teaching.
- Take steps to reduce the frequency of disciplinary problems in the school and truancy, by deploying strategies such as school-wide positive support (see **Strategy 7**) and functional behavioural analysis (**Strategy 18**).

 The evidence

✓ In a large-scale meta-analysis, instructional quantity was ranked as the fourth highest influence on learning, with an effect size of 0.84. This was across all learners, not specifically those with special educational needs.[12]

✓ In keeping with this analysis, a New Zealand study found that the amount of time to interact with relevant curriculum content was strongly related to learning for high-, medium- and **low-achieving** nine year olds in science lessons.[13]

✓ A US study of 47 **mildly handicapped** learners during reading instruction found that, irrespective of their placement in regular or inclusive classes, they experienced significantly less academic engaged time with opportunities to respond than their non-handicapped peers (N = 30).[14]

✓ In another US study, 26 students with **learning disabilities** in different types of special education services were found to receive less than 45 minutes per day in opportunities for active academic responding (i.e., time spent making active, observable learning responses, not including passive listening). This was seen as a concern, given the positive relationship between active academic responding and achievement.[15]

✓ A further US study investigated the influence of educator wait-time and the duration of the time between trials on various tasks and wait-time durations on the performance of four **multiply handicapped** learners. The results showed that learners' performances were superior under the long wait-time conditions irrespective of the length of the inter-trial interval.[16]

✓ In another study of wait-time, an Australian investigation found that when wait-time was greater than three seconds, changes in educator and learner discourse took place and higher cognitive level achievement was obtained in elementary, middle and high school science classes. This finding was attributed to both educators and learners having additional time to think.[17]

✓ In a small-scale English study, the Pause, Prompt, Praise approach was used with same-age peer tutors in a secondary special school catering for learners with **moderate learning difficulties** who were working in Key Stage 4 (an English description covering 15–16-year-old students). The findings showed that tutees' rates of self-correction began to rise and the tutors showed improved skills and confidence.[18]

✓ In a US study, school-wide behavioural support was implemented over a two-year period. As a result of decreased student behaviour problems, instructional time across the school increased by 72.7 learner-days in the first year and 86.2 learner-days over baseline in the second year.[19]

✓ There is evidence to show that fourth- and fifth-grade students with **learning disabilities** can be trained to implement three-second time delays in peer tutoring and that this was effective in teaching spelling.[20]

 Addressing risks

The main risk is that in attending to the quantity of learning time, the quality of instruction that takes place in that time could be neglected. Learning time is a necessary, but not sufficient condition for learning to take place.

 Conclusion

Opportunity to learn means not only providing an adequate quantity of time for students to learn what is contained in the curriculum, but also, critically, ensuring that these opportunities are of the highest possible quality. A corollary to opportunity to *learn* is opportunity to *teach*, which means that educators have the skills and resources required to be effective teachers of learners with special educational needs, in other words to implement the strategies outlined in this book.

Key references

1 Brophy, J.E. and Good, T.L. (1986). 'Teacher behavior and student achievement'. In M.C. Wittrock (ed.), *Handbook of research on teaching*. 3rd edn. New York: Macmillan.

2 South Africa Human Rights Commission (2006). *Report of the public hearing on the right to basic education*. Pretoria: South Africa Human Rights Commission.

3 Nelson Mandela Foundation (2005). *Emerging voices: A report on education in South African rural communities*. A report researched by the Human Sciences Research Council (HSRC) and the Education Policy Consortium (EPC). Pretoria: HSRC Press.

4 National Commission on Teaching and America's Future (1996). *What matters most: Teaching for America's future*. New York: Author.

5 Arlin, M. (1984). 'Time, equality, and mastery learning'. *Review of Educational Research*, 54(1), 65–86; Gaskins, R.W. (1998). 'The missing ingredients: Time on task, direct instruction and writing'. *The Reading Teacher*, 41(8), 750–755; Newmann, F., Marks, H.M. and Gamoran, A. (1996). 'Authentic pedagogy and student performance'. *American Journal of Education*, 104(4), 280–312; Yair, G. (2000). 'Not just about time: Instructional practices and productive time in schools'. *Educational Administration Quarterly*, 36(4), 485–512; and Ysseldyke, J. and Christensen, S. (1993–1998). *The Instructional Environment System – II: A system to identify a student's instructional needs*. Fifth Printing. Longmont, CA: Sopris West.

6 Christenson, S.L., Ysseldyke, J.E. and Thurlow, M.L. (1989). 'Critical instructional factors for students with mild handicaps: An integrative review'. *Remedial and Special Education*, 10(5), 21–31.

7 Dunlap, G., Dyer, K. and Koegel, R.L. (1983). 'Autistic self-stimulation and intertrial interval duration'. *American Journal on Mental Deficiency*, 88(2), 194–202.

8 See a review by Stahl, R.J. (1994). 'Using "think-time" and "wait-time" skilfully in the classroom'. ERIC ED370885. In particular, note the originator of the wait-time idea: Rowe, M.B. (1986). 'Wait-time: slowing down might be a way of speeding up!' *Journal of Teacher Education*, 37(1), 43–50.

9 DfES (2004). *Primary National Strategy excellence and enjoyment: Learning and teaching in the primary years*. Cambridge: Cambridge University Press.

10 For example, see Glynn, T. (1995). 'Pause, prompt, praise: Reading tutoring procedures for home and school partnerships'. In S. Wofendale and K. Topping (eds), *Parent involvement in literacy: Effective partnerships in education*. London: Cassell.

11 Ysseldyke and Christensen, op. cit.; Englert, C.S., Tarrant, K.L. and Mariage, T.V. (1992). 'Defining and redefining instructional practices in special education: Perspectives on good teaching'. *Teacher Education and Special Education*, 5(2), 62–86; Stanovich, P.J. and Jordan, A. (2000). *Exemplary teaching in inclusive classrooms*. Paper presented at the Annual Meeting of the Council for Exceptional Children, Vancouver, Canada, April 2000; and McIntosh, K., Herman, K., Sanford, A., McGraw, K. and Florence, K. (2004). 'Teaching transitions: Techniques for promoting success between lessons'. *TEACHING Exceptional Children,* 37(1), 32–38.

12 Hattie, J. (1999). *Influences on student learning*. Inaugural lecture, University of Auckland, Auckland, New Zealand.

13 Alton-Lee, A. and Nuthall, G. (1990). 'Pupil experiences and pupil learning in the elementary classroom: An illustration of generative methodology'. *Teaching and Teacher Education: An International Journal of Research and Studies*, 6(1), 27–46.

14 O'Sullivan, P.J., Ysseldyke, J.E., Christensen, S.L. and Thurlow, M.L. (1990). 'Mildly handicapped elementary students' opportunity to learn during reading instruction in mainstream and special education settings'. *Reading Research Quarterly*, 25(2), 131–146.

15 Thurlow, M.L., Ysseldyke, J.E., Graden, J. and Algozzine, B. (1984). 'Opportunity to learn for LD students receiving different levels of special education services'. *Learning Disability Quarterly*, 7(1), 55–67.

16 Valcante, G., Roberson, W., Reid, W.R. and Wolking, W.D. (1989). 'Effects of wait-time and intertrial interval durations on learning by children with multiple handicaps'. *Journal of Applied Behavior Analysis*, 22(1), 43–55.

17 Tobin, K. (1987). 'The role of wait time in higher cognitive level learning'. *Review of Educational Research*, 37(1), 69–95.

18 Burns, E. (2006). 'Pause, prompt and praise: Peer tutored reading for pupils with learning difficulties'. *British Journal of Special Education*, 33(2), 62–67.
19 Scott, T.M. and Barrett, S.B. (2004). 'Using staff and student time engaged in disciplinary procedures to evaluate the impact of school-wide PBS'. *Journal of Positive Behavior Interventions*, 61(1), 21–27.
20 Telecsan, B.L., Slaton, D.B. and Stevens, K.B. (1999). 'Peer tutoring: Teaching students with learning disabilities to deliver time delay instruction'. *Journal of Behavioral Education*, 9(2), 133–154.

Index

Note: for multiple-authored sources, only the first-named author is included.

ABAB design 5
ability groups/grouping 46–9, 151, 190
acceptance, of learners, 34
accessibility, of research 7; of
    classrooms 34; of curriculum 30,
    225; of education 225
accountability, in groups 44
acoustics 95–6, 98–9
Adams, G.L. 194n10
Adams, M.J. 160, 161n2
Adelman, H.S. 67n9, 67n11, 110n1
adequate yearly progress 1
advance organisers 174
aggressive learners 46, 163, 167,
    169
Agran, M. 138n5
Ainscow, M. 39, 41n9
Alba, L. 161n6
Allcock, J. 102n29
Alton-Lee, A. 199n9, 230n13
ambient noise 95
American Speech-Language-Hearing
    Association 223n22
Ames, C. 25n1
Ames, R. 111n14
Anastopolous, A.D. 76n13
Anderman, E.M. 25n5
Anderson, A.
Andrews, J. 39
Anshel, J.R. 100n9
antecedent-based intervention 88, 173,
    174, 182, 183, 226
Antia, S.D. 51n9

anti-social behaviour 73, 168
anxiety disorders 163, 169
applied behaviour analysis see
    behavioural strategies
apraxia 216
Archibald, L.M.D. 26n10
Arlin, M. 230n5
ASHA Working Group on Classroom
    Acoustics 100n11
Ashman, A.F. 25n1, 130, 130n1
assessment, adapted 31
assistive technology 69, 207–15,
    226
Association for Direct Instruction
    193
asthma 94
at-risk learners 37, 56, 135, 150, 158,
    159
attention, learners' 33, 144
attention deficit hyperactivity disorder
    (ADHD) 74, 95, 169, 212
audio books 209
augmentative and alternative
    communication 207, 216–23,
    226
autism/autistic spectrum disorder 7, 38,
    55, 118, 136, 179, 180, 216, 220,
    221

Ballard, K. 75
Baron-Cohen, S. 120n11
Barrett, P.M. 171n16
BBB Autism Support Network 181n6

Beaman, R. 181n3
Beck, Aaron 294
Becker, W. 349n7
behavioural parent training 72
behavioural strategies/approaches 69,
    84, 173–81, 182, 183–5, 188, 219
behaviour disorders/problems 36, 38,
    49, 55, 87–8, 118, 135, 186, 220
behaviour modification *see* behavioural
    strategies
behaviour therapy *see* behavioural
    strategies
Bennerson, D. 146n6
Bennetts, L.K. 101n15, 101n27
Bereiter, C. 188, 194n2
Best Evidence Encyclopedia 12n3
Beukelman, D.R. 222, 222n4, 223n24,
    n25
biological structures and functions 18,
    207, 216
bipolar disorders 169
Bishop, R. 112n31
Black, R.S. 120n2
Blake, P. 101n14
blind/visually impaired 7, 93, 208–9,
    218
Bloom, L.A. 206n13
Blumenfeld, P.C. 25n6
Bondy, A. 222n8, 223n18
Booth, T. 39
Borkowski, J.G. 25n1
Bransford, J. 130n9
Breslin, C. 171n12
Brestan, E.V. 12n7, 76n9
British Association for Counselling and
    Psychotherapy 170
Bronzaft, A.I. 102n33
Brophy, J.E. 41n10, 181n11, 229n1
Brown, G. 206n4
Buckley, S. 42n18
Bulgren, J.A. 146n11
Burns, E. 231n18
Buzan, T. 146n14

Cafiero, J.M. 223n12
Cameron, J. 181n4
Campbell, D.M. 205
Carlberg, C. 42n23

Carnine, D. 193
Carr, E.G. 89n2, 91n21, 187n4
Carr, J. 181
Carter, M. 223n13
cerebral palsy 216, 220
chaining 177–8
Chambless, D.L. 12n5
Chandler, L.K. 186
Chard, D. 199n7
choral responding, in direct instruction
    190
Christensen, S.L. 230n6
chunking 145
Churchill, Winston 92
Clarke, C. 82n6
Clarke, M. 223n14
classroom environment/climate 17, 32,
    44, 78, 103–12, 226
class size 80–1
class-wide peer tutoring 52, 54–6
Clendon, S. 161n11
Cochrane review 168
cognitive-behavioural therapy 65, 74,
    122, 163–72, 173, 185, 226
cognitive strategies/cognition 122, 147,
    164
cognitive strategy instruction 122–31,
    134, 165–6, 191, 226
Cohen, P.A. 58n5
collaborative consultation 36, 60,
    63
Collaborative for High Performance
    Schools, the 100n6
collaborative teaching 60–7, 71, 84–5,
    212, 219, 226
Collett-Klingenberg, L. 120n5
communication 33, 158
community of practice *see* collaborative
    teaching
comprehension skills 148–9, 150
Compton, S.N.B. 171n10, n11
computer adaptations 209–10
computer-assisted instruction/learning
    48, 207
Computer Vision Syndrome 98
concept mapping 144–5
conduct disorders 73
conflict, coping with 115

Conroy, M.A. 181n2
contamination, in studies 5
context, of learning 17, 43, 60, 78, 83, 92, 103, 113
Cooper, H. 200n10, n11
Cooperative Educational Service Agency 12 and FBA Task Force 187, 187n6
cooperative group teaching 32, 36, 43–51, 52, 226
cooperative learning *see* cooperative group teaching
Cooperative Reading and Composition (CIRC) 47
corporal punishment 180
co-teaching 60, 62–3
Cotton, K. 111n9, 112n30
Council for Exceptional Children 100n2, 199n5
Coyne, M.D. 25n3, 152n6, 161n10
criterion-referenced assessment 31
Crone, D.A. 187
cross-age tutoring 52
Crowther, I. 100n5, 101n17
cultural factors 32
curriculum adaptations 30, 84

deaf/hearing impaired 7, 35, 38, 47, 55, 65, 93, 96, 98
De La Paz, S. 130n8
delinquent learners 118, 192
Denham, A. 121n16
Department of Education, New Zealand 76n5
Department of Education, South Africa 41n6, 67n10
depression 163, 167
Detterman, D.K. 25n1
DfEE 66n3
DfES 230n9
developmental disabilities 98, 186
Dieker, L.A. 66n5
differential reinforcement 177
direct instruction 129, 173, 179, 188–94, 226
disabilities 2, 36, 81, 136–7, 185–6, 191, 212, 221
discipline problems 87

disruptive behaviour/learners 46, 74, 75, 109, 135
Distar Language Kit 192
distinctive teaching strategies, for learners with special educational needs 7–8, 11
distributed practice 195–6
Dockrell, J. 13n16, 25n1, 26n11, 130
Dorman, J. 112n26
Down syndrome 37, 98
Doyle, W. 181n10
drill 18, 192
Dunlap, G. 230n7
Dunne, E. 50
Dunst, C.J. 128
Dweck, C.S. 25n6
Dyslexia Association of Ireland 222n6
Dyson, A. 39, 42n19

Education of All Handicapped Children Act (1975) 28
Edyburn, D. 213
effect size 4, 13n11
Elliott, D. 66n6
Ellis, Albert 164, 171n4
Ellis, E.S. 130n5
emotional disorders/problems 38, 49, 118, 135, 136, 142, 186
emotions 14, 19, 20, 104, 133
engaging with the same idea 196
Engelbrecht, P. 42n22
Engelman, S. 188, 194n3
Englert, C.S. 41n7, 111n15, 205n2
Erchul, W.P. 67n17
Ervin, R.A. 187n7
Erwin, P.G. 121n17
Etsheidt, S. 171n6
evidence-based teaching, general x, 85; criteria 3–7
executive system 15, 21, 24, 132, 133, 147, 154, 164
expanded keyboard 208
expectations 80, 86, 106
external responses 68, 83, 174, 188, 201
external task demands 68, 83, 174, 188, 201

extinction 176
Eyberg, S.M. 76n7

fading 178
Farrell, P. 120n9
Fazio, B. 199n8
feedback 24, 31, 54, 116, 197, 202,
    203–4, 205
Fielding, R. 101n24
Fisher, M. 41n16, 120n7
Fitzgerald, G. 214n11
Flexer, C. 101n28
Florian, L. 101n18, 206n2
flow charts 145
FM systems 209
Ford, M.E. 25n1, n2, 111n4, n11
formative assessment and feedback 31,
    201–6, 226
Forness, S. 181n7
Fraser, B.J. 110, 110n2, 111n21,
    112n28
Freeman, R. 90n7
Freiberg, H.J. 111
French, N.K. 66n8
Freschi, D.F. 66n8
Friend, M. 66n4
friendship skills 115
Fryxell, D. 41n15
Fuchs, D. 58n7, n10
Fuchs, L.A. 206n7, n14
Fulk, B.J.M. 146n10
Fulk, K.57
functional behavioural assessment 88,
    90, 173, 182–7, 226, 228
furniture and equipment 93

Gamoran, A. 51n16
Ganz, J.B. 223n20
Gardner, R. 180
generalization 23, 179, 195
Gersten, R. 130n10, 194n15
gestures 217–8
Gilberts, G.H. 138n18
Gillies, R.M. 51n13
Gillon, G. 161n13, 162n14
Glass, G. 12n9
Glynn, T. 230n10
goals, learners' 19–20, 105, 133

Goldstein, H. 12n7, 223n11
Goldsworthy, C.L. 160, 161n7, n9
Graham, S. 131n23, 138n8
graphic sign systems 218–19
Greaney, K. 162n18
Greeno, J. 199n5
Greenspan, S.R. 120n2
Greenwood, C.R. 58n1, n14
Gresham, F.M. 121n15
Grossman, D.C. 90n14
group process skills 45–6, 49, 115
group tasks 45

Haertel, G.D. 111n22
Hall, L.J. 223n16
Hall, T. 58n13
Hallam, S. 51n16
Hargreaves, D. 12n7
Haring, T.G. 58n8
Harris, K.R. 25n8, 130n7, 131n27, n28,
    138n13, 146n15
Harrower, J.K. 42n24, 138n15
Hattie, J. 12n6, 82n10, 131n19, 194n11,
    206n3, n10, 230n12
Hawken, L.S. 89n3, 90n16
head pointer 208
Heckaman, K 187n9
Heimann, M. 214n12
Heller, M.F. 82n2
Heschong Mahone Group 101n25
Heward, W. 12n4, 200n12
Hidi, S. 25n4
Higgins, S. 99, 101n22
High Scope 191
Hirsch, E.D. 13n13, 146nn12
Hoagwood, K. 67n16
Hoek, D.J. 131n13, n14
homework 197–8, 199
Hood, K.K. 77n15
Hornby, G. 58n4, 76
Horner, R.H. 89n1, 181n8
Houtveen, T. 50n4, 51n15
Howlin, P. 120n12
Hughes, C. 131n24, 138n17
Hunt, P. 51
Hurford, D.P. 162n16
Hutchinson, N.L. 131n12
hyperactivity 167

Idol, L. 66, 66n1, n7, 131n17
inclusive education 27–42, 60, 78, 80, 226
Index for Inclusion 38, 39
individual education plans (IEPs) 31, 227
Individuals with Disabilities Education Act (IDEA) 182, 214
indoor environmental quality 92–102, 226
integration, cf. inclusion 27
intellectual disabilities 7
interdependence of learners 44, 45, 132
Ireson, J. 51
Iwata, B.A. 187n10

Jackson, L. 111n8
James, A. 171n15
Jenkins, J.R. 131
jig-saw puzzle groups 44–5
Johnson, D.W. 50, 50n1, 51n10
Jones, K. 57
Jönsson, T. 41n5
Juniper Gardens Children's Project 53

Kalkowski, P. 59
Kame'enui, E.J. 194n5
Kamps, D.M. 58n9
Karsten, S. 42n17
Karten, T.J. 39
Katz, J. 41n11
Kauffman, J.M. 76n2
Kaufman, M. 51n7
Kavale, K.A. 58n16
Kazdin, A.E. 76n6
Kehle 111n16, n20
Kelly, L. 200n13
Kelly, M. 152n5, 153n14
Kendall, P.C. 303
Kern, L. 138n14
key-guards for computer 208
keyword strategy 140
Kintsch, A. 214n5, 215n17
Klinger, J.K. 153n15
Kluwin, T.N. 42n25
Kotahitanga 109–10, 112
Kounin, J.S. 112n29

Krantz, P.J. 77n18
Kratochwill, T.R. 13n14

Lancaster, Joseph 44, 53
Lang, D. 100n3
language disabilities/impairments 95, 142, 158, 197, 212
LaNunziata, L. 194n4
Larkin, M.J. 152, 152n6, n7
leadership, for inclusive education 35, 78–9, 81
Learning and Teaching Model 14–26
Learning Disabilities Association of America 161n5, n9
learning disabled/disability/difficulties 35–6, 38, 39, 47, 48, 55, 56, 95, 123, 127, 128, 129, 130, 135, 136, 140, 142, 143, 150, 151, 158, 191, 192, 197, 209, 213, 228, 229
learning time 227–8
Lederer, J. 152n5
Le Fevre, D.M. 152n13
letter strategy 141
Lewis, A. 13n19
Lewis, T.J. 89, 89n3, 90n4, 91n20
lighting 94, 97–8
Lindsay, G. 82n1, n5
Lipsey, M.W. 12n8, 13n15, 51n14, 171n13
listening strategies 156
Lloyd, J.W. 12n8, 146n7
Lovett, M.W. 131n18
low-achieving learners 46, 48-9, 128, 204
Luckner, J.L. 67n18
Lue, M.S. 222n1
Luiselli, J.K. 91n18
Lund, S.K. 222n3, 223n15
Lysakowski, R.S. 206n11

McCart, M.R. 76n6, n11
McConnell, S. 120, 121n18
McCormick, C. 160
McDonald, N. 215n14
McDonnell, J. 58n11
McGrath, H. 120n3
McGregor, G. 13n16, 40
McIntosh, D.E. 41n8, 6n14

McIntosh, K. 230n11
McIntosh, R. 145n3
MacIver, D.J. 50n5, 111n10
Maheady, G.F. 58n13
mainstreaming *see* inclusive education
Maori students 109–10
Marchand-Martella, N.E. 193, 194n4
Margolis, H. 120n6
Marks, S.U. 66n8
Markus, H.R. 137n2
mass practice 196
mastery, in direct instruction 190
Mastropieri, M.A. 131n16, 145n5,
    146n9
Mathes, P. 59n17
Mathur, S.R. 120n1, 121n13
Matson, J.L. 77n17, 138n15, 181n9
Mayrowetz, D. 82n3, n8
Medcalf, J. 58n12
Medway, F.J. 67n13
Meichenbaum, D.H. 165, 171n2, n5
memory, long-term 15, 23, 139, 195;
    primary 15, 18, 139, 144, 145,
    195–6; short-term 15, 22–3, 139
mentally retarded/mental retardation
    35–6, 38, 47, 55, 135, 136, 142,
    212
mental representations 144–5
meta-analyses 4
metacognition 123
Merrell, K.W. 120n7
Meyer, L. 194n8
Meyer, R.E. 162n15
Millar, D. 222n5
Miller, J.A. 187n4, n5
mind mapping 145
Mills, P.E. 194n14
Mirenda, P. 223n17, n23
Mitchell, D. x-xi, 40n4, 41n9, 76n3
mixed ability groups/grouping 43, 45,
    46–7, 129, 149
Miyake, A. 26n9
mnemonics and other memory strategies
    139–43, 179, 226
modelling 192
Montague, M. 131n11
Moore, D. 152n5
Moos, R.H. 110n3

Mostert, M.P. 12n4, n8
motivation 15, 19–21, 68, 106, 113,
    164
mouth-stick 208
multi-modal approach 219
multiple-baseline design 5
multiple sclerosis 94, 216
multiply handicapped learners 228
mutual assistance groups 44

Nakken, H. 41n11
National Association of Cognitive-
    Behavioral Therapists 171n1
National Center for Educational
    Statistics 100n1, 101n21
National Clearing House for
    Educational Facilities 99
National Commission on Teaching and
    America's Future 229n4
National Institute for Direct Instruction
    193
National Reading Panel 161n12
negative reinforcement 176
Nelson Mandela Foundation
    229n3
Newmann, F. 230n5
New Zealand Ministry of Education
    13n18
Nirje, B. 40n1
Nisbet, P. 214n4, n9
No Child Left Behind Act (2001) 1,
    11n1
normalization 28
Norwich, B. 13n19
Nuthall, G. 120n8, 199n3

OECD 108, 111n6, 112n24
office referrals 87
Okano, K. 111n5
Oliver, C. 181n6
One Laptop Per Child 214n2
operant conditioning *see* behavioural
    strategies
opportunities to learn 84, 224–31
oppositional behaviours 74
OSEP Center on Positive Behavioral
    Interventions and Supports 89, 89n3,
    90n7, 91n22, 187n3

O'Sullivan, P.J. 230n14
Oswald, K. 90n17
overcrowded schools 93, 97

Pacchiano, D.M. 199n4
pace, of lessons 189, 193, 227
Palincsar, A.S. 152, 152n1, n5, n7, n10
paraprofessionals 34, 63
parents/caregivers 34
parent–child interaction therapy 72–3
parent involvement 36, 68–77, 81, 84,
    226
parent management training 168
Paris, S.G. 137, 138n3, n4
Pattison, S. 171n7, n9
Pause, Prompt, Praise 54, 227, 229
Pavlov, Ivan 173
Pavuluri, M.N. 171n18
Peabody Language Kit 192
peer-assisted learning strategies (PALS)
    55
peer review 6
peers' influence 2, 17
peer tutoring 9, 32, 52–9, 118, 149,
    226
pegword strategy 140–1
personal agency belief 14, 20–1
pharmacological treatments 8
phonemic awareness 155
phonemic/rhyming strategies 157
phonological awareness and
    phonological processing 154–62,
    226
physical disabilities 7, 93
Picture Exchange Communication
    System 218–19, 221
picture strategy 141–2, 219
Pierce, K.L. 138n16
positive behavioural support *see* school-
    wide positive behaviour support
positive reinforcement 174–5
post-traumatic stress disorders 163
practice 190, 193
Presley, M. 130, 272n7
prevention 85
principals, leadership 35
problem-solving 133
Project Follow Through 188, 191

proleptic teaching 148
prompts 174, 192
Public Law 105–17 187n2
punishment 74, 175–6
Purdie, N. 231n6

quality of life ix, 1, 132
Quinn, M.M. 121n14

Rainforth, B. 66n2
Ramsay, P. 41n7, 111n7
randomized controlled studies 5
Raskind, M.H. 215n15
reading difficulties/disabilities 53–4,
    128, 150, 151, 154–62, 158, 159
reciprocal teaching 147–53, 226
Reeve, P.T. 66n5
rehearsal 144
Reid, R. 187n8
Reinecke, M.A. 170
reinforcement 24, 74, 86, 88, 119,
    178–81
resources, for inclusive education 35
retrieval, of responses 15, 24
review and practice 195–200, 226
Reynolds, A. 111n15
Rivera-Batiz, F.L. 101n19
Robinson, T.R. 171n8
Rosenberg, G.G. 102n30
Rosenshine, B. 152n3, n9, n11, 199n1,
    n4
rote learning 18, 198
Rouse, M. 41n7, 42n20
routines 228
Rowe, M.B. 230n8
rules, classroom 107

safe environment 104
Saint-Laurent, L. 41n13
Salamanca Statement 28, 40n2
Salend, S.J. 41n11
Sanders, M. 76n8, 77n16
Sasso, G.M. 12n4, 42n26
scaffolding 148, 149, 190, 193
Scherer, M.J. 214n6, 215n16
Schlosser, R.W. 222, 223n10
Schmidt, C. 100n10
Schmidt, M. 214n10

School Consultation Research Project 65

school culture/environment/ethos 17, 44, 78–82, 84, 103, 226

school phobia 74

school refusal 163

school-wide positive behaviour support 83–91, 173, 182, 185, 226, 228, 229

Schunk, D.H. 206n5

Schwab Learning 214n4

Schwartz, I. 223n19

Schweinhart, L. 194n13

Scott, B.J. 41n7

Scott, T.M. 91n19, 231n19

scripts, in direct instruction 189

Scruggs, T.E. 130n4, 145n1, 146n8

self-awareness 133

self-beliefs 33

self-concept 19

self-harm 168, 186

self-monitoring 24, 119, 133

self-regulated learning 122, 132–8, 164

Self-Regulated Strategy Development 135

SENCOs 34, 60

Serketich, W.J. 76n10

setting 49

shaping 177

Shapiro, E.S. 187

Sharpe, M.N. 42n21

Shaw, R. 215n13

Sheridan, S.M. 67n12

Shield, B. 102n31, n32

side effects, in intervention 5–6

Sigafoos, J. 223n9

sign language 218

signal-to-noise ratio 95

Simeonsson, R.J. 13n12

Simonides of Ceos 140

single-case studies 5

Sipert, D.J. 111n12

Skinner, B.F. 173

Slavin, R.E. 11n1, 12n3, 50n6

Smith, H. 206n12

Smith, S.B. 161n3, n4

social construction of knowledge 44, 61, 164

social skills training 46, 65, 84, 86, 87, 113–21, 185, 226

Society for the Treatment of Autism 181n6

sound-field amplification 95–6, 98, 207

sound reverberation 95, 100n13

South Africa 30, 64, 225

South Africa Human Rights Commission 229n2

special educational needs, learners with ix, 2–3, 48, 80, 99, 134–5, 142, 191

special friends programme 55

speech/language difficulties 7, 216–23

speech synthesizers 209

Spence, S.H. 76n12

Sprague, J. 90n3

SRA/McGraw Hill 194n4

Stage, S.A. 138n7

Stahl, R.J. 230n8

Stanovich, P.J. 41n7, 82n9, 206n2, 230n11

Steege, M.W. 187

Stevens, R. 51n8

sticky keys 208

structured lessons, in direct instruction 189

successive approximations 177

success rates 189–90

Sugden, D. 25n7, 26n13, 130n2

Sugai, G. 89, 90n13, 187n2

summative assessment 201–2

supports, for inclusive education 34

Sutherland, K.S. 51n18

Swanson, H.L. 26n12, 51n19, 131n26, 152nn6, 194n12, 199n6

Swing, S.R. 131n20

syllable strategies 157

talking calculators 209

task completion 32–3

task demands/difficulty 15, 17–18, 45, 174

Taylor-Greene, S. 90n11, n12

teacher aides 34, 63

Teacher Training Agency 111n13

team-based services *see* collaborative teaching

Technology-Related Assistance for
  Individuals with Disabilities Act
  (1998) 214n3
Telescan, B.L. 58n15, 231n20
theory of mind 117
Thorndike, Edward 173
Thurlow, M.L. 230n15
time-out 176
Tobin, K. 230n15
Topping, K.J. 50n2, 57, 58n2, n6
Torgesen, J. 160n1, 161n7
transitions 107, 227–8
traumatized children 170
treatment fidelity 3
Triple P-Positive Parenting Programme
  73, 75
Troia, G.A. 130n3, 131n21
Troutman, A. 181
trust, in environment 19, 104
Tunmer, W.E. 161n8, 162n19
Turnbull, A.P. 76, 90n9, n10

underachievement 80, 128
UNESCO 40, 40n2
United Nations Convention on the
  Rights of Disabled Persons 28, 40n3,
  217, 222
United States Surgeon General 174
University of Kansas Center for
  Research on Learning 130
US Department of Health and Human
  Services 181n1

Valcante, G. 230n16
Van de Wiel, N. 12n7, 171n3, n14
Van Wijk, C.J.F. 13n16
ventilation 94
vision, for inclusion 29
visualization 145
voice output communication aids 217,
  218
voice recognition programmes 208
voice synthesizers 218

von Tetzchner, S. 222n7
Vygotsky L. S. 147–8, 152n2

Wade, S. 40
wait time 227, 228
Waldron, N.L. 41n14
Walter-Thomas, C. 66n5
Wang, M.C. 41n12, 112n23
Watson, J.B. 173
Webber, J. 138n6
Web sites access 210–11
Wehmeyer, M.L. 137, 138n9, n10
Wertsch, J.V. 152n3
What Works Clearinghouse 12n3, 159,
  162n20
Wheldall, K. 13n17, 58n3
White, W.A.T. 181n7, 194n9
whole language 155–6
Wilson, B.A. 120n4
Wolery M. 12n7, 82n4
Wolfe, L.H. 138n12
Wong, B.Y.L. 131n22
Wood, D.J. 152n4
Wood, J. 152n4
Wood, S.J. 138n11
Woodward, J. 131n25, 199n2, 206n6
World Health Organisation 95, 100n13
word-level strategies 156–7
Wubbels, T. 112n25

Xin, J.F. 51n12

Yair, G. 230n5
Yates, F.A. 145n2
Yocum, D.J. 67n14
Ysseldyke, J. 199n5, 206n8, n15,
  230n5, n11

Zaidman-Zait, A. 214n7, n8
Zimmerman, B.J. 137n1
Zirpoli, T.J. 187n1
Zollers, N.J. 82n7
zone of proximal development 147–8